CHF

D1349139

C016312850

EAT Mexico

RECIPES FROM MEXICO CITY'S
STREETS, MARKETS & FONDAS

LESLEY TÉLLEZ

PHOTOGRAPHS BY
PENNY DE LOS SANTOS

KYLE BOOKS

For my parents and grandparents

Published in Great Britain in 2017 by
Kyle Books; an imprint of Kyle Cathie Ltd
192–198 Vauxhall Bridge Road
London SW1V 1DX
general.enquiries@kylebooks.com
www.kylebooks.co.uk

First published in America in 2015 by Kyle Books

10 9 8 7 6 5 4 3 2 1

ISBN 978-0-85783-387-7

Text © 2015 Lesley Téllez
Photography © 2015 Penny De Los Santos
Design © 2015 Kyle Books Ltd

Designer: Little Mule Studio
Project editor: Anja Schmidt
Photographer: Penny De Los Santos
Food styling: Adrienne Anderson
Prop styling: Marina Malchin
Copy editor: Sarah Scheffel
Editorial Adaptation: Jo Richardson
Production: Nic Jones, Gemma John and Lisa Pinnell

A Cataloguing in Publication record for this title is available from
the British Library.

Colour reproduction by ALTA London
Printed and bound in China by C&C Offset Printing Co., Ltd.

TABLE OF CONTENTS

INTRODUCTION 7

CHAPTER 1
ON THE STREETS 19

CHAPTER 2
IN THE MARKETS 57

CHAPTER 3
IN THE FONDAS 93

CHAPTER 4
IN THE COUNTRY 127

CHAPTER 5
AT HOME 159

INDEX 188

ACKNOWLEDGEMENTS 192

SIEMPRE "CON TODO"

The first thing that struck me when I moved to Mexico City in 2009 was that I didn't recognise any of the food. I grew up in Southern California, one of the North American epicentres of Mexican food. But these Mexico City tacos – the ones that abounded on street corners, and in markets and in *taquerías* whose lights stayed on until well past 2am – these tacos were gorgeous and wild and raw, like some species of animal long extinct.

At the slow-cooked beef *suadero* stalls, a *taquero*, or taco maker, would lift a hunk of meat out of a caramel-coloured moat of fat, revealing beef transformed into a glistening, crispy-edged confit. He'd chop it to bits with a large cleaver – *whack! whack! whack!* – and slap a tortilla on the grill, drizzling on a little extra fat like a kiss good-bye. 'Con todo?' he'd ask. *With everything?* I learnt to say yes. (For the love of God, yes. Always *con todo*.) He'd sprinkle on raw onion and fresh coriander and place the taco on a plastic plate lined with a square of grey paper. Other hunks of meat remained bubbling in the fatty moat.

On almost every other street corner, a *trompo*, or roasting spit, lay stacked with orangey-red marinated pork, cooked until juicy and blackened in spots. Men in aprons and triangular hats worked fast, slicing meat off the cylinder of pork and catching it in cupped hands lined with tortillas. 'Con todo?' Yes, please. On went pineapple and a pinch of coriander and onion. Underneath went the grey paper and plastic plate.

At the *tlacoyo* stands, women with long grey plaits stuffed balls of masa with beans or cheese like an empanada, then pressed it into a oval-shaped patty. The *tlacoyos* cooked on *comales* – a round sheet of metal propped on a square grill – until crisp and freckled on both sides. 'Con todo, señorita?' They added diced cactus, onion, coriander, grated cheese and a spoonful of salsa.

We moved to Mexico City for my husband's job; I quit my own newspaper job without much of an idea of what I'd do next. We'd both wanted to move to Mexico for years, mostly to improve our Spanish, and I was confident that I'd figure something out. That something turned out to be studying food.

EATING MEXICO FROM BORDER TO BORDER

The neighbourhood markets in Mexico City were full of produce I'd never seen before. *Huitlacoche*, the purplish-grey corn fungus once eaten by the Aztecs, lay in pebbly, damp piles. Fresh cactus paddles sat on mounds of herbs. Clay pots overflowed with cold salads of *nopal* (cactus), *pata* (pig's trotters) and *haba* (broad or fava beans). Vendors cried out, 'Qué le damos, guerita?' (What can we give you, light-skinned girl?) or 'Qué buscaba?' (What are you looking for?) when I walked by. I didn't know whether I was supposed to answer or keep on walking.

In a city that suffered from crippling traffic, crumbling infrastructure and occasionally fetid air, somehow food was universally adored. Relished, even. *Chilangos*, the local word for people who live in Mexico City, ate on busy avenues and street corners, gulping down tacos, homemade fried potato crisps and exhaust. They ate baroque fruit salad sculptures covered in dollops of whipped cream in the markets. They slurped bowls of *barbacoa* consommé at the weekends underneath plastic tarpaulins, and they bought sweet bread from bike-riding vendors.

Residents of Mexico City and the nearby outskirts have created a unique food economy that doesn't exist anywhere else in the country. Immigrants from all over Mexico have flocked to the capital to work, and, depending on the neighbourhood and snacks sold, setting up a food business requires relatively little capital. Only in Mexico City can one find food from Puebla, the Yucatán, Oaxaca, Guerrero, Tlaxcala, Baja California and Veracruz, co-existing, side by side. The cuisine of Mexico City historically focused on Central Mexico, but modern Mexico City cuisine boasts a sort of pan-identity, embracing influences and ingredients that extend from Mexico's northern border to Guatemala. It is a chaotic, energising and overwhelming place to learn about Mexican food.

Deep down my passion for exploring the tastes of Mexico City was about more than just the food – I was eager to connect with a culture I wanted to know better. My great-grandparents had been born in Sonora, Chihuahua and Guanajuato, but the language and most of the cultural customs hadn't made it to my generation. I had struggled occasionally with my cultural identity in my twenties. Growing close to Mexican food opened up a new door, connecting me to my family and my ancestors in ways I couldn't have predicted.

ABOUT THIS BOOK

This cookbook is an earnest attempt to capture Mexico City's informal food scene, which has continued to fascinate me since those early days in 2009 when I arrived. What this book is *not* is a definitive guide to all of Mexico City's food. There are plenty of well-known local dishes that aren't included here because of time and space constraints. (I'm sorry, *caldo de gallina*.) I'm also hyper-conscious of taking on the herculean task of translating a cuisine that isn't native to me. My sources for the recipes in this book are the same Mexican street, market and *fonda* vendors who've inspired me; collections of popular Mexican recipes (particularly cookbooks by Josefina Velázquez de León); and many other cookbooks and books about Mexican food culture found in Mexico City's lovely Biblioteca de la Gastronomía Mexicana (Library of Mexican Gastronomy) at the Fundación Herdez in the Centro Histórico.

Many of the recipes in this book require some patience to prepare. There are very few shortcuts in Mexican cooking, which is one of the things I like about it! Early in my time in Mexico City, I took a 14-month cooking course at the Escuela de Gastronomía Mexicana. It was a diploma programme devoted to Mexican cooking, and during our three- to four-hour weekly cooking and lecture sessions, I tried to suppress the gringa side of me that told me to hurry, hurry, hurry. When preparing Mexican food, it's not about speed or how perfect the plate looks in the end – it's about the steps themselves, and taking pleasure in both the process and the result.

POBLANO

HABANERO

ÁRBOL

GUAJILLO

MULATO

PASILLA

ÁRBOL
FRESCO

CHIPOTLE
MECO

ANCHO

COSTEÑO

SERRANO

JALAPEÑO

CHILE
MORA

MUST-HAVE MEXICAN INGREDIENTS

Here's a quick guide to the ingredients I use most frequently in this book. You can find these, and many of the other specialist ingredients used in this book, in Mexican and other speciality food stores and markets or online. Some items may also be found in major supermarkets, particularly the 'world foods' section. Throughout the book, I've suggested sources for other hard-to-find ingredients, in some cases Latin American, Caribbean and Asian grocery stores or online suppliers.

ANCHO CHILLI: A large dried chilli with a fruity aroma, the ancho is used most often in moles, adobos and *chiles rellenos*. Sometimes vendors will toss in mulatos with the anchos. To tell them apart, hold an ancho chilli up near the light. It should have a reddish tint, possibly near the stem. It should also smell much fruitier than the mulato, which tends to smell more raisiny and prune-like. The ancho is known as a poblano chilli when fresh. You can find them in major supermarkets or from online suppliers.

ÁRBOL CHILLI (FRESH): A pencil-thin, long green chilli, the fresh chilli de árbol is consistently hotter than both serranos and jalapeños, which can be forgettable depending on the season and where you buy them. You can find fresh árbols at Mexican grocery stores.

ÁRBOL CHILLI (DRIED): Skinny, dried árbol chillies are a deep crimson colour and about the same length as the fresh chillies, around 7.5–10cm long. When purchasing, make sure they have their stems intact. If they don't, they could be chilli japonés, which has a different flavour profile. Dried árbol chillies are very hot and best used in table salsas – condiments that sit on the table, for drizzling.

ACHIOTE: Annatto seeds in English, *achiote* is sold either ground or in seed form. Ground achiote in Mexico City is most commonly pre-mixed with vinegar and spices and packaged in small rectangular bars. These bars are often used for marinades for *taco al pastor* and *cochinita pibil*. You can buy the bars or the whole seeds from Mexican grocery stores or Mexican or online specialist food suppliers.

BEANS (DRIED): A staple in the Mexican kitchen. Using the best-quality beans you can find matters; old beans may not soften during cooking or can have off flavours. Most of the beans called for in this book are black (turtle) beans or brown pinto beans – the latter is my substitute for *bayos*, a creamy brown Mexican bean that's difficult to source dried – both available from major supermarkets and other food stores and online. For most recipes in this book, any Mexican bean will do. I'd encourage you to try as many varieties as possible.

MEXICAN BAY LEAF: I call for dried Mexican bay leaves (*Litsea glaucescens* or *hojas de laurel*) in some of my recipes. The flavour is a bit more subtle than the Mediterranean bay leaf, and the leaf itself is narrower. You can order them from online Mexican food suppliers.

CORIANDER (FRESH): Fresh coriander (*Coriandrum sativum*) is an essential condiment in Mexican cooking, often mixed with onion and added to tacos, or chopped and added to salsas. It should taste sharp and herbal, with wide, flat leaves that are a bit broader and rounder than flat-leaf parsley. Use both the leaves and stems for maximum flavour.

CHICKEN STOCK: Mexican chicken stock is not the same as the variety found outside Mexico. It tends to be lighter in taste, generally because it's made with only chicken, onion, garlic and perhaps a bay leaf and salt. If you have time to make your own, it's worth it (page 98). Be careful when using chicken stock cubes or powder – the flavours may be overly chickeny, and they can ruin a good sauce or mole.

CHIPOTLE CHILLIES (DRIED): Brown and leathery, dried chipotle chillies (known in Mexico City as '*chipotle meco*') are medium-hot and somewhat smoky, and often used in salsas or *mole poblano*. They are jalapeños when fresh. Available from major supermarkets and Mexican and specialist food suppliers.

CHIPOTLES IN ADOBO SAUCE (CANNED): Canned chipotle chillies are spicier than their dried counterparts, since they are smothered in a sauce that's made from additional chillies (usually anchos). They're a bit fruitier than dried chipotles and freeze very well.

MEXICAN CINNAMON: Also known as true or Ceylon cinnamon, Mexican cinnamon (*Cinnamomum verum*) is much more sharp and flavourful than the cassia bark usually on sale in US supermarkets. But it is the type that's routinely sold in the UK.

CORN HUSKS (DRIED): Dried corn husks are essential in making tamales. The husks are generally sold by Mexican grocery stores and specialist food suppliers in packages of flat, thick, triangular-shaped leaves. I find them difficult to fold and truthfully too manicured for my tastes. I much prefer the stacks of husks sold nestled inside each other in round, rectangular packages, usually also available from the same sources. These rectangular husks have naturally raised edges and are thinner and more papery, which makes them much easier to fold than the flat ones. If you can't find corn husks and are dead set on making tamales, you can use baking parchment instead, but the flavour and shape will not be the same.

CREMA: A lightly acidic cream made from cow's milk, Mexican *crema* is usually used to cool off hot or astringent flavours, particularly in enchiladas, *chilaquiles*, tacos or tostadas. *Crema* is sometimes referred to as 'soured cream' at Mexican restaurants, but that's not exactly accurate, as standard soured cream is much more sour. You may find *crema* at Mexican or Latin American grocery stores, but if you can't find it, you can try making Homemade Crema (page 139) or use soured cream thinned down with a little milk.

EPAZOTE: This pungent herb (*Dysphania ambrosioides*) is so abundant in Mexico City, market vendors often give it to me for free. When fresh, it has an intense medicinal flavour. (Bonus: It also has anti-parasitic properties.) While fresh epazote is much preferred over dried, the fresh variety sold outside of Mexican can taste quite mild. If you get a mild batch – so mild you can use it as salad leaves – if you're using dried, keep adding it to the dish until the flavour becomes noticeable. You should only eat the leaves, not the stems. Look for fresh epazote at Mexican grocery stores; any leftovers can be frozen for future use. Dried epazote is available online.

GUAJILLO CHILLI (DRIED): A medium-hot chilli with a thick, maroon-coloured skin, the versatile guajillo is one of my favourite dried chillies. Once hydrated and blended, it paints anything it touches a deep red colour, and the flavour is subtle and slightly herbaceous. The guajillo is wonderful in table salsas, adobos, moles and marinades. Be careful when buying them, though – I've seen some grocery stores mislabel chilli colorados as guajillos. Colorados are sweeter, longer in length and have a lighter, shinier, more berry-coloured skin. A true guajillo will have a rounded tip and thick, dark-red matt skin, and it will taste slightly more acidic and complex.

HABANERO CHILLI (FRESH): A small, extremely hot chilli, the habanero is perhaps the hottest fresh chilli found in Mexico. It's very popular in Yucatecan cooking and in the occasional table salsa in Mexico City. You can find it at most Mexican grocery stores and online from chilli producers. A Scotch bonnet chilli is an acceptable substitute, although it won't have the same floral perfume as the habanero.

JALAPEÑO CHILLI: Jalapeños in Mexico City are also known as *cuaresmeños*, although they're called jalapeños in other areas of the country, including Xalapa, Veracruz, where the chilli originates. (If you have an opportunity to eat the amazing jalapeños of Xalapa, by all means do it!) Sadly, jalapeños outside Mexico often lack flavour. I'd recommend substituting serranos in cases where you want more heat.

LARD: Mexicans have used lard to fry and *guisar* (stew) for generations, and it's still extremely common. I use it with abandon in this book because it produces the best flavour. The lard I'm referring to is either white or a very light brown in colour and freshly rendered, often sold in plastic containers at Mexican grocery stores or available from quality butchers. Avoid the standard hard, hydrogenated blocks of lard sold at supermarkets, which are tasteless.

MASA HARINA: This is my catch-all term for dehydrated, nixtamalised corn flour, meaning that the corn has been soaked and cooked in an alkaline solution such as limewater. Fresh masa tastes better every time, but reconstituting this flour with water will offer an acceptable substitute. This flour is sold under several brand names including Maseca, Minsa and Quaker, available from Mexican and specialist food stores and suppliers. It's important to note that masa made with dehydrated flour will not be as flexible and soft as true masa. If you're making *tlacoyos* or *huaraches* or any other masa snacks – or tamales – it's worth seeking out real masa made from freshly ground, nixtamalised corn. Cornmeal or standard cornflour should not be substituted.

MORITA CHILLI (DRIED): This small, hot, very wrinkled chipotle chilli has a smoky flavour, with slightly fruity undertones. Moritas have more bite than the standard chipotle meco, so they work wonderfully in table salsas. If they're too brittle to slice open and remove the seeds, try softening them on a *comal* or in a non-stick frying pan first. Available from Mexican and specialist food suppliers.

MULATO CHILLI (DRIED): The mulato – a large, flat, dark-purple dried chilli – is used most often in moles or meat sauces. It's medium hot and smells raisiny and prune-like. You can find mulatos at most Mexican grocery stores or specialist food suppliers online.

NOPAL: Nopal refers to the prickly pear cactus paddle, which is sold either with spines or (if you're lucky) already cleaned at Mexican grocery stores. Cactus has a natural slime, but it's reportedly very nutritious. If you hate the slime, dice the cactus and cook on the hob until tender, then increase the heat and reduce until the slime has evaporated.

ONION, WHITE: All of my recipes call for white onion, unless explicitly stated. They're sharper tasting than yellow onions and the traditional aromatic in Mexican cooking.

MEXICAN OREGANO: Used in soups, marinades, *guisados* and more, Mexican oregano (*Lippia berlandieri Schauer*) isn't related to the sharper, spicier, more familiar Mediterranean oregano. Several states in Mexico actually have their own varieties of oregano, and several sub-varieties. You can find it at Mexican grocery stores or online.

PASILLA CHILLI (DRIED): This long, skinny, dark chocolate-coloured chilli is medium spicy, with a slightly sweet and faintly tobacco-ish aroma. The pasilla is a chilaca chilli when fresh; when dried, it is most often used in moles, adobos, salsas and soups. You get it from Mexican and specialist food stores and suppliers.

POBLANO CHILLI (FRESH): A large, fresh chilli, the dark-green poblano is most often used either stuffed or roasted and cut into strips called *rajas*. The poblanos in Mexico tend to be more flavourful and hotter than those found elsewhere. At their peak in the late summer and early autumn months, they're peppery and buttery, and a natural complement to ingredients like cheese and cream. You may see them labelled in some Mexican grocery stores as 'fresh pasilla'.

QUESO FRESCO: The words 'queso fresco' in my recipes refer to a fresh, white cheese, lightly salty and creamy, available from Mexican grocery stores or online suppliers. Don't buy Colombian cheese as a substitute if you see it at a Latin or South American grocery store – it's much saltier.

QUESO AÑEJO: A catch-all term for a hard, aged cow's milk cheese, queso añejo is most often crumbled onto tacos, enchiladas and more. It may be difficult to find, although some Mexican grocery stores sell a salty, slightly aged cheese they call Cotija (which unfortunately I can't recommend, having tasted the real Cotija from Michoacán). Substituting another aged cheese such as ricotta salata or Pecorino Romano works.

SALT: I use coarse-ground salt because I prefer the flavour over ordinary table salt. To substitute table salt, which is saltier, start out with less than what's called for in the recipe.

SERRANO CHILLI (FRESH): The dark-green serrano is hotter than a jalapeño, but not as hot as a fresh árbol chilli. Its bright, grassy flavour is just about perfect in seafood dishes, stews, sauces and salsas. The serranos available outside Mexico can be larger than they are in Mexico. I much prefer their flavour over the sometimes less-hot jalapeño.

MEXICAN SQUASH: A plump variety of courgette with mottled, greenish-grey skin (sometimes called 'grey zucchini'), Mexican squash may be found at Mexican grocery stores, but standard dark-green courgettes are a fine substitute.

TOMATOES: Tomatoes, both fresh and cooked, are a staple in Mexican cooking. All the tomatoes I use in this book, unless specifically noted, are rectangular plum tomatoes, usually the Italian or Roma variety. That said, if the recipe calls for raw tomatoes, it's worth seeking out the best, freshest tomatoes you can find. If locating fresh, ripe tomatoes isn't possible, particularly during the winter, canned or cherry tomatoes are an acceptable substitute.

TOMATILLOS: Related to the Cape gooseberry, these small, acidic fruits are wrapped in a papery husk. Look for them at Latin American food stores and select supermarkets.

TORTILLAS: I use the standard-sized corn tortillas sold by most Mexican grocery stores and online suppliers, measuring 14–15cm in diameter. If using smaller tortillas, adjust your portion sizes accordingly.

ESSENTIAL EQUIPMENT

To make the recipes in this book, you'll need a few items that you may not already own.
Buy from good kitchenware stores or suppliers, or Mexican grocery stores or online suppliers.

BLENDER: The blender is the workhorse of the Mexican kitchen, used to make table salsas, meat sauces, moles, adobos and more. It replaces the much older-school *molcajete* (lava rock mortar and pestle) and *metate* (sloped lava rock tablet and rolling pin), both of which still produce excellent food, but take much longer to do so. Tip: If you're loading the blender with hot food or sauce, place kitchen paper over the lid and press down firmly to hold the lid in place. Otherwise the top may pop off and you'll find yourself with sauce all over the ceiling.

COMAL: A round, thin sheet of metal or clay, the *comal* conducts an insane amount of heat, which means it's perfect for lightly charring tomatoes for salsas, toasting garlic or warming several tortillas at a time. A non-stick frying pan is a more or less acceptable substitute, but if you think you may be cooking Mexican recipes more than once, a *comal* is worth the modest investment.

LARGE PANS: Many of the recipes in this book call for boiling a kilogram or more of meat at a time, and some call for cooking large cuts of meat slowly in lard. It's helpful to have at least one large, heavy-based (at least 11.5-litre) pan to be able to cook the dishes such as Carnitas (page 38), Turkey Tortas (page 48), Pozole (page 65) and Mole (page 124). Particularly with mole, a heavier pan is essential, otherwise the mole will stick and burn.

SPICE GRINDER: An electric spice grinder, or a coffee grinder, comes in very handy when making mole, or other sauces or marinades that call for grinding a large number of spices and nuts. For smaller quantities, or times when your sauce may not need to be so velvety smooth, a mortar and pestle work just fine.

SIEVE: A fine-mesh sieve – preferably a large, deep one – is essential for straining the pesky seeds and skin out of tomato sauces; making moles and adobos velvety smooth; straining coffee grounds out of Café de Olla (page 61); or even for straining out big pineapple chunks from your Tepache (page 63).

TORTILLA PRESS: Unless you're already skilled at patting out tortillas by hand, it's necessary to have a tortilla press on hand to flatten your tortillas to an acceptable thinness. Your other option would be two sheets of shopping-bag plastic and a rolling pin, although tortillas made this way may not come out perfectly circular.

CHAPTER 1

ON THE STREETS

My love for the street food of Mexico City bloomed out of necessity. It was 2009, my second week in town, and as I made my way along the pavements, I found myself growing progressively weak, my growling stomach about to chomp through my intestines. My health-conscious American gringa side – the same side that had enrolled in fitness bootcamps for two years – told me to buy a granola bar at a convenience store. But I didn't want a granola bar. Not when I had fried meat smells coming at me from all directions. I found a taco stand, bought something with meat, drizzled it with salsa and wolfed it down, ignoring the inner voice that warned I'd regret it.

Now, I still eat on the street at least once a week when I'm in Mexico. I love the sense of community and ritual involved, and the feeling of comfort amid the chaos of the streets. Upon arrival, customers always say 'Buenos días' or 'Buenas tardes'. Folks who are about to leave tell the others to enjoy their meal – *provecho* – while the remaining eaters chorus back 'Gracias!' (I have several times choked down bites of taco just to say 'Gracias!') Most street stalls offer small comforts: plastic overturned buckets or stools to sit on – old ladies always get first dibs – and if not napkins, squares of grey paper to wipe your hands.

Street food breaches many of Mexico City's socio-economic boundaries, but there's a general conception that it's not fit for the wealthy class. Foreigners aren't prone to wandering the city's blue-collar neighbourhoods, so it may seem a little strange to *chilangos* that my favourite place to walk and observe is Calle López, a dirty, pothole-ridden street about a block west of Eje Central. The area is technically considered the Centro Histórico, but it is not the Centro Histórico frequented by tourists. Crumbling Art Deco apartment buildings share the landscape with dozens of raw chicken vendors and small kitchens selling cheap home-style cuisine. There is an egg shop, a *tortillería*, a handful of taco stands, a market and some kitchen stores.

The upmarket Mercado San Juan, where Mexico City's top chefs buy their groceries, lies just down the street.

Calle López doesn't really wake up until 10am, when the *fondas* begin emitting cooking smells, and pots of chicken stock and deep-red sauces bubble on stoves. Women from far-flung pueblos in the State of Mexico arrive and lay down their edible merchandise on the pavement, squeezing into an uneven space next to a row of parked cars. During lunch hour, it's nearly impossible to walk freely. Across from the San Juan Arcos de Belén Market, petite pavement delis offer tortillas, cooked vegetable *guisados* and produce trucked in from local farms. A woman with grey plaits tied with a black ribbon hand-pats tortillas and *tlacoyos*, and lays them gently on the *comal,* while another woman further down the block stands in front of a clay cauldron of rust-red chorizo, spooning it into corn tortillas.

The largest street food stalls in the neighbourhood lie at the head of Calle López and a narrower street named Aranda. By 2pm, this area – essentially a large patch of concrete, shaded by plastic tarpaulins –

blares full blast. Horns shriek and tubas thump from an unseen radio. A man's loudspeaker voice declares that one herbal supplement will solve all your health woes. A breeze lifts the air from the sewers, mixes in odours of grease and coriander, and tosses the cocktail up your nose.

Many of the pavement stalls on Calle López are staffed by women. I have tried to get to know them, but many are suspicious of people asking too many questions. Then one afternoon, Maria Luisa Gonzalez, a stout, middle-aged woman with a thick black plait and the standard female street vendor's chequered smock, opened up to me. She's staffed her pavement stall for six years; someone from her town has held the location for more than 50.

Gonzalez sells homemade foods prepared by her sister, arranging bowls of cactus and broad bean salads, stewed greens, platters of *chiles rellenos*, cauliflower fritters and homemade blue and white corn tortillas. Like other vendors in this area, she does not live in the neighbourhood; she lives in San Francisco Xochicuautla, located about halfway between Mexico City and Toluca. She wakes up at 4am every day to make it to the stall by 9.30am.

Mexico City officials have tried to clean up parts of the Centro, sweeping away the street vendors near the Zócalo, or public square, and even bringing in police with plastic riot shields to prevent any sellers from coming back. But the Calle López vendors remain, mostly undisturbed.

One vegetable stall near the corner of López and Delicias looks like it hasn't changed in 50 years. A table barely larger than a TV tray displays items of food as if they were jewels. Twenty-carat-sized habaneros sit next to a bundle of six serrano chillies, a pyramid of three thin-skinned criollo avocados and one lonely bunch of herbs. The woman who operates the stall never greets me when I walk by and stare. She knows my favourite thing to do is look.

TORTILLAS DE MAÍZ
HOMEMADE CORN TORTILLAS

In one of my first cooking classes in Mexico City, we students crowded around a *comal*, watching our baby tortillas puff up into starchy yellow bubbles.

Someone said, 'Mira, se infló! Ya te puedes casar.' (Look it inflated! Now you can get married.)

It was a joke, an old wives' tale, but the implication stuck with me: tortillas were an important part of the Mexican diet, but how you make them, your skill, mattered too.

As a gringa learning how to make Mexican food in Mexico, I could not ignore the tortilla, even if I was happily married. I studied the history of corn and spent two and a half hours in class grinding my own masa on the *metate*, an ancient lava-rock tablet and rolling pin. I took extra tortilla-making classes, and befriended a lovely woman who ran a *tortillería* in the Centro Histórico. She didn't mind when I peppered her with questions about where the corn and the masa came from, and how the tortilla machine worked.

In urban Mexico City, the tradition of making corn tortillas has not changed much in at least a few hundred years. The dough is ground by volcanic stone in corn mills now, not by women hunched over a *metate*, but it is still ground fresh daily. (Although fluctuating corn prices mean that many *tortillerías* now used dried nixtamalised corn flour instead of fresh corn.) Every day around 1 or 2pm, people queue up to buy their portion, clutching tea towels to wrap their tortillas and take them home.

Since corn and masa are so integral to the Mexican diet – they've been eaten for millennia – it's worth it to make your own fresh masa at least once in your life, just to witness the journey from kernel to dough. You can find dried corn for making tortillas online (don't use popcorn or dried sweetcorn!), or you can buy some in Mexico and bring it back in your suitcase.

To grind the corn at home, I like a tabletop electric mill such as the Nixtamatic, which is designed specifically for nixtamal. Unfortunately, it's currently only sold in Mexico. An alternative option is to use a hand-cranked mill designed specifically for wet-grinding corn, such as the Victorio model (sold online). You may need to pass the masa through a few times to reach the desired smooth texture.

As someone who's made dozens of sticky, too-thick, too-thin, burnt, raw, dry and gummy tortillas, I can definitively say that there is no magical set of instructions that will get you perfect tortillas every time. A steady, hot heat is important, as is well-kneaded, hydrated masa. But I still stand over the *comal* with a furrowed brow, willing the tortillas to puff up. Sometimes they don't and that's okay. This is a lifelong journey – for Mexicans and anyone seeking to truly understand their cuisine.

HACIENDO TORTILLAS
MAKING TORTILLAS

175g masa harina or 450g tortilla masa, ground from
    fresh nixtamal (page 25)
270ml warm water

1   If using masa harina, place in a large, deep bowl and slowly add the water. Knead for about 3 minutes until you have a moist, cohesive dough that cleanly pulls away from the bowl and no longer feels sticky or thin. To test whether the masa is adequately hydrated, grab a piece, roll it into a ball and flatten it. If the sides crack, the masa needs more water. The final texture should be slightly damp, like cold clay. Once the masa is ready, cover it with a damp tea towel and leave to rest for 15 minutes, which will result in a softer, more pliable dough.

2   If using fresh tortilla masa, sprinkle a little water, a tablespoon at a time, onto the masa and knead firmly until soft and pliable. You should need 60ml water at the most, depending on how dry and crumbly the masa is.

3   Heat a *comal* or non-stick frying pan to medium-low.

4   Break off a knob of masa and roll it into a smooth ball, about the size of a golf ball. Cover the rest of the dough with a damp tea towel.

5   Flatten the dough ball between your palms, so it's about 1cm thick. Place on one side of a tortilla press lined with square sheets of plastic (these can be cut from plain shopping bags, but avoid those with lettering or illustration, as the colouring could leach onto the tortillas). Make sure the dough circle sits smoothly between the plastic sheets, then close the press. Push down the lever. (See photos on page 24.)

6   Open the press and rotate the tortilla a quarter-turn, keeping the sheets intact. Close and push down on the lever again. Continue to rotate the tortilla until it's evenly pressed into a round about 3mm thick. (If you have a heavy press that will make a thin, even tortilla every time, you can skip the rotating routine.)

7   Open the tortilla press and peel back the top plastic sheet. Place the tortilla face down in your open palm so that about half of it sits in the centre of your hand, the other half hanging

off. Gently peel back the remaining plastic sheet. The dough should not stick to the plastic or your hands. If it does, you've added too much water and need to begin again. (See 'Troubleshooting Homemade Corn Tortillas' on page 24.)

8   Thicker tortillas will be easy to place on the *comal*. Tortillas made with fresh masa, however, take some practice. With half the tortilla resting in your open palm, and the other half hanging off the side, stand over the *comal* and slowly move your hand in a horizontal fashion, spreading the tortilla so that the underside hits the *comal* first.

9   Flip – with a heatproof spatula or your calloused fingers – as soon as the outer edges of the tortilla start to darken and look less moist, after about 45 seconds. The tortilla should have some dark-brown freckles at this point. If it doesn't, increase the heat. Or if it's blackened, reduce the heat.

10   Flip the tortilla again as soon as small air bubbles start to appear on the freckled surface, after about 35 seconds. At this point, after the second flip, the tortilla might inflate. Cook the tortilla for a further 25 seconds, and then push it to the side of the *comal*, away from hot direct heat, and cook for another 25 seconds. Flip once more and cook for a final 45 seconds, for a total of roughly 3 minutes per tortilla, depending on how hot your hob is. Place the tortilla in a tea towel or covered basket to keep warm.

11   Repeat steps 4–10. Serve the tortillas warm and store any leftovers in an airtight container in the fridge for up to a week, or alternatively freeze for longer storage. To reheat, place the defrosted tortillas on a *comal*, or reheat individually on a gas hob.

COOKING TIP: Cal, *the Spanish word for calcium hydroxide, is an alkaline solution needed for nixtamalising corn. In Mexico you can occasionally find it in rock form, but elsewhere it's generally white and powdery, and available online.*

TROUBLESHOOTING HOMEMADE CORN TORTILLAS

Be aware that masa made from masa harina and masa made from fresh nixtamal do not feel the same. Masa composed from dehydrated flour is stiffer and denser; because of that, it is more difficult to press a thin tortilla with masa harina. Just be patient and persistent, and do the best you can.

If you're using masa harina and the resulting dough is too sticky, sprinkle a little more masa harina on top and knead until smooth and moist. Try to make another tortilla and see if it sticks to your hands or the plastic; if it does, you need a bit more.

If you're making your own nixtamal, the kneading may take much longer, 15–20 minutes, to reach the desired soft texture. Grinding your own nixtamal also requires more water, around 240ml for 1.3kg of freshly ground dough.

For tlacoyos or huaraches, you will need to add more water, as they take longer to cook and they'll dry out if not sufficiently hydrated.

The water temperature does matter. When making tortillas with masa harina, warm water results in a more malleable, pliable dough. Cold or room temperature water is fine for fresh masa.

It's impossible to over-knead tortilla dough. So go ahead. Get your aggressions out as you knead, or peacefully stare into the middle distance.

Dividing the masa into individual balls first may dry it out, even if it's sitting under a damp tea towel. Instead I like to knead the masa with damp hands and pull off portions as needed, as they do on the streets.

Most tortillerías in Mexico City do not add salt to their masa, so I don't salt mine either. I don't miss it, particularly since I often add salsa to whatever I'm eating with the tortillas anyway.

The printed instructions on bags of masa harina are not always correct. Using visual and tactile cues is a much more reliable method.

FRESH NIXTAMAL

This makes quite a bit of masa – around 1.3kg – but if making fresh nixtamal is new for you, you'll want to have some leftover dough for use later. I prefer to freeze extra dough in 450g balls, in sealed plastic bags, or, if I have a friend on hand to help, we'll make tortillas or tlacoyos and freeze those. Masa or frozen tortillas should last at least a few months in the freezer, tightly sealed.

1   Pick over the corn carefully, removing any stones or bits of matter.

2   Pour the water into a large saucepan. Add the calcium hydroxide and stir until dissolved. Bring this mixture to a vigorous boil.

3   Stir in the corn, making sure that it does not stick to the base of the pan. Reduce the heat to medium and simmer for 7–10 minutes until the outer skin of the corn barely scrapes off with your fingernail. The corn will still be hard at this point. Do not overcook it, otherwise your masa will be too gummy.

4   Remove from the heat and cover. Leave to stand for at least 6 hours or overnight.

5   The next day, drain the corn. Wash the kernels well, rubbing them between your hands to loosen and discard any errant skins. This may take 5–10 minutes, depending on how many of the skins came loose in the pan.

6   At this point the corn is ready to be ground. (The kernels must be cool or room temperature in order to do so.) Once the corn has been ground into tortilla masa, it must be sufficiently hydrated and kneaded (see 'Troubleshooting Homemade Corn Tortillas' opposite for detailed instructions). Then the masa is ready to be shaped into tortillas.

900g dried corn for making tortillas/masa (see page 25)
2.8 litres cold water
1 tablespoon plus 1 teaspoon powdered food-grade calcium hydroxide, also known as 'pickling lime' or *cal*

SALSA VERDE CRUDA
RAW TOMATILLO SALSA

Green salsas run the gamut on Mexico City streets. They can be boiled, pea green and soupy; they can be charred and thick and flecked with blackened bits of tomatillo. They can also be astonishingly hot, which is why it's always good to ask the street vendor, 'Cuál salsa pica más?' (Which salsa is hotter?) This is my favourite version of all: a raw, acidic, chunky purée that slices through anything fatty; I like to serve it with Slow-cooked Pork (page 38), Crispy Carrot Tacos (page 115), Tlacoyos (page 42), Mexican-style Eggs (page 86) and almost anything else.

9 fresh árbol chillies, or
    4–5 serrano chillies
1 large garlic clove, peeled
275g tomatillos, husked and
    rinsed (see below)
2 tablespoons cold water
55g onion, diced
1 tablespoon chopped coriander,
    or more to taste
juice of ½ large lime, optional
½ teaspoon salt, or more to taste
½ medium Hass avocado,
    peeled, optional

1   Chop the chillies and garlic roughly, then place in a blender. Whizz until they are mostly chopped.

2   Cut the tomatillos in half and add to the blender with the water. Whizz until the salsa transforms into a thick, chunky sauce.

3   Pour into a bowl and stir in the onion and coriander. Taste and see if you like it as is, or if you'd prefer more acidity, salt or creaminess. Add the lime juice, if using, and the avocado if desired. Blitz until creamy and taste again for salt if necessary.

4   The salsa (minus the avocado) will keep for about a week in a sealed container in the fridge.

COOKING TIP: *As with every salsa in Mexico, it's really the cook's touch that gives it personality. Feel free to add more water if you want it thinner, and – even though some Mexicans probably wouldn't agree – you can even omit the salt, which creates a brighter, sweeter salsa that's almost like a relish. If you own a powerful blender, no need to chop anything first. Just toss it into the blender jug whole.*

HOW TO BUY AND PREPARE TOMATILLOS

Small tomatillos, occasionally labelled miltomates *in Latin American grocery stores, tend to be more flavourful than the larger ones. In Mexico City cooks generally use the larger tomatillos, known as tomate verde, in sauces and smaller tomatillos in table salsas.*

Choose tomatillos that are firm and not loose in their husks. While bright yellow and hunter-green criollo varieties are available in Mexico, elsewhere around the world the tomatillos should be a light lime-green colour, or perhaps lime green splotched with purple. Avoid tomatillos that look wrinkly or pale and colourless. It's best to buy a bit more than you think you'll need, as you may discard a few later.

To clean, remove the husk and rinse in water to scrub off any dirt. Some cooks in Central Mexico reserve the husks and boil them in water with tequesquite, *a type of salt that grows on the highland lakes which is also traditionally used as a leavening agent for tamales instead of baking powder.*

SALSA ROJA TAQUERA
RED TACO-STAND STYLE SALSA

The best red salsas I've had on the street are a deep, rusty brick colour, and they taste definitively of dried chillies, acid and salt. Most people use a combination of dried árbol chillies – the hottest dried chilli in the markets – and guajillo or cascabel, which paint the salsa a gorgeous deep-red colour. In this simple version, I keep the tomatoes to a minimum and omit onion so that the chillies can shine brighter. It's tongue-swellingly hot, which makes it perfect on just about anything. I've called for eight dried árbol chillies, but you can bump it up to ten for even more fire.

1   Snip off the stems of the chillies and shake out their seeds as best you can. If the chillies are too dry and brittle, warm them slightly on a gently heated *comal* or non-stick frying pan and then remove the seeds. Alternatively, keep the seeds in to make a very hot salsa.

2   Heat the *comal* or frying pan over a low to medium-low heat and place the unpeeled garlic cloves near the edge of the pan, away from direct heat. Turn occasionally for 5–7 minutes until soft and blackened in spots. Peel the garlic cloves once cool enough to handle and set aside in a blender.

3   To toast the chillies, work with one at a time so that they don't burn. Place each chilli near the edge of the pan – again, away from the hottest part of the pan – and turn constantly for 5–10 seconds, pressing any wrinkled or folded spots lightly so that all parts of the chilli skin come into contact with the pan. They are done when the colour lightens up in spots and they emit a spicy aroma. (This is a very quick process!) Remove all toasted chillies to a separate bowl and cover with water. Leave to soak for 15 minutes or until the skins are soft. Drain, reserving the soaking water.

4   While the chillies soak, heat the *comal* or frying pan to medium or medium-high. Cook the whole tomatoes, turning often with tongs, until soft and blackened in spots. Transfer to a bowl and set aside.

5   Add the hydrated chillies to the blender (with the garlic), with 2 tablespoons of the reserved chilli water and a generous 60ml water. Blend until smooth. Add the tomatoes and another 2 tablespoons water, plus ¾ teaspoon salt. Blend again, adding more water and salt if desired. (Note that the saltiness will mute when the still-warm salsa cools.) Serve at room temperature.

8–10 dried árbol chillies
2 guajillo chillies
3 medium garlic cloves, unpeeled
2 ripe plum tomatoes
salt

COOKING TIP: *Just make sure you choose real guajillos and not, as can occasionally happen, colorados mislabelled as guajillos. The thinner-skinned colorados will make the salsa taste too sweet, and the colour won't be as deep red; see page 12 in the Ingredients section.*

Whether you use a blender or a molcajete (a lava-rock mortar and pestle), it's easy to start creating your own homemade salsas. Salsas are generally comprised of four things:

- *Dried or fresh chillies*
- *Aromatics, such as garlic or onion*
- *Acids, such as tomatoes, tomatillos or lime juice*
- *Salt*

All of these items, save for the salt of course, can be prepared in the following ways: roasted on a comal or in a non-stick frying pan, boiled or used raw. At that point they can be chopped, mashed in a molcajete or blended. The combinations are endless, particularly when you start adding in things like fresh herbs, peanuts or other native Mexican ingredients like xoconostles (sour cactus fruit) or guaje seeds.

Here are some more guidelines to follow:

- *Taste as you go, so you can see how the flavours stack up along the way.*

- *Good salsa needs salt. If your batch of salsa lacks oomph, add a hefty pinch of salt and taste again.*

- *Warm ingredients amplify the saltiness. You have to wait until a salsa reaches room temperature to truly know what it tastes like.*

- *Good salsa needs acid. So you've salted it, but it's still flat and boring. Does it need lime juice? Maybe a splash of vinegar?*

- *If you lack a high-powered blender, blend garlic or onion and chillies first. This helps you control the texture later on, particularly if you're creating a salsa with chunky bits of tomatoes or tomatillos, which break down quickly in a blender. Likewise, if you're working in a molcajete, mash the aromatics first – they'll break down the easiest, and they'll impart a flavourful coating for the later ingredients.*

SALSA DE CHILE DE ÁRBOL CON CACAHUATE
ÁRBOL CHILLI AND PEANUT SALSA

Peanut salsas aren't exactly common on the street, but you can find them at the more creative stalls and taquerías. With so much competition, a taco stand truly is only as good as its salsas. The fried peanuts in this salsa lend a silky texture, backed up by a killer combo of fried garlic and vinegar. It's great on any taco, roasted vegetables, eggs, potatoes or dipped with homemade tortilla chips. This salsa is hottest when eaten within a few days. After that, the flavour mellows considerably.

1   Heat the oil in a medium frying pan over a medium-low heat. Fry the árbol chillies first, turning often with tongs, for 1–3 minutes until they soften, toast and start to release a spicy aroma, trying not to burn them so that they don't impart a bitter flavour. Remove to a bowl and then fry the guajillos, cooking until the skin puffs up, shines and brightens in colour. Transfer to the same bowl.

2   Fry the peanuts in the same pan, stirring constantly, for 3–4 minutes until they toast to an even golden brown on all sides. (If you notice them start to burn or blacken in spots, reduce the heat.) Transfer to the same bowl as the chillies.

3   Increase the heat to medium. Fry the garlic cloves in the same pan until blistered and dark golden on all sides. Transfer to the bowl.

4   Cut the chillies into smaller pieces. Put the chilli mixture in a blender, discarding any leftover oil. Add the water, salt and vinegar. Blend on high for at least 2–3 minutes until very smooth and silky. Serve at room temperature. Refrigerate any leftovers in an airtight container.

2 tablespoons rapeseed oil
10 dried árbol chillies, de-stemmed and deseeded
7 guajillo chillies, de-stemmed and deseeded
2 tablespoons raw unsalted peanuts
2 medium garlic cloves, peeled
330ml water
2½ teaspoons salt
3–4 teaspoons cider vinegar, or more to taste

CEBOLLAS ENCURTIDAS
PICKLED ONIONS AND HABANERO

Pickled onions are a must-have condiment on any street taco, although they're probably best known at the tacos de canasta *stalls and Yucatecan-style* fondas *that serve* cochinita pibil *(page 121). The power duo of habaneros and vinegar marries perfectly with anything greasy, while the raw onion adds crunch. Another bonus: they don't take long to make. This tastes best if left in the fridge overnight before eating. You can store these for at least a week.*

1   Slice the onion into slivers, place in a medium bowl and cover with boiling water. Leave to soak for 10 minutes, then drain.

2   Return the onions to the bowl and add the remaining ingredients. Cover with an airtight lid and leave to sit for at least 2 hours or, even better, overnight before serving.

COOKING TIPS: *Feel free to add more habaneros if you want more heat, or substitute the larger Scotch bonnet chilli if you can't find them. Just don't touch your eyes, nose or mouth after handling.*

1 medium onion
120ml distilled white vinegar
2 large habanero chillies, de-stemmed, deseeded and sliced into slivers
½ teaspoon dried thyme
¼ teaspoon dried Mexican oregano
1 teaspoon salt
⅛ teaspoon ground black pepper

QUESADILLAS DE HONGOS
MUSHROOM QUESADILLAS

Mushrooms stewed in garlic, chilli and epazote are a fixture at the tlacoyo and quesadilla stalls that set up along city pavements. The vendors, most often women, make their stews – also known as guisados – the day before at their homes, and then bring them to work in plastic containers. The food sells out most often around 4pm. The epazote in this recipe is key. The bitter herb, which grows like a weed in Mexico City (you sometimes actually see it sprouting from pavements), has a distinct flavour that for me encapsulates Central Mexican cooking. Serve these with a salsa of your choice.

450g chestnut mushrooms
2 medium garlic cloves, very finely chopped
1 serrano chilli, very finely chopped with seeds
2 tablespoons olive oil
¼ large onion, chopped
¼ teaspoon salt
4 tablespoons chopped epazote leaves
115–225g Monterey Jack or other mild, meltable cheese, grated
8–12 corn tortillas

COOKING TIPS: *The epazote I've bought in New York tends to be less pungent than the Mexican variety, so I've added quite a bit here. I've also browned the mushrooms, something the vendors don't normally do, as they make their fillings the night before.*

1   Rub any dirt from the mushrooms with damp kitchen paper. Do not discard the stems. Slice the mushrooms into 3mm pieces.

2   Mix the garlic and chilli together in a small bowl and set aside.

3   Heat 1 tablespoon of the oil in a large, deep frying pan to medium-high. Cook half the onion for about 3 minutes until translucent. Add half the garlic and chilli mixture and cook, stirring constantly, for about 1 minute until aromatic and slightly soft.

4   Stir in half the mushrooms, tossing in the oil to coat. Reduce the heat slightly so that the garlic doesn't burn and cook, undisturbed, for at least 2 minutes until the mushrooms begin to release their juices. Increase the heat to high and cook for 4–5 minutes until the mushrooms turn a darker golden brown on one side. Carefully stir and cook until both sides are evenly browned and most of the moisture has evaporated.

5   Stir in half the salt and epazote, then transfer the mixture to a bowl while you cook the second batch.

6   Create a work space near the hob with the mushrooms, cheese and tortillas at the ready. Warm a large (25–28cm) *comal* or non-stick frying pan over a medium heat. Line with three tortillas. Heat the tortillas, flipping perhaps three or four times, until soft and pliable. Transfer to your work space.

7   Place 3–4 tablespoons of the cheese on one side of the tortilla, plus about 2 heaped tablespoons of the mushrooms. Fold over into a half-moon shape and return each quesadilla to the *comal* or frying pan with the cheese side closest to the heat. Press down on each with a heatproof spatula for about 10 seconds so that they stay closed.

8   Flip the quesadillas after about 2–3 minutes once the underside has turned slightly crispy and freckled in parts. (If they burn, turn the heat down slightly; conversely, if they are still limp after 3–4 minutes, turn the heat up.) Cook for about 4 minutes in total until crisp and melty. Tip: If the pan is very hot, move the quesadillas after the initial few flips to the outer edges, away from direct heat.

9   Serve immediately, or transfer to the oven, warmed at the lowest setting, until all the quesadillas have been cooked.

HUITLACOCHE QUESADILLAS
CORN SMUT QUESADILLAS

Huitlacoche (wheat-lah-COE-chay) is the Nahuatl-derived word for the puffy, purplish-blue fungus that grows on top of corn. It's widely eaten in Mexico City and the surrounding states, where it's most often spooned into quesadillas or crêpes. Huitlacoche is at its peak during the rainy season (June to September), when suddenly buckets of it pop up in local markets. The best kind is light in colour and free of any black mould. The flavour mixes the earthiness of mushrooms with the slight sweetness of sweetcorn. Serve these with a salsa of your choice. The cheese is up to you as well – in Mexico I use Chihuahua, which is mild and melty, but outside of the country good-quality Chihuahua cheese may be hard to find. Monterey Jack makes a good substitute.

1   Heat the oil in a medium frying pan over a medium-high heat. Add the onion and cook for about 3 minutes until translucent. Add the garlic and chilli and cook for about 1 minute until the garlic starts to release its aromas.

2   Stir in the sweetcorn, huitlacoche, 120ml water and salt to taste. Reduce the heat slightly, cover and cook, stirring occasionally, for about 10 minutes until the corn and huiltacoche are both tender. If the corn is not tender and all the liquid has evaporated, add more water and keep cooking. (Alternatively, if the corn is tender and the mixture appears soupy, increase the heat to high and reduce the liquid.) Add more salt to taste and remove from the heat.

3   Heat a large, heavy-based frying pan or *comal* over a medium heat. Place a plate and the cheese nearby. Warm a few tortillas at a time, depending on the size of your pan, until soft and pliable. Remove to the plate and place about 4 tablespoons of the cheese on one side of each tortilla, and add 2 heaped tablespoons of filling to each. Fold over into a half-moon shape and return to the hot pan. Press down for perhaps 20 seconds with the underside of a spatula (or your hand) until each quesadilla keeps its shape. Cook, flipping three or four times, for about 4–5 minutes until both sides are lightly crisp – I actually like mine very crisp – and the cheese is oozy. If the pan is very hot, move the quesadillas after the initial few flips to the outer edges, away from direct heat.

4   Repeat with the remaining tortillas, cheese and filling.

5   Serve straight away, or transfer to the oven, warmed at the lowest setting, until all the quesadillas have been cooked.

3 teaspoons rapeseed oil

85g onion, chopped

1 large garlic clove, very finely chopped

½–1 serrano chilli, very finely chopped with seeds

165g fresh sweetcorn kernels

450g fresh huitlacoche (see Tip)

12 corn tortillas

115–225g Monterey Jack or Chihuahua cheese, grated

salt

COOKING TIP: *Fresh huitlacoche is still rare outside Mexico. Musky, gloppy canned huitlacoche tastes nothing like the real thing, so please don't use it as a substitute. Higher-quality huitlacoche in jars is just starting to enter the gourmet food market (available online) and is a more flavourful option, if you don't have access to fresh.*

CHICKEN TINGA
CHICKEN IN CHIPOTLE-TOMATO SAUCE

This is another one of those classic guisados, *or stewed mixtures, sold at local quesadilla and* tlacoyo *stalls. Shredded chicken is simmered in a light tomato sauce with a touch of smoky chipotle. Usually it's served in a warm, freshly made corn tortilla, with or without cheese. The dish originated in the state of Puebla, but it's become popular in Mexico City and the surrounding states. I've included a tostada version here, which is a bit more fun to eat. Of course, a warm corn tortilla works just as well too.*

1   Remove any excess fat from the chicken, including the skin. Place in a large, heavy-based pan and just cover with cold water. Add the onion, bay leaf and garlic and bring to the boil. Reduce the heat to its lowest setting, cover and simmer for about 25 minutes or until the chicken is thoroughly cooked. Remove from the pan and leave to cool. Shred into pieces with your fingers. Strain the broth, reserving 240ml, and freeze the rest.

2   Make the sauce. If using fresh tomatoes, cut in half and remove the seeds, then roughly chop. If using canned tomatoes, drain them well, then pulse in a food processor into coarse, chunky pieces. Drain again if they're very juicy.

3   Heat the oil in a large frying pan over a medium-high heat. When hot, add the onion and cook for 3–5 minutes until soft and translucent. Stir in the garlic and cook for 30 seconds–1 minute until aromatic. Add the tomatoes, cooking for about 5 minutes if using fresh (you want a thick, chunky paste) or about 3 minutes for canned to allow the flavours to meld, stirring occasionally.

4   Stir in the shredded chicken, chipotle and adobo sauce, oregano, the chicken stock or 60ml of the reserved broth (see step 1) and ½ teaspoon salt. (If using fresh tomatoes, you'll need to add more than 60ml liquid so that the *tinga* doesn't stick to the base of the pan as it cooks. The ideal texture should be juicy, but not soupy.)

5   The chipotle should be noticeable but not too punchy. Taste and add more if necessary. Bring to the boil, then reduce the heat, cover and simmer for about 10 minutes. Uncover and add salt to taste. If the *tinga* still looks soupy, increase the heat and reduce the juices a bit more.

6   To serve as tostadas, slather a thin layer of crema on each tortilla. (For more amped-up chipotle flavour, mix a little of the adobo sauce into the crema.) Add a few spoonfuls of *tinga*, a slice of white onion and two slivers of avocado to each. Top with the crumbled cheese.

VARIATION: *Oyster mushrooms are a great vegetarian substitution here, although mushroom* tinga *is not necessarily authentic to the streets of Mexico. Prepare the* tinga *the same way, using 450g oyster mushrooms, shredded into strips, and substituting 120ml vegetable stock or water. Leave the lid off while cooking and turn the heat up after about 5 minutes to reduce some of the juices.*

900g bone-in chicken breasts
¼ small onion
1 dried Mexican bay leaf
1 medium garlic clove, unpeeled

For the *tinga* sauce:
6 fresh ripe plum tomatoes, or
    2 × 400g cans whole peeled
    plum tomatoes
1 tablespoon rapeseed oil
190g onion, chopped
1 medium garlic clove, very finely
    chopped
2 chipotles in adobo sauce from
    a can, very finely chopped
    with seeds, plus 2 teaspoons
    adobo sauce, or more as
    needed
½ teaspoon dried Mexican
    oregano
60ml Basic Homemade Chicken
    Stock (page 98), plus more if
    needed
480g Homemade Crema
    (page 139)
12 tostadas or tortillas
1 onion, sliced
1 avocado, peeled, stoned and
    sliced
queso añejo or another aged,
    crumbly cheese, crumbled
salt

BASIC SAVOURY COARSE-GROUND MASA FOR TAMALES

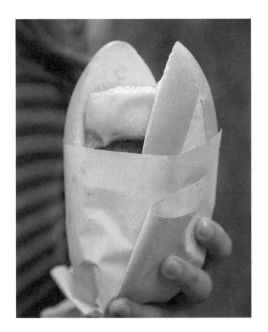

Tamales in Mexico City are notoriously dense with masa, the idea being that such a substantive meal will stave off hunger for hours. Tricycle-riding vendors sell them just as most commuters are making their way to work, from 6 to 10am. The vendors come back out when the sun sets.

Not all street tamales have the same texture. The city's banana-leaf tamales, an influence from the Gulf Coast and Oaxaca, tend to be smoother and firmer and are made with tortilla masa. Steamed corn-husk tamales are made from tamal masa, a coarse-ground masa that's grainier than the tortilla.

For many Mexico City cooks, coarse-ground masa often starts with dried, nixtamalised corn flour, sold by the kilo in neighbourhood markets. Select mills in the city – fewer and fewer, but they still exist – also sell freshly ground nixtamalised corn flour, which feels damp and moist like soil. The latter produces the lightest, fluffiest tamales I've tasted.

Both flours are hydrated with fat (almost always lard) and stock, which adds flavour and makes them puff up like steamed puddings.

For home cooks inexperienced with masa, making a good batch can rely on several factors: the type of fat you use, whether you beat the lard or simply stir it a few times, whether you're using fresh nixtamalised masa or masa harina and how much stock you use for both; and even, some Mexican cooks say, whether you're angry when you're making them, which could lead to half-cooked tamales. (In cooking school, we peeled off strips of corn husk and tied bows on the steamer pan handles so that the pan would be happy and our tamales would turn out nicely.)

All of that said, tamales can also be forgiving, in the sense that they'll nuzzle and steam whatever you place inside them. And as a cooking instructor once told me, 'They should be eaten out of the husk, or else you don't know how to eat tamales.'

This recipe, for a coarse-ground tamal dough, can be used for almost anything you like. Just make sure you incorporate air into the masa. Aerate the lard by beating it thoroughly first, then incorporate more air as you add the moistened masa bit by bit, which will result in a lighter, fluffier tamal. The tamales will be very soft when you remove them from the steamer. Give them about 15 minutes to firm up before serving.

HACIENDO TAMALES
MAKING TAMALES

1   If using masa harina, whisk the flour together with the baking powder and salt in a large, deep mixing bowl. Working first with a spoon or spatula, and then with your hands, gradually add 720ml stock, stirring and then kneading lightly, until all the liquid has been absorbed. Set aside and leave to sit for 10 minutes to allow the liquid to fully soak into the flour. If using fresh masa, moisten the dough with about 60ml stock, and knead well until soft and pliable. Add more liquid only if the masa still seems dry. (You will add the baking powder and salt later.)

2   Meanwhile, in a stand mixer fitted with the paddle attachment, beat the lard on a medium speed for about 5 minutes until it's smooth, glossy and much more aerated.

3   With the stand mixer running on high (or using your hands), incorporate small, golf-ball-sized pieces of masa into the lard a little at a time, mixing well after each addition, until a cohesive, very sticky dough forms. It should look similar to a thick muffin batter. Add more liquid if the dough looks too dry.

4   If using fresh masa, sprinkle the baking powder and salt onto the dough. Mix well for several more minutes, and taste to see if the masa needs more salt. If so, add and keep mixing until a cohesive, very sticky dough forms. The dough should feel rather light. If it's very heavy and dense, add a little more liquid and the extra 25g lard and keep mixing.

5   Store the dough made with masa harina in the fridge, tightly covered, for up to 24 hours. Dough made with fresh masa must be used the very same day or it will turn sour. (Masa harina sucks up liquid quickly, so this dough may need a bit more stock before using it if you've stored it for several hours.)

460g masa harina, or 1.3kg
    fresh tamal masa
2 teaspoons baking powder
½ teaspoon salt, or more to taste
60–720ml room-temperature chicken,
    beef or vegetable stock, depending
    on the type of masa
340g lard, plus 25g if using fresh masa

COOKING TIP: *To test whether the dough is ready to place inside the husk, remove a 2cm piece of masa to a cup of water. If it floats, the masa is ready. If it sinks, you should keep mixing, or perhaps add a bit more lard.*

TAMALES DE RAJAS
ROASTED POBLANO CHILLI TAMALES

In this popular street tamal, stewed strips of jalapeño lie in a bed of savoury corn masa, oozy with cheese and bits of stewed tomato. My version doesn't exactly mimic the street version, which counts on the availability of flavourful tomatoes year round. Instead, I char the tomatoes on the comal, fry the mixture with a good bit of garlic and onion and mix that directly into the masa. It's not exactly traditional, but it captures the spirit of a tamal that stands on its own. If you prefer less heat, you can use poblano chillies (charred, skinned, deseeded and sliced) instead of jalapeños. (Char the jalapeños the same way as poblanos, over an open gas flame.) Serve in the husk, with plenty of salsa.

36 dried corn husks, plus more
    if needed
6 large jalapeño chillies, or 3
    poblano chillies
9 plum tomatoes, roasted on a
    comal or non-stick frying pan
    and set aside to cool, or
    2 × 400g cans chopped
    tomatoes
1 tablespoon olive oil
50g onion, chopped
2 garlic cloves, very finely
    chopped
2 tablespoons chicken or
    vegetable stock
½ teaspoon salt
¼ teaspoon ground black pepper
1 batch Savoury Coarse-Ground
    Masa (page 34)
225g Monterey Jack, or another
    mild, melty cheese, cut into
    3 × 1cm pieces

1   Place the corn husks in a 7.5–11.5-litre pan of warm water to soak, pulling them apart as they soften.

2   Char, deseed and peel the jalapeños (see the panel opposite). Cut the chillies into slivers, toss with a few pinches of salt and set aside.

3   Place the tomatoes in a food processor and pulse until chunky. (If you're using winter tomatoes, you'll want to remove any awful-looking white tomato cores.) Drain through a sieve, tapping the edge to remove the excess juice. Save the juice for another use, such as a Bloody Mary or Michelada, and place the drained tomatoes in a bowl. Set aside.

4   Heat the oil in a large frying pan over a medium heat. When shimmering, add the onion and stir quickly, cooking for 3–4 minutes until translucent and soft but not browned. Add the garlic and stir until aromatic. Pour in the tomatoes, stock, salt and pepper. Bring to the boil, then reduce the heat to medium and cook for 5–7 minutes, stirring occasionally, until the flavours meld. Leave to cool to room temperature, then stir into the masa. At this point, if you made your masa with masa harina, you can reserve the dough for up to 24 hours. Dough made with fresh masa must be used the same day, or it will turn sour.

5   Lift some of the husks out of the pan and shake off the excess water. Arrange a work space with the *rajas* (charred chillies), cheese, masa and moist husks at the ready.

6   The husks will have two ends: one rounded end that curves upwards, almost cup-like, and one thin and pointy. Hold the husk with the rounded end towards you. Add about 4 tablespoons of the masa to the moist husk and spread it, using the underside of the spoon, into a longish rectangle. The rectangle should be wide enough to enclose the filling, once you add it. The masa should come to about 2.5cm from the bottom of the rounded end. As for the pointy-end side, make sure you leave enough room to fold the husk over. It's best to leave at least a forefinger's length of space on that side.

7   Add two or three pieces of the chillies and some cheese. Clutch both sides of the husk and fold them together so that the masa covers the filling like a little empanada. Pay attention to the natural way the husk folds in on itself; one side usually feels more natural as the 'top' fold. The tamal should fold cleanly and securely, and the filling should not drip out. If it does, you've added too much filling. (You can open the husk and add more masa, if so.)

8 Once closed, fold down the narrower end of the corn husk and press along the fold to seal. Ensure that there aren't any holes where masa could seep out during cooking. If there are holes, wrap the *tamal* in another leaf. The finished tamal should look elongated, like a slightly flattened sausage (see page 143 for photos). Set aside on a baking tray and repeat to make about 24 tamales.

9 When you've stuffed and folded all the tamales, add water to the steamer pan and place a coin in the bottom. The coin will rattle when the water starts to boil.

10 Very carefully, using tongs, place the tamales in a loose vertical position in the steamer pan, with the folded sides touching the pan floor. Don't place them too tightly or they won't have room to expand, and they'll turn out too thick and dense. Cover with more husks, then a layer of clingfilm, then the steamer pan lid. If the pan has a side opening for the purpose of adding water, cover that as well, with foil.

11 Steam for 50 minutes–1 hour over a high heat. Listen to the pan occasionally to ensure that the coin keeps rattling. Add more water if the coin is silent, taking extreme care not to dampen the tamales.

12 To check for doneness, remove one tamal and open the husk. If it peels back cleanly, without sticking, the tamal is done. Leave to cool for at least 15 minutes before serving.

COOKING TIP: *If you don't have a 10-litre steamer pan, you can use a stockpot with a heat-proof bowl set over it and a heatproof plate placed snugly on top. It will be difficult to add more water if you use this method, so fill the lower chamber of the 'steamer' with plenty of water.*

HOW TO PROPERLY CHAR POBLANO CHILLIES

In Mexico City, charred poblano chillies – known colloquially as 'rajas', after the shape in which they're cut – jazz up just about everything they touch. Their grassy, buttery notes pair especially well with cheese, eggs and cream.

Poblanos are rarely eaten raw. They are roasted on a comal*, peeled and deseeded, then either stuffed or sliced into strips. The best way to char the chillies is on your hob, if you have a gas one. Here's how to do it:*

Place the chillies directly on top of a gas burner, turning with tongs until blackened in spots. Be careful not to overcook them, or the flesh, once you remove the skin, will turn slimy.

Place in a tea towel – I've found that three or four fit well in the average one – and wrap into a bundle. This forces the chillies to sweat, which makes the skin easier to remove. (Placing them in a plastic bag or even a covered bowl may cause them to overcook; tea towels let them breathe.) Leave for 15–20 minutes.

Working with one chilli at a time, slough off the charred skin with the pads of your fingers. Do not run under water; this removes all the fantastic charred flavour. Use a sharp knife to carefully remove the poblanos' stems and inner seeds. If you are preparing chiles rellenos, *cut an incision from tip to end, leaving about 2.5cm of space at either end. If you are making* rajas, *cut the chillies all the way open, and, using a small spoon or paring knife, remove all the seeds as well as any stringy veins.*

The flesh should still feel somewhat firm, particularly if you're going to cook them later in a guisado or tamal, and retain a dark-green colour. If the flesh is greenish-yellow, the chillies are overcooked.

I don't recommend using an oven to roast poblanos, unless you're roasting dozens at a time. The oven blasts them with too much heat and leaches out the flavour. Likewise with an overhead grill, unless you place the chillies very close to the heat source.

Charring the chillies in a non-stick frying pan or comal *is an option if you don't have access to a gas hob.*

CARNITAS
SLOW-COOKED PORK

I'd been visiting a carnitas *stall in the Colonia Roma for about three years when I finally worked up the courage to ask the owner, Victor Hugo Quiroz Pérez, if he could show me the process from start to finish. He told me to show up at his shop at 6am on a weekday morning. At about 6.30, Quiroz appeared from an apartment building door directly adjacent to the* carnitas *stall: 'Buenos días!'*

We walked inside the dark shop. The glass display cases in the front lay empty, to be filled later with glistening pig parts. Quiroz washed his hands in a small sink and then walked over to a huge metal cauldron, already filled with a pool of caramel-coloured, melted lard, the same lard used to fry yesterday's carnitas. *Once the lard was warm, he put the* vísceras, *or offal, in first; then the shoulder, or* espaldilla.

He took a raw pig's head and carefully sliced the skin off. 'Esta es la máscara,' he said. (This part is the mask.) Using a small blowtorch, he gently burnt off any errant hairs from the thin, limp piece of fat. He whacked the head with a cleaver and prised the two halves apart with his hands. They opened with a loud crack, and he scooped out the soft brains with his fingers, to be used in quesadillas later. (Pig brain quesadillas are a delicacy at carnitas *stalls.) Quiroz placed the butterflied head softly into the lard. The skin, or* cuero, *would be added an hour later, along with the ribs.*

Quiroz learnt the carnitas *trade from his Michoacán-born father, which made sense: most* carnitas *in Mexico City are modelled after those in Michoacán, a state whose capital, Morelia, lies about four hours away by bus. Chilango* carnitas *are almost always prepared in the same manner: the pork is slow-cooked for several hours in lard, then chopped and served in a warm corn tortilla. The only accompaniments are lime juice and a bright, hot salsa.*

Unfortunately I didn't have time to stay until the meat finished cooking, but Quiroz insisted that there was no magic to the recipe, beyond adding in a little garlic, orange juice and salt. He was right. When I made the recipe at home, I was astonished by how good it was and how little hands-on work was involved.

3.2kg lard (see Tip)
3.2kg pork shoulder
7 garlic cloves, peeled
60ml fresh-squeezed orange
    juice, zest of ½ orange
    reserved
2 teaspoons salt
16–20 corn tortillas
lime wedges, for serving
Salsa Verde Cruda (page 26),
    or salsa of choice

1   Melt the lard in a 11.5-litre pan over a medium-low heat.

2   Add the pork, making sure that the meat is covered with the hot fat (cut it into three pieces if need be). Increase the heat and bring to a rapid boil.

3   Reduce the heat to a simmer – the lard should be a bit foamy – and cook for 1½ hours, uncovered. The lard surface should show consistent, small, gentle bubbles; if it doesn't, increase the heat. Conversely, if it bubbles too roughly and begins to crackle, reduce the heat.

4   Meanwhile, mash the garlic in a *molcajete* or mortar with about 1 tablespoon of the orange juice. (Or toss the garlic and 60ml orange juice into a food processor.) Scrape into a small bowl and set aside.

5   After the meat has cooked for 1½ hours, add the garlic paste, the juiced orange half (zest and all) and the salt.

6 Continue simmering another 1½ hours, for a total cook time of about 3½ hours, or until the meat is tender and falls apart when pierced with a fork. (Note: this may take less than 3 hours if using meat in pieces, rather than one large shoulder.)

7 Transfer the meat to a wire rack set over a baking tray to cool. Strain the lard, leave to cool and store in the fridge for future use, such as refrying beans.

8 About 10 minutes before serving, warm the tortillas on a *comal* or non-stick frying pan, then wrap in a tea towel to keep warm.

9 Chop the meat against the grain – don't shred, or else it will become chewy – and serve on a platter, accompanied by the tortillas, lots of lime wedges and the salsa.

COOKING TIP: *You may be tempted to use oil instead of lard, but that would make every* carnitas *vendor in Mexico (and me) weep. If you can't find 3.2kg pork shoulder, you can use less, as long as you use the equal weight of lard.*

QUESADILLAS DE CAMARÓN
PRAWN QUESADILLAS WITH AVOCADO

Quesadillas in Mexico City come in several shapes, sizes and preparations. Many don't contain cheese, to which most people beyond Mexico would respond, 'Well, isn't that just a taco?' Without delving too much into what constitutes a taco versus a quesadilla on Mexico City's streets (the biggest cues are the size and shape of the tortilla), the truth is that this snack – a fried, crackly shell of prawn and creamy avocado – makes you forget cheese and the semantic debate altogether.

This particular version is inspired by one of my favourite street stalls, which, like others, sells variations on popular Gulf Coast dishes: tostadas with fresh seafood, seafood empanadas and caldo de camarón, a spicy, pungent broth made from dried prawns (and a hangover cure). The trick here is to keep the oil hot, or else the tortillas won't be crisp enough. Serve with a tart, vinegary salsa such as Valentina sauce, or the Árbol Chilli and Peanut Salsa (page 29), to cut some of the fat.

1   Place the bay leaf, garlic clove, onion and two pinches of salt in a saucepan of water. Bring to the boil and add the prawns. Cook briefly – about 30 seconds – until the prawns just turn pink and the flesh firms up. (Don't worry about undercooking because you will fry these later.) Discard the aromatics and drain the broth, reserving for future use if desired. Place the prawns in a bowl and toss with ¼ teaspoon salt and the pepper.

2   Place a wire rack on a baking tray in the oven and heat to 120°C/gas mark ½, or the lowest setting on your oven. (For people with crazy-hot ovens, you can preheat the oven to 120°C/gas mark ½, and then turn it off.)

3   Pour the oil into a deep pan and heat to 150–160°C. In a 11.5-litre pan, the oil will come to about 2.5cm high; in a smaller 4-litre pan, perhaps 7.5cm. The oil is ready when a 2cm piece of tortilla dropped into the pan sizzles and turns golden brown within 20–30 seconds. If the tortilla piece turns dark brown, your oil is too hot.

4   While the oil heats, warm three tortillas on a *comal* or non-stick frying pan until soft and easy to fold. (Don't overcrisp them or else they won't fold at all, and the cocktail sticks won't insert correctly.) Place two or three prawns on one side of each tortilla and fold, securing closed with three cocktail sticks: one at each corner and one in the centre.

5   Once the oil is hot enough, add the quesadillas and fry for 2 minutes or less on each side until slightly golden brown, depending on how hot your oil is. Transfer to the wire rack inside the warmed oven. Repeat with the rest of the tortillas and prawns, frying two or three quesadillas at a time, depending on the size of the pan.

6   Once all the quesadillas have been fried, peel and stone the avocado, then cut into about 5mm slices. Cut the rest of the onion into slivers.

7   Leave the quesadillas to cool slightly, then carefully – taking care not to break the shell – remove the cocktail sticks and open each slightly, just wide enough to wedge in four or five slivers of onion and a slice of avocado. Serve immediately with lime and salsa.

1 dried Mexican bay leaf
1 garlic clove, unpeeled
⅛ small onion, the rest sliced
    for garnish
450g raw prawns, peeled and
    deveined
⅛ teaspoon ground white pepper
1–1.4 litres vegetable oil
12 corn tortillas, or more if using
    smaller prawns
1 ripe Haas avocado
salt

To serve
lime wedges
Valentina sauce or other tart,
    spicy salsa

TLACOYOS DE FRIJOL Y REQUESÓN
BEAN AND CHEESE TLACOYOS

Tlacoyos are small, flat patties about the size of your hand, made from corn masa that's been stuffed with mashed beans, requesón *(a salty, spreadable cheese similar to ricotta) or broad (fava) beans, and cooked until crisp on a comal. Once you leave Mexico City,* tlacoyos *take on other shapes and names. In some areas of Puebla, for instance, they're called* tlayoyos.

For a long time, my tlacoyo *dream was to find a mayora – an older, respected Mexican cook – who could teach me how to make them. In 2013, I finally was able to learn with Señora Rosa Peña Sotres, who graciously invited me into her home and spent a full Sunday teaching me patiently how to stuff and fold. 'Ya aprendió!' (You've learnt!), she declared, as I placed a small, misshapen* tlacoyito *on her charcoal-fired comal.*

Patting them out by hand isn't easy if you're a beginner, but you'll get it down with practice. It's fun to gather a group of friends and make them con calma *(Spanish for 'without hurry'), particularly if someone brings the ready-made masa. Don't skimp on the garnishes. If you can't find cactus, which Mexican grocery stores or online suppliers generally stock, try shredded raw cabbage or carrots.*

1 teaspoon lard
¼ small onion, the rest chopped for garnish
1 medium garlic clove, peeled
450g cooked beans (any kind will do), at least 120ml cooking liquid reserved, or 400g can beans, liquid drained and reserved
450g fresh tortilla masa, or 175g masa harina
240–360ml warm water
250g Homemade Requesón (page 64)
460g jar pickled cactus strips, or 4 large cactus paddles, diced (see pages 76 and 146) and blanched in boiling salted water for 3–5 minutes, until just tender
chopped fresh coriander
crumbled queso fresco
salsa of choice
salt

1 Heat the lard in a frying pan over a medium heat. When hot, add the onion wedge and garlic. Fry, turning occasionally, until blistered and deep golden brown.

2 Add the beans and mash roughly using the base of a heatproof cup. You don't want them too pasty and smooth. In Spanish, they call the desired texture *martajada*. Add a little bean liquid if they look too dry. Cook for about 5 minutes until the flavours combine, adding more bean liquid as needed. Season with salt. Transfer to a bowl.

3 If you're using masa harina, place in a deep bowl and pour 240ml of the warm water on top. Knead together for about 5 minutes to form a thick, pliable dough. To check whether the dough is sufficiently moist, break off a small ball and flatten it. If the edges crack, you need more water – up to 120ml. (The masa should be moister than the average tortilla masa, as it will cook longer than a tortilla and shouldn't dry out.) If using fresh tortilla masa, sprinkle with a few drops of water and knead firmly for about 5 minutes, adding the water a teaspoon at a time, until the masa is very soft and creamy. (For fresh masa you will only need perhaps 60ml water in total.) Grab a piece of masa and cover the rest with a damp tea towel to keep it hydrated.

4 Roll the masa into a ball just larger than a golf ball, and using your palm, flatten into a disc about 5mm thick. (You can also place the ball on a tortilla press, but be careful not to press it too thin.) Fresh masa will be much easier to work with than masa harina, but if you're using the latter, keep working and patting, pressing firmly on the masa ball to form a circular shape.

5 Holding the disc in your palm, add 1–2 tablespoons beans or requesón to the centre, spreading the filling into a longish rectangle, without hitting the top or bottom edges. The filling amount really depends on how big your disc is – if the filling spills out when you try to close the *tlacoyo*, you have too much.

6 Fold both sides of the *tlacoyo* towards the centre to enclose the filling. Press the seams together, pinching them closed with your thumbs. Set aside on a baking tray and repeat with the remaining masa and filling.

7 Warm a *comal* or non-stick frying pan over a medium heat. Place the *tlacoyo* in the pan, without oil, and cook until the sides start to dry slightly, then turn it over. If you don't start to see golden-brown freckles, increase the heat; if you see burnt spots, reduce the heat. Keep turning at intervals and cook for about 10–12 minutes in total until both sides are freckled and crisp, and the edges have puffed a bit.

8 Garnish with the cactus, coriander, cheese, salsa and onion. Serve warm.

BURRITOS DE FLOR DE CALABAZA
SQUASH FLOWER BURRITOS

Burritos are much more a Northern Mexican snack than a chilango one, but they're gaining in popularity in Mexico City at bars and small cafés. These are not the burritos generally seen outside Mexico. They are smaller – you can hold them with one hand and the filling will not spill out – and they include ingredients like poblano chillies, avocado, steak and cheese. They contain beans but no rice. This recipe is inspired by my favourite street stall in the Zona Rosa, where my go-to order is squash flowers, cheese and beans with Chilli Morita Salsa.

1 batch Quick Refried Beans
  (see opposite)
1 batch Creamy Chilli Morita
  Salsa (see opposite)
4 large (30cm) flour tortillas
2 tablespoons rapeseed oil
150g onion, chopped
185g chopped plum tomatoes,
  or any other fresh, ripe tomato
30 courgette flowers, stems
  removed and torn in half
115g Chihuahua cheese, or any
  other mild melting cheese,
  grated
salt

1   Prepare the refried beans and chilli morita salsa, and place in bowls on a clean work surface, next to four dinner plates. Place the tortillas near the hob.

2   Heat 1 tablespoon of the oil in a large, heavy-based frying pan. Working in batches, add half the onion and cook for 3–5 minutes until translucent. Add half the tomatoes and season with salt; cook for about 4 minutes until the tomatoes have slightly softened.

3   Meanwhile, warm two flour tortillas on a large griddle or frying pan. Wrap in a tea towel to keep warm.

4   Add half the courgette flowers to the pan, plus a little more salt to taste. Stir and cook for about 3 minutes until the flowers have wilted slightly. Separate the mixture into two long, rectangular-shaped piles. Sprinkle a quarter of the cheese onto each pile, covering the filling evenly. Leave undisturbed for about a minute until the cheese melts.

5   Place the two warm tortillas on plates and smear about 2 tablespoons beans in a rectangular shape that spans the length of each tortilla.

6   Using a spatula, carefully scoop one batch of the cheesy courgette-flower filling onto a bean-smeared tortilla. Repeat with the second tortilla.

7   Add about 2 teaspoons of the salsa to each tortilla and fold the tortilla over itself, tuck in the sides and roll into a burrito.

8   Repeat with the remaining tortillas and filling.

COOKING TIP: *If you can't find courgette flowers, try substituting a vegetable mixture that sounds good to you, like corn, mushrooms and Swiss chard.*

QUICK REFRIED BEANS

Refried beans are used in all sorts of Mexican recipes, and not just as a side dish. I like them in Stuffed Cactus Paddles (page 172) or Squash Flower Huaraches (page 74), or smeared into a tortilla with a little salsa.

1 teaspoon lard
1 small piece onion (about half a 1cm-thick slice)
1 medium garlic clove, peeled
350g cooked beans, preferably black or pinto,plus
   120ml cooking liquid reserved, or 550g canned
   black beans, about half the liquid drained
salt

1   Heat a medium frying pan to a medium-high heat. Add the lard, and when hot, add the onion and garlic. Cook for about 3 minutes until golden and blistered on all sides. Add the beans and bean liquid quickly (the liquid may splatter, so don't get too close), and mash with a masher or the base of a heatproof cup.

2   Stir and keep mashing until the beans form a semi-chunky paste. If there is too much liquid, increase the heat and reduce, stirring often so that the beans don't burn. If the beans look too dry, add more liquid. Cook for 7–10 minutes until the beans start to congeal and pull easily away from the sides and base of the pan. Remove from the heat, season with salt if needed and set aside until ready to use.

CREAMY CHILLI MORITA SALSA

This smoky, creamy salsa goes perfectly with the squash flowers. It shouldn't be too hot, though, or else it will overwhelm their delicate flavours. Any leftovers can be stored in an airtight container in the fridge for up to two days. You can eat it on fish tacos, with quesadillas, pizza (if you're into that) or anything else that calls for a salsa.

2 medium garlic cloves, unpeeled
5 morita chillies
3 tablespoons mayonnaise, thinned with 1 tablespoon
   milk and mixed with a squeeze of lime juice
salt

1   Heat a *comal* or non-stick frying pan to a medium heat and add the garlic at the outer edges, away from direct heat so that they don't burn. Cook for 5–7 minutes until blackened in spots and slightly squishy.

2   Lightly toast the chillies for 30–60 seconds per side until they release their aroma. Transfer to a bowl of hot water and leave to soak for 15–20 minutes or until the skins soften.

3   Remove the chilli stems and slice three of the chillies open to remove the seeds. Place all the chillies in a blender with the lime-accented mayonnaise, 150ml water and ½ teaspoon salt. Blend until smooth. If the salsa is too hot, add more mayonnaise and water. Transfer to a bowl and set aside or refrigerate until ready to use.

TACOS DE CANASTA
STEAMED TACOS

Bike-riding vendors sell these tacos across the city from little baskets that sit above their back wheels. Fished out warm from a nest of paper and cloth, the taco is supremely satisfying – a soft, greasy half-moon filled with refried beans, or mashed and fried potato. In other areas of Mexico they're known as tacos al vapor or tacos sudados.

This dish is not the easiest to make at home, but if you've got a basket, it's a fun activity to do with friends and makes great party food. (I highly recommend making these with friends; it's a lot of work for one person.) You'll need to line the basket with a large cloth, then a layer of sturdy plastic such as shopping bags or a dust sheet and finally a layer of baking parchment, plain packaging paper or newspaper. Only the paper should directly touch the food.

For the potato filling:
900g Yukon Gold or Maris Piper potatoes, rinsed and peeled
25g lard
½ medium onion, cut into 5cm slivers
2 medium garlic cloves, peeled and very finely chopped
1 teaspoon salt

For the bean filling:
20g lard
⅛ medium white onion, chopped
1 garlic clove, peeled
450g dried beans, such as pinto or black, soaked and cooked according to the packet instructions until soft, plus 240ml cooking liquid reserved, or 2 × 400g cans black or pinto beans, liquid drained and reserved
1 teaspoon salt, or more to taste

For the tacos:
140g lard (see Tip)
40 corn tortillas (see Tip)
Pickled Onions and Habanero (page 29)
Raw Tomatillo Salsa (page 26)
Árbol Chilli and Peanut Salsa (page 29)

1   To make the potato filling, place the potatoes in a large saucepan and cover with 5cm cold water. Bring to the boil, then reduce the heat to medium and cover the pan halfway. Simmer for about 45 minutes until very tender and the outer flesh sloughs off slightly. Remove the potatoes from the water to cool, reserving 120ml of the potato water. Once cooled to room temperature, mash the potatoes to a smooth purée with your hands, a potato ricer or a food mill. Set aside.

2   Heat the lard in a large frying pan over a medium heat. When hot, add the onion and cook, stirring constantly, for 2–3 minutes until translucent. Add the garlic and cook until aromatic. Stir in the potatoes, reserved potato water and salt. Once warmed through, remove from the heat and cover to keep warm.

3   To make the bean filling, heat the lard in a large frying pan over a medium-high heat. When hot, add the onion and garlic – they should sizzle when they hit the pan – and fry for 3–5 minutes until golden and blistered on all sides. Add the beans and bean liquid quickly, as they may splatter. Stir in the salt and reduce the heat to medium-low. Mash the beans with a bean masher or the base of a heatproof cup until you have a textured paste. Cook until most of the liquid has been absorbed. If the beans look too dry, add more bean liquid. (The ideal texture should be creamy and soft and perhaps the slightest bit runny.) Season with more salt, if needed. Remove the pan from the heat and set aside. Reserve extra cooking liquid as the beans may dry out the longer they sit.

4   For the tacos, melt 85g of the lard in a small saucepan and keep warm over a very low heat. Nearby, assemble a work space with a pastry brush, the potato filling, bean filling and lined basket.

5   Warm the tortillas two or three at a time on a *comal* or in a non-stick frying pan heated to medium until soft and pliable. Don't overheat, otherwise they will be too crispy to fold. Keep warm in a tea towel or tortilla warmer.

6 Place 2–3 tablespoons filling on one half of a tortilla. Fold and brush with the warm melted lard, then pat down slightly so that the taco lays flat. Place in the basket, the edges of each taco overlapping slightly. Repeat until you have an even layer, brush with lard again, then stack another layer on top, brushing each layer with more lard. (It's helpful to assign one filling to a specific side of the basket so that you know what you're getting when you reach in later.)

7 Once all the tacos have been prepared, heat the remaining 55g lard over a high heat. When smoking, after about a minute, quickly pour on top of the tacos. They should sizzle. Wrap tightly with the layers of paper, plastic and cloth. The tacos will keep warm for at least 3 hours. Serve with the salsas.

COOKING TIP: *Don't skimp on the fat. Lard is the most flavourful, although vegetable oil will work at a pinch. Both must be heated to smoking before the basket is closed, otherwise the tacos will not stay warm. Also, make sure that the potatoes are well cooked – you want as smooth a texture as possible.*

Because this dish is so simple, it really matters that you use the best tortillas you can find, ideally ones made from fresh nixtamalised masa. Any leftovers crisp up nicely on the comal.

TORTAS DE PAVO
TURKEY TORTAS WITH CHIPOTLE SALSA

Turkey tortas – sandwiches stacked with oven-baked or slow-fried turkey – are immensely popular in the Downtown Historic Centre, and elsewhere around Mexico City. It's not surprising given the turkey's long history in Mexico: the animal was first domesticated there, several hundred years before the Spaniards arrived.

My favourite stall sits not too far from the famed San Juan Market. The owner, Luis Buenrostro Gutiérrez, has sold his sandwich in the same way for more than 40 years. Turkey simmers for hours in a large cauldron of lard, and then chunks are sliced off, barbecued and placed on an open-faced telera roll smeared with ripe avocado. Vinegary, tart chipotle salsa and a few leaves of pungent, peppery pápaloquelite, a native Mexican herb, finish it off. He gave me this recipe with the strict instructions that readers only use lard – 'It must be lard, no ifs, ands or buts!' – and that they do not substitute refried beans for avocado. (He actually looked disgusted at that idea. Even the young guy stacking soda bottles looked at me askance.) These are surprisingly easy to make at home, assuming you can find enough lard.

2.7kg lard
1.8kg turkey legs
200g can chipotles in adobo
    sauce
1 medium jalapeño chilli, roughly
    chopped with seeds
2½ tablespoons cider vinegar
rapeseed oil
4–6 *telera* rolls (see Tip)
1 large Haas avocado
1 bunch pápaloquelite, leaves
    only, optional
salt

COOKING TIPS: *If you can't find* telera, *the flat roll traditionally used for tortas in Mexico, try substituting a buttery hamburger bun. If you can't find pápalo, which may be found at some Latin American grocery stores, leave it out.*

Strive for the most even heat possible when cooking the turkey. The lard should bubble gently – the heat shouldn't be so low that it does not bubble at all.

1 Melt the lard over a low heat in a large stockpot. Add the turkey legs so that they're submerged in the fat and increase the heat to high. Don't disturb them for about 10 minutes until the lard starts to boil and foam.

2 Using tongs, carefully turn the legs in the lard and turn the heat to low. Cook for 1 hour, undisturbed, and then sprinkle ¾ teaspoon salt into the pan. Do not stir.

3 Carefully turn the legs, making sure that they're submerged in the lard again, and cook for a further 45 minutes. Turn the legs again and cook for about another hour more, for a total of 2 hours and 45 minutes, or until very tender.

4 Clutching the bone-end with tongs (trying to lift them out by the meaty end will cause the leg to fall apart), place the turkey legs on a rimmed baking tray lined with a wire rack and leave to cool for about 45 minutes until room temperature. At this point you can store the meat in an airtight container for up to a week. Strain the lard, leave it to cool and refrigerate for future use.

5 To prepare the salsa, place the chipotles in adobo, jalapeño, vinegar, 2 teaspoons water and ½ teaspoon salt in a blender and pulse until thick and chunky. Remove to a small bowl and set aside.

6 Grease a *comal* or non-stick frying pan lightly with the oil and heat to medium. Cut open the rolls and toast for about 1 minute per side. Scrape off any crumbs from the pan and place the rolls on a work surface. Slather one-quarter of the avocado on one side like a paste, and top with 2 teaspoons salsa and a sprinkle of pápalo leaves, if using.

7 Cut the turkey legs into small pieces against the grain, and then place the meat in the heated pan for 30 seconds–1 minute to crisp lightly. Transfer to the empty pieces of bread, placing the avocado-laden bread on top to close. Cut in half and serve immediately.

TACOS AL PASTOR
MARINATED, SPIT-ROASTED TACOS

Tacos al pastor – *made from marinated pork that's been roasted on a vertical spit – are wildly popular in Mexico City, particularly at night. The best taqueros put on a show, slicing off bits of caramelised meat and catching it in one hand (or behind their back!), and then reaching above the meat to slice off a piece of warm, juicy pineapple. According to city folklore, these tacos were invented in the capital. The dish is a direct descendant of shawarma, brought by Lebanese immigrants who arrived in Mexico in the early 20th century.*

The marinade in this recipe comes from Tacos Don Guero in the Cuauhtémoc neighbourhood, whose taqueros were kind enough to explain their ingredients to me at 6am one weekday morning. Obviously very few people at home will have a vertical spit – part of what gives tacos al pastor its signature flavour – but a barbecue would work well, or a blazing-hot cast-iron frying pan or griddle greased with a little lard.

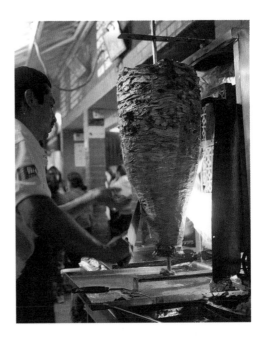

1   The day before you plan to eat, place the pork in a large bowl and toss with the lime juice and salt. Heat a *comal* or non-stick frying pan to a medium-high heat. Add the onion wedge and garlic, placing the garlic near the edge, away from direct heat. Cook for about 7 minutes until soft and blackened in spots, turning occasionally. Peel the garlic and place both items in a blender. Crumble the achiote paste into the blender and add the vinegar, cumin seeds, peanuts, bay leaf, cinnamon stick, cloves and allspice. Blend until smooth. Pour the marinade over the meat and toss to coat. Cover with clingfilm and refrigerate for 24 hours.

2   The next day, prepare the garnishes. Chop the pineapple, slice the limes into wedges, prepare the salsa and chop the coriander and onion.

3   Heat a large, heavy-based frying pan to high and add 1 teaspoon lard. When smoking, add one piece of marinated steak. The meat should sizzle and smoke, so make sure that you have a working extractor fan above your hob. Cook for 2–3 minutes until the meat starts to release its juices and lighten slightly in colour, then flip and cook a further 2–3 minutes. Both sides should have dark-brown charred spots; if they don't, increase the heat further. Transfer to a chopping board and repeat with the remaining steaks, scraping the pan well to remove any burnt bits between frying.

4   Scrape out the pan once more and cook the pineapple until soft and charred in spots. Remove to a bowl.

5   Warm the tortillas on a *comal* or in a non-stick frying pan. Place in a tea towel to keep warm. Cut the meat into small pieces. Serve on a platter for guests to feed themselves, passing round the tortillas and garnishes.

900g pork butt (upper shoulder), sliced into
   very thin steaks
60ml fresh lime juice
¾ teaspoon salt
¼ medium onion, plus 150g chopped
2 large garlic cloves, unpeeled
½ × 100g bar achiote paste
5 tablespoons cider vinegar
½ heaped teaspoon cumin seeds, toasted
2 tablespoons raw unsalted peanuts, toasted
1 small fresh Mexican bay leaf
5cm piece of cinnamon stick
2 cloves
2 allspice berries
330g fresh pineapple flesh, chopped
5 limes, cut into wedges
salsa of choice
50g fresh coriander, chopped
lard or vegetable oil
24 corn tortillas

ENCHILADAS VERDES
GREEN CHICKEN ENCHILADAS

Typical Mexican enchiladas arrive rolled up and stuffed, but at my favourite enchilada street stall – the inspiration for this recipe – they're stacked in a messy, luxurious pile, with separate individual layers of corn tortillas, fresh coriander and onion, green enchilada sauce, grated cheese and chicken. The whole thing is topped with a blanket of crema and more cheese. It's almost like a deconstructed lasagne. The dish is enough to make you fall deeply in love with Mexico City – particularly when the corn tortillas are homemade, and the green sauce is prepared with a slow-simmering pot of fresh chicken stock.

1.3kg skinless chicken
    legs, thighs and breasts,
    fat trimmed
450g chicken carcass,
    fat trimmed
3 medium garlic cloves,
    unpeeled
1 dried Mexican bay leaf
5 black peppercorns
1 medium onion, quartered
1¾ teaspoons salt
¼ teaspoon freshly ground
    black pepper
900g tomatillos, husked
    and rinsed
2 large serrano chillies
35g lard or 1 tablespoon plus
    2 teaspoons rapeseed oil
24 corn tortillas
25g fresh coriander, chopped
480g Homemade Crema
    (page 139)
115g mild cheese, such as
    Monterey Jack, grated

1 At least 2 hours before you'd like to eat, place the chicken, 1 garlic clove, the bay leaf, peppercorns and a quarter of the onion in a large stockpot. Cover with cold water and bring to the boil. Reduce the heat to very low, cover and simmer for 25 minutes. Remove the chicken legs, thighs and breasts with tongs or a slotted spoon and leave to cool. Discard the chicken carcass and strain the stock; set aside.

2 Once cool enough to handle, shred the meat and season with ¾ teaspoon salt and the ground black pepper. Set aside.

3 Place the tomatillos in a large saucepan. Add the remaining 2 garlic cloves, peeled, and 2 quarters of the onion. Cover with cold water. Bring to the boil, then simmer on a medium heat for about 12 minutes until the tomatillos turn pea green and soften. Transfer to a bowl and leave to cool. (Vegetarians can reserve the cooking water, increase the heat and reduce for 15–20 minutes to use instead of the chicken stock.)

4 De-stem the chillies and roughly chop with the cooked garlic. Add to a blender with half the tomatillo mixture and 120ml of the strained chicken stock. (If you have a high-powered blender, toss all the ingredients in at once.) Blend until smooth. Add the remaining tomatillo-onion mixture and 1 teaspoon salt, and blend again until smooth.

5 Warm 15g of the lard or 1 tablespoon of the oil in a large frying pan over a medium heat. When hot, add the sauce in one quick pour, being careful as it might splatter. Cook for about 5 minutes until the flavours meld.

6 Heat the remaining 10g lard or 2 teaspoons oil in a small frying pan over a medium heat and swirl to coat the base of the pan. Fry the tortillas lightly, one at a time, for about 30 seconds per side until slightly tougher but still pliable. (They shouldn't be crisp.) As you work, remove the fried tortillas to serving plates – I like to serve four per person. Fold the tortillas in a half-moon shape and ensure that they sit in an even layer on each plate.

7 Dice the remaining quarter of onion. Ladle 180ml of the sauce over each serving of tortillas, spreading it slightly so that the tortillas are entirely smothered in sauce. Add a layer of diced onion and coriander, a layer of grated cheese, a layer of chicken, some crema and another layer of sauce. Top with another light sprinkling of diced onion.

COOKING TIP: *I recommend making your own light stock here, using the water in which you've cooked the chicken; see recipe on page 98. Mexican cooks consider that a hen, as opposed to a cockerel, makes the most flavourful stock base. If you're vegetarian, this dish can still be pretty wonderful, especially if you use homemade vegetable stock.*

ESQUITES
STREET CORN IN A CUP

Chilango *street corn vendors come out at dusk only, and they sell two snacks:* elote – *a big, starchy ear of corn, crusted with mayonnaise, slightly funky* añejo *cheese and chilli powder – and* esquites, *a mix of corn stewed with epazote and spices, and served in a cup with mayo, lime juice and chilli powder. The latter is my favourite, particularly for its dense, hearty Mexican corn kernels, which taste nothing like sweetcorn. To recreate that corn's same chewy heft when I'm not in Mexico, I use* mote, *a dried lightly nixtamalised Andean corn. It cooks for at least an hour so that the broth has more time to develop flavour. The result is so warm and comforting, I think it works on its own as a main dish.*

400g *mote* corn (maize), or 900g frozen sweetcorn (see Tip)
2 tablespoons rapeseed oil
½ medium onion, chopped
2 medium garlic cloves, very finely chopped
12–15 sprigs of epazote, or less if very pungent
1 dried árbol chilli, toasted, de-stemmed and deseeded
2 teaspoons salt
2 large limes, cut in half
chilli piquín powder
mayonnaise, optional
good-quality crumbled aged-cheese, such as *queso añejo*, ricotta salata or Romano, optional

1   If using *mote*, the night before, place it in a large pan and cover with cold water. Leave to soak overnight. The next day, drain and cover with 7.5cm of fresh water, then bring to the boil. Reduce the heat, and once the cooking surface is only gently bubbling, cover and simmer over a low heat for 30 minutes. Drain and reserve the cooking liquid.

2   Heat the oil in a heavy-based pan over a medium-low heat. Add the onion and garlic and cook for about 3 minutes until the onion is translucent. If using *mote*, add to the pan with 1.2 litres of the reserved cooking liquid, or a mixture of cooking liquid and water. If using frozen sweetcorn, add to the pot with 960ml water. Add the epazote and dried chilli, increase the heat and bring to the boil. Stir in the salt, reduce the heat and simmer until the corn is tender – for *mote*, 30–35 minutes, or until the kernel is translucent when cut in half. For frozen corn, this takes about 10 minutes.

3   To serve, fill a standard-sized mug or shallow bowl halfway with corn. Squeeze lime juice on top and cover with more corn. Top with more lime juice, chilli powder, and mayo and cheese if desired. Serve immediately.

COOKING TIPS: *You can find* mote *at Latin American grocery stores or online suppliers. If not available, dried, nixtamalised pozole corn would work (this generally has a smaller kernel than* mote*), or fresh or frozen sweetcorn as a last option. Skip the mayo if you like, but the lime juice here is essential.*

GORDITAS DE NATA
SWEET CREAM BISCUITS

You can find these tiny, golden-brown biscuits near the Basilica de Guadalupe, Mexico's oldest and most famous religious site. They're hard to ignore: vendors cry out for you to try a sample, and an enticing yellow-cake smell wafts around them at all times. Similar versions are sold in other parts of Mexico, including Michoacán.

The main ingredient is nata, or clotted cream. Dense and rich – and still small enough to fit in the palm of your hand – these biscuits are unbeatable in the morning with coffee, or as a sweet side to something like Mexican-style Eggs (page 86).

1   In a medium bowl, whisk together the flour, baking powder, bicarbonate of soda and salt. Set aside.

2   In a large bowl, stir together the clotted cream, sugar and vanilla.

3   Add the flour mixture, a little at a time, to the clotted cream mixture, stirring with a rubber spatula and then kneading with your hands until a cohesive dough forms. Add the milk if the mixture looks too dry.

4   Divide the dough in half and transfer one half to a floured surface. Roll out to 5mm thick. Cut into small rounds using a 5cm biscuit cutter. Cook on an ungreased *comal* or in a non-stick frying pan heated to low, flipping occasionally, for about 5 minutes until golden brown and crisp on both sides, and no longer doughy at the edges.

5   Serve warm with butter if desired, or any leftover clotted cream. Reheat any leftover *gorditas* on the hob.

250g plain flour
1 teaspoon baking powder
½ teaspoon bicarbonate of soda
¼ teaspoon salt
175g clotted cream
50g sugar
½ teaspoon vanilla extract
1–2 tablespoons milk, or more if necessary

COOKING TIP: *These cook on the hob, so ensure that the heat is very low and that they're not rolled out too thin. The ideal texture is soft and chewy.*

Just in case you can't lay your hands on any clotted cream, see my recipe for a handy substitute below.

CLOTTED CREAM SUBSTITUTE

Whip the heavy cream until soft peaks form. Fold in the soured cream and sugar. Use immediately, or place in a sieve set over a bowl, and store in the fridge for up to 3 days.

240g double cream
75g soured cream
1 tablespoon icing sugar

CHAMPURRADO
THICKENED MEXICAN HOT CHOCOLATE

This is a thicker, more decadent version of the warm chocolate-flavoured beverage that's sold on the streets to accompany tamales. You can find versions of it all around Mexico, but the base tends to have some sort of combination of chocolate, corn (either masa or a toasted ground corn called pinole) and sugar. My version is so rich that I think it works as dessert. (Or, if you are me, a 3pm snack.) The masa flavour isn't extremely noticeable, so if you'd like more of a corn boost, add more masa or stir in some pinole, *which can be found at some Mexican grocery stores or online.*

1   If using masa harina, add 180ml warm water to a small bowl and sprinkle in the masa a little bit at a time, whisking after each addition until it forms a thick batter. If using fresh masa, add 120ml water to a blender and crumble the masa into small pieces. Blend on a low speed into a thick paste. Strain the fresh masa paste into another bowl, pushing on the bottom of the sieve with a spatula.

2   For the masa harina version, bring 300ml water and the cinnamon stick, if using, to the boil in a medium saucepan. (For fresh masa, use 480ml water.) Add the masa batter and immediately whisk until dissolved. Reduce the heat to medium or medium-low and cook for 3–5 minutes until thick and very bubbly.

3   Over a medium heat, add the milk, chocolate, sugar and salt. Simmer, stirring constantly and scraping the base of the pan, for 15–20 minutes until it thickens more deeply.

4   Discard the cinnamon stick, if using, and serve warm, ladled into mugs. To reheat, add more milk to thin down, and warm on the hob over a low heat.

75g masa harina, or 110g fresh
   tortilla masa
7.5cm piece of cinnamon stick,
   optional
720ml full-fat milk
150g good-quality Mexican
   chocolate
1 tablespoon sugar
1 pinch salt

COOKING TIP: *Using good-quality Mexican chocolate matters. Taza is available online, and other recommended brands are Rancho Gordo, Hernán and Susana Trilling's Season of My Heart if you should come across them. The quantity of cinnamon and sugar varies in each chocolate, so taste a small piece first and then decide whether you'd like to add the cinnamon stick, or use more or less sugar.*

CHAPTER 2

IN THE MARKETS

In Mexico City, there are two types of markets: *mercados*, generally boxy buildings full of produce stalls and eateries, and *tianguis* (tee-AHN-geese), outdoor markets that move to different neighbourhoods throughout the week. Many *mercado* buildings in Mexico City were constructed in the middle of the 20th century, and there's a sense, stepping inside, that things haven't changed much.

Vendors own their stalls and treat them like small pieces of real estate. They sell neatly arranged piles of tropical fruits, shaggy heads of purple-tinged and curly leaf lettuce, tangles of coriander, sacks of dried beans in various colours. Some stalls specialise in herbal remedies and teas (a vestige of Mexico's indigenous past), and the bushy herbs are stacked so high that you can barely see the vendor's face. Other stalls sell paper plates and styrofoam cups, or cat, dog and bird food.

At the butchers' counters, bright yellow chickens lie in neat rows, open-air, on the countertops. Steak and pork vendors have refrigerated cases, but they leave items out to lure in customers: large, crinkled sheets of *chicharrón* (pork crackling) and reddish wedges of oily *chicharrón prensado*, a type of terrine made from leftover pig parts. The lard, white and whipped and sold by the kilo, always reminds me of cake icing.

MERCADOS VS TIANGUIS

The *mercado* is as much about eating as it is shopping. Every market offers prepared food, sold either at lunch counters or small restaurants, and all of it is cooked daily or à la minute. You can find fresh juices and tortas, *guisados* and tacos, and pitchers of *agua frescas*. Eating there, your market bags resting at your feet, the strum of a guitar or some other music in your ear from a wandering musician – it's hard not to romanticise the experience, particularly when you've spent your life shopping at bland supermarkets.

The *tianguis*, from the Nahuatl word 'tianquitzli', meaning plaza or market, is an open-air market that usually spans several blocks, with stalls offering fresh produce, prepared food, clothes, shoes and other odds and ends. The vibe is wilder than the *mercado* – vendors don't hesitate to yell out their wares at passers by. 'Limón limón limón limón!' Limes limes limes limes! 'Papaya papaya papayaaaaa!' There are ambulant vendors too: men toting big glass jars of honey and pollen, flat baskets of fresh herbs, coolers of homemade tamales, fresh cheeses or stacks of wooden hangers.

It's interesting to ponder how long all of this will go on, as Mexican demographics have changed. More women now work outside the home and families report having less time to cook. The *mercados* and *tianguis* are only open during business hours, so they don't fit the average working person's schedule. Some *mercados* have lost most of their tenants, leaving huge, half-empty shells in otherwise bustling residential neighbourhoods.

I don't take my market experience for granted. One of my favourite ways to spend an afternoon is at my local *mercado* in the Roma neighbourhood, greeting the vendors who know my face and asking for recipes for ingredients I've never seen before. Every single vendor I have ever asked for a recipe has given me one. Their instructions almost always start with, 'Sofríe su ajito, cebollita, y chilito para darle sabor...' (You fry garlic, onion and a little chilli to give it flavour...) With the vendors' help, the recipes that follow reflect the snacks, tacos and prepared dishes found at markets I've loved.

CAFÉ DE OLLA
SWEET CINNAMON-SPIKED COFFEE

Café de olla – *literally 'coffee from the pot' – is typically served for breakfast at markets across the city and across Mexico, comprising coffee that's been mixed with* piloncillo, *a type of unrefined Mexican cane sugar, and cinnamon. The beverage is traditionally brewed in a clay pot. I'm not generally a fan of sweetened coffee, but this drink pairs perfectly with heavy, spicy Mexican breakfasts. The* piloncillo *is warm and molasses-y, and cinnamon and cloves add a bit more depth of flavour than you'd find in standard coffee.*

1   Pour 1.4 litres water into a large stainless steel saucepan or clay pot, and then add the *piloncillo*, cinnamon stick and cloves. Heat on high and cook until the *piloncillo* completely dissolves. Bring the mixture to the boil, add the ground coffee and return to the boil.

2   Reduce the heat to medium and simmer for about 3 minutes. Turn off the heat, cover the pan and leave for 10–15 minutes until the grounds settle to the bottom.

3   Strain the coffee using a fine-mesh sieve or muslin. Discard the coffee grounds, cinnamon stick and cloves. Serve warm, ladling into individual mugs.

80g *piloncillo*, chopped or grated, or dark brown sugar
1 cinnamon stick
4 cloves
6 tablespoons medium or dark roast coffee, ground

COOKING TIP: *In Mexico City,* piloncillo *is sold in small, unwrapped cones or in small nuggets. In other parts of Mexico, the sugar may come in blocks or circular discs called* panela *or* panocha. *You can buy* piloncillo *from Mexican grocery stores or online suppliers, but you can substitute brown sugar at a pinch.*

This is not an overly strong coffee, and it's always served plain, without milk. But if you want it weaker, add more water. Leftovers can be stored in the fridge for up to two days. It's delicious hot or cold.

HOW TO GRATE OR CHOP PILONCILLO

A sharp knife works best to cut piloncillo. *To do so, turn the cone upside down and grab it by the wider end. Tilt it at a 45-degree angle and, using your knife, cut the* piloncillo *at the narrower end, slicing through at a slight angle. The pieces should slice off more or less cleanly. If the* piloncillo *is very hard, keep clutching the* piloncillo *by the wider end and use your knife to flake off small bits. Do not put the* piloncillo *in your food processor, or you might break the machine.*

LICUADO DE MAMEY
MAMEY MILKSHAKE

Mamey, pronounced 'mah-MAY', was the first Mexican tropical fruit to completely bewitch me. The American football-shaped fruit has a creamy, sunset-coloured flesh, and tastes like a mix of pumpkins and cherries. Most chilangos *eat mamey raw or blend it with milk to make a thick shake called a* licuado. *At local markets,* licuado *stalls carry a selection of grains, herbs and nuts, and they'll make any combination the customer wants. I include my preference below for puffed amaranth and raw oats, which add a nuttiness to mamey's sweet flavour.*

720ml full-fat milk

350g fresh mamey, chopped, or 400g frozen mamey pulp, defrosted

25g rolled oats

2 tablespoons puffed amaranth (amaranth popcorn)

1 tablespoon honey or other desired sweetener, optional

Place the milk, mamey, oats and amaranth in a blender and blend on a high speed until smooth. Add more mamey if desired, or honey. (Fresh mamey may not need any sweetener.) Pour into two glasses – or one if you're especially hungry – and serve.

COOKING TIP: *Look for frozen mamey pulp in Mexican or Caribbean grocery stores, and some may also stock fresh mamey seasonally. If you can't find mamey, don't substitute anything else, as the flavour won't be the same. Health food stores or online suppliers sell ready-puffed amaranth (sometimes as 'amaranth popcorn') or amaranth 'grain' for puffing your own (see page 163 for instructions).*

TEPACHE
SWEETENED FERMENTED PINEAPPLE JUICE

On a hot, early spring Mexico City day, before the summer rains arrive to clean the air and cool everything down, there's nothing better than an icy glass of tepache, *or sweet, fermented pineapple juice. It's sold at markets and street stalls across the city, sometimes in little plastic bags wrapped around a straw. The taste is sweet and floral and slightly funky, almost like a very mild fruit beer. (The alcohol level here is minimal.) This makes a great party punch, or a refreshing drink on a hot day.*

1   About three days before you wish to drink the *tepache*, wash the pineapple well and cut it into pieces, keeping the rind on. Place the pineapple in a large pan with 3.8 litres water and the cloves, allspice and cinnamon stick. Leave it for two days, covered loosely with a double layer of muslin. (Feel free to peek at the *tepache* while it sits; it won't hurt the drink.) On the second day, you should start to smell some pineapple funk emitting from the pan.

2   Place the *piloncillo* cones in a small saucepan and pour 240ml water over them. Cook over a low heat, stirring often, until the cones dissolve completely. Remove from the heat and leave to cool for about 30 minutes. Stir the cooled *piloncillo* syrup into the pineapple, along with the beer. Cover and leave to sit for another day.

3   On the last day, you may notice some white mould spots on the liquid's surface. That's okay. Ignore them. Strain the liquid into a large serving container, and discard the pineapple chunks and spices. Stir and serve over ice.

1 very ripe, soft pineapple, about 1.3–1.8kg
2 cloves
2 allspice berries
7.5cm piece of cinnamon stick
2 *piloncillo* cones (about 450g in total), or light soft brown sugar
355ml bottle light or lager-style beer, such as Modelo Especial

COOKING TIP: *To ferment the pineapple, you need a large (10-litre) pan and some muslin. The drink needs to interact with the air in order for it to start fermenting – don't cover it tightly with a lid. If you like sweeter drinks, add more sugar. For a more fermented taste, leave the pan to sit longer than three days. The drink will keep in an airtight container in the fridge for up to five days, but warning: it may get boozier as it sits.*

REQUESÓN
HOMEMADE REQUESÓN CHEESE

Requesón is a salty, spreadable cheese sold at markets around the city. It tastes like a creamier, more acidic version of ricotta. Making it from scratch is easy: you curdle milk with vinegar or another acid such as lime juice, and then warm it and watch the curds form. Most street vendors use it as a tlacoyo filling but you can use requesón for all sorts of things – stirred into scrambled eggs and tomatoes, smeared into a corn tortilla with salsa or, less authentically Mexican, spread onto a piece of toast with honey or mixed in a dip of fresh herbs and olive oil.

3.8 litres full-fat milk
120ml distilled white vinegar
1 teaspoon salt

1   Stir together the milk and vinegar in a large, heavy-based pan. Cook over a medium-high heat until large, thick curds form on the milk's surface and the curds have clearly separated from the thinner, clearer whey, 35–40 minutes if using cold milk directly from the fridge, or slightly less if using room-temperature milk. The curds won't necessarily look big and lumpy – think more of a layer of algae on a lake. Try not to disturb the milk too much while it cooks, in order to give the curds more time to come together.

2   Remove the pan from the heat and leave to sit, uncovered, for 10 minutes, to allow the curds to continue to thicken.

3   Line a fine-mesh sieve with a layer of muslin and set over a bowl. Using a slotted spoon, transfer the curds to the muslin and leave to sit for 45 minutes–1 hour or until room temperature. (This gives the cheese time to set and cool off.)

4   Transfer the cheese to a bowl or airtight container. Stir in the salt, mixing until thoroughly combined. Use immediately, or chill first in the fridge.

COOKING TIP: *Homogenised, pasteurised milk works fine here, but make sure the milk is not ultra-homogenised, otherwise the curds may not come together. This recipe also divides and multiplies easily. Leftovers can be stored in an airtight container in the fridge for up to three days.*

POZOLE BLANCO
WHITE POZOLE

Several varieties of pozole, a pork and hominy stew, exist all over Mexico, but only in the capital can you find so many of them in one place, from green pumpkin-seed-thickened pozole from Guerrero to spicy red pozole from Jalisco. Mexico City's markets and fondas sell large, steaming bowls, accompanied by the typical garnishes: radishes, Mexican oregano, chopped onion, chilli powder, tostadas. My favourite is the simple, restorative pozole blanco. I start by cooking pork ribs, shoulder and pig's trotters for a few hours in an aromatic broth, then stew hominy in the same broth until the kernels burst open. The result is a rich, satisfying soup, elevated further by contrasting accompaniments. Pozole reheats beautifully and you can store leftovers in the freezer.

1 The night before you wish to eat, place the hominy in a large pan, cover with cold water and leave to soak overnight.

2 The next day, rinse the pig's trotters well and place in a large bowl. Cover with cold water and leave to soak for 1 hour. (Opinions vary on whether soaking pig's trotters is necessary; I'm doing it here, because that's the way I learnt to prepare them.)

3 Rinse the pig's trotters and place them in a large, deep pan with the pork shoulder, ribs, onion wedge and garlic. Cover with cold water and bring to the boil. Skim off any scum that floats to the surface. Reduce the heat to medium and simmer for about 2½ hours until the meat is tender, adding more water when the meat is no longer submerged.

4 Remove the meat from the pan, reserving the pan and liquid, and leave to cool, then shred or cut into small pieces; set aside. (Note: the pig's trotters will not have much meat, but they help add a gelatinous quality to the broth.)

5 Drain the hominy and discard the soaking water. Add the kernels to the pan containing the meat broth. Bring to the boil and cook, stirring occasionally, for 1–1½ hours until the kernels just begin to split apart into a flower-like shape. The kernels may not flower evenly, which is okay.

6 Return the meat to the pan and stir in the salt, tasting for more if needed. Cook over a medium heat for 10–15 minutes until the flavours meld.

7 Serve warm in large, deep bowls, accompanied by all the garnishes: tostadas, to be slathered in a layer of crema; a plate of shredded lettuce or cabbage; and small bowls of chopped onion, sliced radishes, *chicharrón*, if using, Mexican oregano and chilli powder. Hand round lime wedges and salsa at the table.

COOKING TIPS: *You can buy pozole corn that has already been nixtamalised and dried from Mexican grocery stores or online suppliers, which saves some time. Don't buy canned hominy, which is mushy and lacks flavour. One acceptable substitution would be mote corn, which is also pre-nixtamalised and only requires soaking overnight. You can buy pig's trotters from select supermarkets or butchers.*

450g dried hominy for pozole
2 pig's trotters, weighing about
  1.1–1.3 kg
450g pork shoulder, in one piece
450g pork ribs
½ medium white onion, plus
  230g chopped
2 garlic cloves, peeled
1 tablespoon salt, or more
  to taste
24 tostadas
480g Homemade Crema
  (page 139)
½ iceberg lettuce or cabbage,
  shredded
1 small bunch of radishes, sliced
chicharrón (pork crackling or
  scratchings), broken into
  pieces, optional (page 136)
2 tablespoons dried Mexican
  oregano
1 tablespoon toasted and ground
  dried árbol chilli, or ground
  chilli piquín
5 limes, quartered
hot, vinegary salsa such as
  Valentina or Cholula

CÓCTEL DE CAMARÓN CON PULPO
PRAWNS AND OCTOPUS COCKTAIL

Sweet and slightly tangy, the Mexican version of prawn cocktail is nothing like the version you find in New England. It's softer, lighter – something you can tuck into with a beer while still leaving room for a few tacos. In Mexico City, these citrusy, tomato-based cocktails can be found at market stalls and street stands, inspired by versions sold on Mexico's Gulf Coast. They are often eaten as starters, or as a complement to another heavier fried dish. The base of the sauce is generally tomato ketchup, thinned down with a little citrus and either stock or mineral water. The dish is always garnished with avocado, which marries perfectly with the ketchup.

salt

450g raw octopus, cleaned and cut into 2.5cm pieces

⅛ medium onion, plus 75g chopped

1 dried Mexican bay leaf

450g raw prawns, rinsed, peeled and deveined

180g tomato ketchup

3 tablespoons fresh lime juice, plus 2 limes cut into quarters

25g fresh coriander, roughly chopped

1 ripe Haas avocado, peeled, stoned and sliced

12 tostadas, or 24 saltine crackers

hot, vinegary salsa such as Valentina or Cholula

1   Fill a medium saucepan two-thirds full with water. Bring to a rapid boil and add 1 teaspoon salt. When the salt dissolves, add the octopus. Reduce the heat to medium-low and simmer for about 45 minutes, partially covered and stirring occasionally, until tender. Remove the octopus from the water and drain or freeze the cooking liquid for another use. Set the octopus aside to cool, then refrigerate once it has reached room temperature.

2   Rinse out the pan and again fill two-thirds full with water. Add the onion wedge and bay leaf, and bring to a vigorous boil. Add a hefty pinch of salt, then add the prawns and cook for 1–2 minutes until just tender and pink. Transfer the prawns to a bowl and strain and reserve 180ml of the cooking liquid. Leave the prawns to cool slightly, toss with a little salt and then refrigerate. Leave the cooking liquid to cool before using. (To speed things up, pour it into a measuring jug and set in an ice water bath.)

3   In a medium bowl, whisk together the ketchup, reserved cooking liquid, lime juice and ¼ teaspoon salt.

4   Spoon the prawns and octopus into tall cocktail glasses or shallow bowls. Top each serving with about 4 tablespoons sauce – enough to coat the seafood – and garnish with a small handful of chopped coriander and onion, and two or three slices of avocado.

5   Serve immediately with tostadas or saltines, handing round the lime wedges and hot sauce at the table.

COOKING TIPS: *The cocktail sauce should be thin but not soupy, and the ratios can be tweaked to your personal taste. Drizzling on vinegary hot sauce adds a nice kick, and fresh, diced tomatoes add sweetness and texture. Using fresh seafood instead of frozen boosts the flavour too.*

ENSALADA DE HABA
FRESH BROAD BEAN SALAD

Broad (fava) beans aren't native to Mexico – they were brought by the Spaniards after the conquest – but they've been roundly embraced over the course of hundreds of years. They're often used in soups and stews, but my favourite way to eat them is in this simple salad, where young unpeeled broad beans are tossed with olive oil, salt and coriander. (The amount of coriander here may seem like a lot, but it's what makes the salad shine.). This makes a hearty side dish with a few tacos, or a filling snack.

1   If using whole broad beans still in their pods, remove the pods and place the beans in a bowl, their waxy inner skins intact.

2   Fill a small saucepan halfway with water. Add the onion half and ½ teaspoon salt and bring to the boil.

3   Add the beans and reduce the heat to medium. Cook until the beans are tender, 3–5 minutes, depending on the bean size. Don't overcook them, otherwise the beans will turn mushy. Drain the beans and leave to cool to room temperature.

4   Rinse the diced onion briefly in cold water. Drain and add to the beans, along with the chopped coriander and olive oil. Stir well and season with more salt. Serve immediately.

1.8kg broad beans still in their pods, or 700g podded very young broad beans with the waxy skins still on
½ small onion plus 2 tablespoons diced
12 sprigs of fresh coriander, roughly chopped
2 tablespoons mild olive oil
salt

COOKING TIP: *Older broad beans will taste bitter or leathery if the skins are left on. Young beans have a firm, pleasant bite. Look for beans that have a delicate, almost mint-green colour in the pod and avoid yellowish-green or brown-speckled beans, which are too old and won't taste right. You could also try skinning the beans for this salad, but the flavour will be creamier and nuttier, and might need a spritz of lime juice.*

PAMBAZOS
FRIED CHORIZO AND POTATO SANDWICHES

For a good while after I moved to Mexico City, the pambazo *scared me. It was a decadent, fried sandwich, oozing crema and lumps of chorizo and potatoes, not meant for weight-conscious gringas. But after a year of passing these guajillo-painted rolls, I caved in and ordered one at a market in the Centro Histórico.*

The young woman behind the counter grabbed a roll and placed it in a bubbling fryer. She scooped out the bread with a slotted spoon and transferred it to a chopping board, where she split the bread into two pieces with her fingers. On one side she added a spatula full of chorizo and potato that she had warmed on the grill. 'Con todo?' she asked. I nodded. Over the potato, she poured one spoonful of crema, then a second, then a third. Then she sprinkled on shredded lettuce and finally added the other side of the bread.

I bit into the sandwich. The bread crunched slightly. The meaty, salty filling I'd expected to go down like a sloppy joe tasted somehow light. Cool. I ate the whole thing and my pambazo *fear evaporated, along with any leftover crumbs.*

4 Yukon Gold or any other small waxy potato (700g in total), peeled

2 teaspoons lard or rapeseed oil, plus more for frying

½ small white onion, chopped

2 medium cloves garlic, very finely chopped

225g Mexican chorizo or other cooking chorizo, casings removed

4 day-old Mexican *telera* rolls, or sub or Vienna bread rolls

120g Homemade Crema (page 139)

50–100g iceberg lettuce, shredded

salt

For the sauce:
5 guajillo chillies, deseeded, deveined and toasted briefly on a *comal*

40g onion, chopped

1 small garlic clove, peeled

½ teaspoon salt, or more to taste

1   Place the potatoes in a medium saucepan and cover them with 5cm cold water. Bring to the boil and then simmer over a high heat for about 30 minutes until the potatoes are soft when pierced with a fork. Leave to cool, then drain and dice.

2   Meanwhile, make the sauce. Soak the toasted chillies in water for about 20 minutes until the skins are soft. Transfer, with 120ml of the chilli soaking water (see panel opposite), into a blender with the onion, garlic and salt. Blend until mostly smooth, stopping occasionally to scrape down the sides of the blender jug. The sauce won't be completely silky-smooth. That's okay. Taste again and add more salt if desired.

3   Heat the lard or oil in a large frying pan over a medium heat. Add the onion and cook for about 3 minutes until translucent. Add the garlic and cook, stirring, for about 30 seconds until sizzling and aromatic, then add the chorizo, breaking it apart into small crumbles. Increase the heat to medium-high and cook, stirring often, for about 8–10 minutes until the sausage is cooked through.

4   Stir in the potato and salt to taste. Cook until warmed through, cover and keep warm.

5   Cut each roll in half and remove some of the inner crumb. Brush the outer crust of each roll with a light coating of the chilli sauce. Working in batches, warm 2 teaspoons lard or oil in a cast-iron frying pan over a medium heat. When smoking, add one half of the bread, chilli sauce-side down. Cook for about 3 minutes until dark golden brown and crisp. Remove and add the other piece of bread, also chilli sauce-side down. Repeat with the remaining rolls, draining between batches on a wire rack set on top of a baking tray.

6   To serve, spoon about 8 tablespoons of the chorizo mixture onto one bread half, then top with a layer of crema and a fistful of lettuce. Cover with the other piece of bread. Repeat with the remaining bread. Serve while the bread is still crunchy and hot.

WHY CHILLI WATER INSTEAD OF ORDINARY WATER?

Chilli water is the term I use for the flavourful water left over from soaking dried chillies. I use it often to thin down sauces or salsas, as it adds a slight pop of heat. Be careful, though – if you burn the chillies, the water will taste bitter, and if the chillies are very hot, the water may be too spicy to use. It's best to taste a little before you add it to anything.

COOKING TIPS: *Using a cast-iron frying pan gives the bread an even, golden-brown toast. I chose Yukon Gold potatoes because they're richer than Russets, but the latter will work. Use radish tops and coriander for a more vibrant substitution for the lettuce. Lastly, be careful when selecting Mexican or other chorizo – processed varieties can taste over-seasoned. The best ones are made by the butchers themselves. If you're unsure, ask.*

FLAUTAS DE RES
STEAK FLAUTAS

Flautas, or 'flutes', common to Northern Mexico and Guadalajara, are long, fried corn tortilla tubes, usually topped with a messy handful of lettuce or cabbage and a squirt of lime juice and salsa. They're very common in Mexico City street stalls and markets, with vendors frying them up in huge, bowl-shaped fryers. The filling – bits of simply seasoned shredded steak or chicken – is plain but delicious. You don't need to overthink it, particularly if you have a great salsa on the side. My personal favourite is Chilli Pasilla Salsa, and the recipe opposite is inspired by a local flauta market stall. This will serve at least four with a side such as Basic Cooked Beans (page 107) or Mexican-style Red Rice (page 97).

In the USA, we generally call any sort of fried, tube-shaped taco a taquito. In Mexico City, these snacks have different names, depending on their shape. Longer fried tubes – measuring the length of a dinner plate – are called flautas. Their shorter cousins, made from standard-sized corn tortillas, are called tacos dorados. Taquitos, meanwhile, mean 'small tacos' in Mexico City, and don't refer to a rolled-up snack at all.

700g piece of beef chuck steak
¼ medium onion
1 large garlic clove, unpeeled
15–20 corn tortillas
240ml vegetable oil
480g Homemade Crema
   (page 139)
120g queso fresco, crumbled
Chilli Pasilla Salsa (see opposite)
200g cabbage, chopped
4–5 limes, cut into wedges
salt and freshly ground black
   pepper

1 Place the meat, onion and garlic in a large saucepan and cover with cold water. Bring to the boil and add 1 heaped teaspoon salt. Simmer gently for about 2 hours or until tender when pulled apart with a fork. Transfer the meat to a chopping board until cool enough to handle, then shred the meat finely. Taste and season with salt and pepper. Strain the cooking liquid, discarding the onion and garlic, and save for another use.

2 Warm the corn tortillas a few at a time on a *comal* or non-stick frying pan until soft and pliable. Remove to a tea towel to keep warm.

3 Place one tortilla on your work surface. Grab a small handful of meat and arrange in a long rectangle in the centre of the tortilla. Roll into a tight tube and secure closed with a wooden cocktail stick. Repeat with the remaining tortillas and meat.

4 Set a wire rack on a baking tray next to the hob. Heat the vegetable oil in a large, heavy-based frying pan over a medium-high heat. (To tell when the oil is ready, tear off a 2cm piece of tortilla and add it to the oil; if it bubbles and sizzles, the oil is ready.)

5 Add the *flautas* about four at a time, depending on the size of your pan, and fry about 1 minute per side, turning occasionally with tongs, until golden brown all over. Transfer to the wire rack to drain. Repeat with the remaining *flautas*.

6 Serve warm, topped first with a layer of crema and cheese, then salsa, then cabbage. Pass round the lime wedges at the table.

COOKING TIP: *I use standard-sized corn tortillas here because they're easiest for home cooks to find. Most Mexicans, however, would say that these are no longer* flautas *but* tacos dorados. *Either way, don't overcook the tortillas, or they won't roll. Leftover poached, shredded chicken or brisket would also work swimmingly instead of steak, and you can bake the* flautas *instead of frying them for a toastier, healthier dish.*

CHILLI PASILLA SALSA

The charred, bitter notes of this salsa match wonderfully with steak, but you can also use it on anything else you'd like: eggs, quesadillas or other meat tacos. Store in an airtight container for up to one week. (The salsa will mellow over time.)

1   Heat a *comal*, griddle or frying pan to medium-low heat. Place the chillies at the edge of the pan and turn constantly for 5–10 seconds until coloured and softened. Place the chillies in a bowl of warm water and leave to soak for about 20 minutes until the skins soften. Drain and reserve the soaking water. Meanwhile, place the garlic near the edge of the pan and cook for 5–7 minutes, turning occasionally, until soft and blackened in spots, then set aside to cool. Increase the heat to medium-high, add the tomatoes and cook, turning often with tongs, until soft and blackened in spots.

2   Peel the garlic cloves and place in a blender with the chillies and 60ml of the reserved chilli water. Pulse until a thick paste forms, then scrape down the sides of the blender jug and pulse a bit more. Add the tomatoes and salt. Pulse a few more times until the tomatoes break down but the salsa is still rather chunky. Taste for seasoning and add salt if needed.

3   Pour the salsa into a serving bowl and set on the table for guests to serve themselves extra if desired.

6 pasilla chillies, de-stemmed
   and deseeded
2 large garlic cloves, unpeeled
4 ripe plum tomatoes
1½ teaspoons salt

HUARACHES DE FLOR DE CALABAZA
SQUASH FLOWER HUARACHES

Huaraches – named after their long, oval shape, like the sole of a leather sandal – were invented near Mexico City's Jamaica Market, according to local legend. Shops specialising in huaraches *still operate near the market today. The masa is predominantly shaped by women, who grab handfuls of the sticky corn dough, toss it on the flat-top grill and quickly spread it into shape with their fingers. The modern* huarache *is monstrous: a masa boat the length of a dinner plate, stuffed with a thin layer of black beans and topped with stewed meat or vegetables, crema, avocado and a thick layer of melted cheese. You can order almost any combination of toppings you want, but my favourites usually contain vegetables – mushrooms, squash flowers, poblano chillies. These are fun to serve at dinner parties, once you get comfortable shaping the masa. To do so, you'll need a rolling pin and a plain plastic shopping bag cut into two large pieces.*

1 batch Quick Refried Beans
    (page 45)
1 batch Chilli Morita Salsa (see
    opposite), for serving
4 poblano chillies
900g fresh tortilla masa
60ml room-temperature water,
    plus more as needed
1 tablespoon rapeseed oil
75g onion, chopped
2 medium garlic cloves, very
    finely chopped
1 bunch of courgette flowers,
    stems removed and flowers
    torn in half
225g chestnut mushrooms,
    sliced
½ teaspoon salt, or more to taste
230g quesillo or any other mild,
    melty cheese, grated
480g Homemade Crema
    (page 139)

1   Prepare the refried beans and salsa and set aside.

2   Roast, peel and deseed the poblano chillies (see instructions on page 37). Chop into 4cm by 5mm strips and set aside.

3   Place the masa in a large, deep bowl and add the water a few tablespoons at a time, kneading extensively after each addition until the dough is extremely sticky and stretchy. You may need between 60–120ml water, depending on the humidity, altitude and other factors. Cover the dough with a damp tea towel while you prepare the filling.

4   Heat the oil in a large frying pan over a medium heat. Add the onion and cook for 3 minutes until translucent, then add the garlic and cook for about 30 seconds until aromatic. Add the courgette flowers and mushrooms and cook, stirring occasionally, for 3–5 minutes until the flowers are tender and the mushrooms are cooked through. Stir in the epazote, poblano chillies and salt. Remove from the heat and set aside.

5   Heat a *comal* or griddle over a medium heat. Create a work space with the refried beans, dough, a rolling pin and plastic shopping bags. Dampen your hands with water. Grab a chunk of masa and roll into a ball slightly smaller than a billiard ball. Create a small crater in the ball with your thumbs and fill with a spoonful of refried beans. Press closed by folding the dough around the beans, and roll again into a ball, then flatten into a thick rectangular shape with your palms.

6   Place one sheet of plastic on the chopping board, and put the oval patty in the middle. Cover with a second sheet of plastic. Use a rolling pin to roll out the *huarache* into a long sole-of-your-shoe shape, about 20cm long and 5mm thick.

7   Dampen your hands again. Carefully peel back the top layer of plastic, and flip the *huarache* into your upturned hand, positioning it so that half hangs off. Carefully peel back the top layer of plastic – the *huarache* may stretch a bit while it's hanging there. Moving your hand in a swift left-to-right motion, place the *huarache* on the hot *comal*.

8   Cook for 1–2 minutes until the edges darken slightly, then flip and cook a few minutes more. Reduce the heat and cook, turning occasionally, for 12–15 minutes or slightly longer depending on your hob, until the masa inside is no longer raw and the outside is slightly crisp and speckled with dark-golden spots. (If the centre of the *comal* is very hot, you may need to move the *huarache* away from direct heat.) Test the first one by cutting it in half. If it's raw in the cente, return it to the hob and make a note for next time.

9   Stack the *huaraches* in a clean tea towel and wrap tightly to keep them warm. Repeat filling, shaping and cooking the remaining *huaraches*.

10   To serve, reheat the vegetable filling and lightly warm the *huaraches* on a *comal* if needed. Spread the morita salsa in a thin layer on top of the *huarache*, followed by a thick layer of vegetable filling. Top with grated cheese. If *huaraches* are no longer hot and the cheese doesn't melt right away, place them under the grill for a minute or two. Serve immediately, with extra salsa and the crema on the table.

COOKING TIPS: *Quesillo, an acidic cow's-milk cheese traditional to Oaxaca, is the typical* huarache *topping, but it's hard to find good-quality quesillo outside Mexico. Feel free to use any other mild, melty cheese as a substitute. If you can't find courgette flowers – available during the summer at farmers' markets and specialist food stores and greengrocers – use 330g fresh sweetcorn kernels.*

A moist, almost wet masa is essential here, otherwise the huaraches *will dry out and turn into crackers as they cook. The dough should be much moister than tortillas and it may even stretch a little once it reaches the desired consistency. Damp hands are important, as is a steady even heat. Masa harina is not an adequate substitute here. The flour doesn't soak up the necessary liquid, and the* huaraches *taste crumbly.*

CHILLI MORITA SALSA

This smoky, intense salsa, inspired by a version I tried near the Jamaica Market, jazzes up the huaraches *and pretty much anything else it touches. (It's also fairly salty, but it needs that to stand up to the* huarache *filling.) The salsa will keep in the fridge in an airtight container for up to a week.*

1 small plum tomato
1 medium garlic clove, unpeeled
6 morita chillies
salt

1   Heat a *comal* or non-stick frying pan to medium heat. Add the tomato in the centre and the garlic clove near the edge. Cook for 5–7 minutes until they're soft and blackened in spots.

2   Meanwhile, briefly toast the chillies for about 30 seconds per side, just enough for them to soften and release their aromas. Remove the chillies to a bowl filled with hot water. Leave them to soak for about 20 minutes or until the skins soften.

3   Remove the stems and add the chillies to a blender with the garlic, tomato and 60ml water. Pulse into a thick sauce. Pour into a bowl and season with salt. Serve at room temperature.

ENSALADA DE NOPAL
CACTUS SALAD

Most markets sell a small number of prepared foods to go, like cactus salad, which is made fresh daily and sold by the kilo from big, colourful ceramic platters or clay pots. The salad – a mix of cooked cactus, coriander, onion and Mexican oregano – is most often eaten as a side dish. You can find variations of it in several other Mexican states, including Tlaxcala and Puebla. The dish is so common that there's really no official recipe, but it should taste fresh, bright and balanced, with a hint of spice from the oregano. Some people add fresh chilli, others more cheese, and I've even heard of adding pumpkin seeds, although I personally don't think it needs them. Here, I've added tomatoes.

12 cactus paddles, rinsed, spines removed (see panel)
¼ large onion, sliced into thin slivers
25g fresh coriander, roughly chopped
2 plum tomatoes, deseeded and diced, or 24 cherry tomatoes, sliced in half
2 tablespoons olive oil
½ heaped teaspoon dried Mexican oregano
60g queso fresco, or other mild cheese, crumbled
salt and freshly ground black pepper

COOKING TIP: *Cactus naturally oozes a light slime, similar to that found in okra, but most of it should seep out during cooking.*

1   Bring a saucepan of water to the boil. While you're waiting, cut the cactus paddles into 5mm by 4cm strips.

2   Add the cactus, onion slivers and a pinch of salt to the water and cook them for 6–8 minutes, stirring occasionally, until the cactus is tender and turns a dull green colour. Strain, discarding the cooking water but keeping the onion slivers. Leave the cactus to cool to room temperature.

3   Place the cactus and onion in a serving bowl. Add the coriander, tomatoes, oil, ¼ teaspoon pepper, the oregano and the queso fresco and toss to combine. Taste and add ½ teaspoon salt, then mix again and taste for more salt if necessary.

4   Serve immediately, or chill for up to 2 hours.

HOW TO CLEAN A CACTUS PADDLE

Unless you don't mind the idea of thorns in your skin, wear rubber gloves or wrap your non-dominant hand – the one that holds the cactus paddle – in a tea towel.

1. *With your hands protected, place a cactus paddle on a chopping board, the narrower end towards you.*
2. *Steadying the paddle on the narrow end, carefully cut off the very outer edge of the cactus paddle. (These spines generally are too hard to remove one by one.)*
3. *Pick up the paddle and hold it at a 45-degree angle. Angle a sharp knife and scrape off the spines, cutting so that they fall away from you. Flip to scrape the other side until all spines have been removed.*
4. *Cut off the rough end near the paddle base. Rinse the paddle in cold water.*

See the photos on page 146.

RAJAS CON CREMA
ROASTED POBLANO CHILLIES WITH MEXICAN CREAM

At the same market stalls that sell ready-made cactus and broad (fava) bean salads, you can often find rajas con crema, *a mixture of roasted, peeled poblano chillies, Mexican cream and cheese. As an American, this mix reminds me a lot of what I love about casseroles: it's buttery and comforting, with a touch of heat from the chillies. My version is not as rich as what's sometimes sold in Mexico City, but it communicates the same decadent idea. In Mexico, these are generally eaten in tacos, or with rice and beans or a soup to make it a meal. You could also stir these into pasta, spoon them onto eggs or eat them on hunks of toasted French bread.*

8 poblano chillies, charred and deseeded (page 37)
1–2 tablespoons rapeseed oil
75g onion, chopped
2 medium garlic cloves, very finely chopped
120ml chicken or vegetable stock
6 tablespoons Homemade Crema (page 139)
25g Monterey Jack, or other mild, melty cheese, grated
8–12 corn tortillas
salsa of choice
salt

1   Cut the chillies into 4cm by 5mm strips. (You can prepare the chillies up to 1 day ahead of time.)

2   Heat the oil in a medium frying pan over a medium heat until shimmering. Add the onion and cook for 3–5 minutes until soft and translucent. Add the garlic and cook for 1 minute until aromatic.

3   Stir in the poblano chillies, stock and a few pinches of salt. Cook for 2–3 minutes until the chillies are warmed and a bit more tender. (Don't overcook them, or they'll become limp and slimy.)

4   Mix in the crema and cheese, stirring until the cheese melts. Remove the pan from heat and season the *rajas* with salt, if desired.

5   Allowing at least two to three per person, warm the tortillas on a *comal* or a large griddle or frying pan until soft and pliable. Place the tortillas in a tea towel or basket to keep warm.

6   Heat up the *rajas con crema*, if necessary, and scrape into a serving bowl. Pass the bowl and the warm tortillas around, along with your desired salsa.

QUELITES SUDADOS
'SWEATED' MEXICAN GREENS

Quelite is a catch-all word for any native Mexican green with young, tender leaves. Lambs quarters or fat hen, known in Mexico City as quelite cenizo, are popular in markets, and so are quintoniles, or leaf amaranth (Chinese spinach). They're almost always eaten simply – steamed with a little onion, garlic and chilli, and spooned into freshly made tortillas. One of my favourite things about quelites (besides their nutrient-rich profile) is that they have a thicker texture than, say, spinach. Even after cooking, they retain a certain bite. They also tend to be grassier, slightly sweeter and more aromatic than any other green I've tasted. These work great as a side dish to a meat-heavy meal. They also make a wonderful quesadilla filling; just be sure to warm the cooked greens briefly on a comal or frying pan to evaporate some of the water so that the tortillas don't turn mushy and fall apart.

1   Heat the oil in large frying pan over a medium heat.

2   Add the onion, garlic and chilli and cook, stirring constantly for about 3 minutes until the onions are translucent.

3   Add the *quelites* – in batches, if necessary – and season with salt and pepper to taste. Stir with tongs to coat in the onion mix. Reduce the heat to medium-low, cover tightly, letting the leaves release their natural juices, and cook for 3–5 minutes until they're limp but still somewhat al dente. (Spinach may take less time, about 2 minutes.) Season with more salt and pepper if needed and remove from the heat.

4   Allowing at least two to three per person, warm the tortillas on a *comal* or a large griddle or frying pan until soft and pliable. Place in a tea towel or basket to keep warm.

5   Heat up the *quelites* if needed and transfer to a serving bowl. Pass round the bowl of steamed *quelites* with the warm tortillas, along with desired salsa and lime wedges.

1 tablespoon olive oil
¼ small onion, cut into slivers
2 large garlic cloves, very finely chopped
½ serrano chilli, very finely chopped, with seeds (use less if you don't want any heat)
900g *quelites* (or spinach or Swiss chard; see Tip), rinsed well and drained
8–12 corn tortillas
salsa of choice
lime wedges
salt and freshly ground black pepper

COOKING TIP: *For the* quelites *to steam adequately, you'll need a large frying pan with a lid. Some farmers' markets may sell fat hen or lambs quarters (Chenopodium album) in the spring and summer, or you could forage for it, as it's a common annual weed. Chinese or Asian food stores may also sell Chinese spinach or leaf amaranth (Amaranthus gangeticus). If you can't find* quelites, *substitute ordinary spinach or Swiss chard leaves. (And don't discard the chard stems – they're great chopped and sautéed with the onion.)*

TACOS CAMPECHANOS
STEAK AND CHORIZO TACOS

The word campechano *in Mexican cooking often refers to a mixing of something – light and dark beer, for instance (*una cerveza campechana*); two types of seafood in a cocktail (*un cóctel campechano*); and, perhaps most popularly, in tacos that feature both steak and chorizo. You can find* tacos campechanos *at* taquerías *all over the city, and all over the country. This recipe was inspired by a taco I had at a* tianguis *south of the city centre, where the steak – a thin, salty, aged cut called* cecina *– was cooked on an open flame and topped with crumbly chorizo, a dollop of crema and a handful of Pico de Gallo Salsa. The flavours and textures left an impression, and luckily they're fairly easy to re-create at home.*

375g cooking chorizo
450g Mexican *cecina* steak
   (see Tip)
12 corn tortillas
3 limes, cut into wedges
Pico de Gallo Salsa (see opposite)
120g Homemade Crema
   (page 139)

1   Heat a large cast-iron frying pan over a medium heat. Use a knife to delicately slice into the chorizo's outer casing, then peel off and discard. Add the chorizo to the pan and crumble into small pieces. Cook, uncovered and stirring occasionally, for 8–10 minutes until crisp-edged, firm and darker in colour. Transfer to a plate lined with kitchen paper.

2   Wipe out the same pan with kitchen paper. Heat to medium, and when hot, add one piece of *cecina* and cook for 3 minutes without disturbing or until dark golden brown spots appear on the underside. Flip and repeat. Transfer the meat to a chopping board and leave to rest for 3 minutes. Chop the *cecina* into small pieces and set aside.

3   Heat the tortillas on a *comal* or non-stick frying pan until soft and pliable, and keep warm in a tea towel or covered basket.

4   To serve, place a small handful of chopped *cecina* on the warm tortilla and sprinkle the chorizo on top. Spritz with lime juice, and add a heaped spoonful of pico de gallo. Finish with a dollop of crema. Serve immediately.

COOKING TIP: *Outside of Mexico City,* cecina *is widely consumed in Morelos, Puebla and Oaxaca, among other states. You may find* cecina *in Mexican grocery stores (not to be confused with Spanish* cecina, *which is a smoked cured beef). Buy the thinnest variety you can find and cook it on a barbecue if possible, or, as a second choice, a blazing-hot cast-iron frying pan. If you can't find* cecina, *a thin skirt (bavette) steak would work.*

SALSA DE PICO DE GALLO
FRESH TOMATO SALSA

In Southern California, pico de gallo *refers to the spicy chilli powder sprinkled on cut fruit or jicama. In Mexico City, as in other areas of Mexico, the name means a fresh, chunky salsa of ripe tomatoes, white onion and any sort of fresh green chilli – jalapeño, serrano or fresh árbol chilli, depending on how hot you want it.*

This is a rustic dish, so there's no right way to make it. You want a juicy, tangy, citrusy mix, with plenty of bite from the fresh coriander. This makes quite a bit – but it will disappear faster than you think. I like this on Steak and Chorizo Tacos (see opposite) or spooned onto thick pieces of Homemade Chicharrón (page 136).

1 Place the tomatoes, onion, coriander and chillies in a bowl. (The pieces shouldn't look too perfect – this is a rustic dish.)

2 Pour in the lime juice and mix well. Season with salt, then taste and add more coriander or lime juice if needed. Serve immediately.

COOKING TIP: *This salsa will keep for up to two days in an airtight container in the fridge, although the flavour will mellow and it may release more liquid, depending on how juicy your tomatoes are. Use a slotted spoon to serve, if necessary.*

900g plum tomatoes, or any other ripe, fresh tomato, diced
½ medium onion, roughly chopped
8–12 sprigs of fresh coriander, roughly chopped
3 large jalapeños or 4 serranos, de-stemmed and cut into half-moons, with seeds
60ml fresh lime juice, or more to taste
salt

POLLO ROSTIZADO EN ADOBO
ROASTED CHICKEN IN ADOBO

Roasted chicken, juicy and golden and rotating on a spit, is a neighbourhood speciality in Mexico City. This recipe, for chicken slathered in an aromatic dried-chilli adobo, comes from Alonso Ruvalcaba, a food writer who recently opened his own roasted chicken shop in Condesa. The dish is a little fancier than what's sold in chicken joints and market stalls, but he's captured the essence of what makes Mexican chicken so good: a crisp, flavourful, slightly spicy skin and moist flesh. Serve with warm tortillas, salsa and (if you want to be truly authentic) homemade potato crisps so that your guests can make tacos.

For the chicken and sauce:

1 whole chicken, about 1.8kg, any giblets removed
½ teaspoon salt per 450g of chicken
2 plum tomatoes
½ medium onion
2 garlic cloves, unpeeled
40g raw peanuts
7.5cm piece of cinnamon stick
2 morita chillies
2 guajillo chillies
2 dried árbol chillies
2 dried chipotle chillies
60ml distilled white vinegar
1 tablespoon vanilla extract
1 lemon
1 small bunch of thyme

For the vegetables:

12 garlic cloves, peeled
12 small red or white potatoes, cut in half
6 small beetroots, cut into quarters, or eighths if they're large
2 red onions, peeled and cut into eighths
olive oil
salt and freshly ground black pepper

1   A day ahead, season the chicken generously with the salt and refrigerate in a covered container for about 4 hours.

2   Meanwhile, warm a *comal* or non-stick frying pan to medium-high heat. Add the tomatoes, onion and garlic and cook for 4–8 minutes until soft and blackened in spots.

3   Place 720ml water in a medium saucepan and bring to the boil.

4   Heat a small frying pan over a low heat. Toast the peanuts and cinnamon, stirring constantly, for 2–3 minutes until the peanuts turn golden brown. (If black spots appear, reduce the heat.) Transfer to a bowl. Increase the heat to medium and toast the chillies, in batches, for 5–10 seconds per side or until aromatic, being careful not to burn them.

5   Snip off the chillies' stems and shake out the seeds. Add the chillies to the boiling water and cook for about 20 minutes until the skins soften. Transfer to a blender, discarding the water. Add the charred tomatoes, onion, garlic, peanuts, cinnamon, vinegar and vanilla. Blend on high into a very smooth, thick paste. Season with salt.

6   Remove the chicken from the fridge and drain off any excess liquid. Slather with the adobo sauce, spreading it over and underneath the skin. Place the chicken in a resealable plastic bag and pour any remaining adobo on top. Refrigerate for 24 hours.

7   The next day, bring the chicken to room temperature, uncovered, for about 45 minutes. Preheat the oven to 230°C/gas mark 8.

8   Place the chicken, breast-side up, on a V-shaped rack set over a roasting tin. Cut the lemon in half and place it and the thyme in the chicken's cavity. Set the chicken on the centre shelf of your oven and roast for 20 minutes.

9   Toss the vegetables with olive oil and season with salt and pepper, then add to the roasting tin. Reduce the temperature to 220°C/gas mark 7 and roast for about a further hour until the chicken is crispy and the juices run clear, or the internal temperature measures 74°C, turning the vegetables occasionally so that they don't burn.

10   Leave the chicken to rest for 15 minutes before serving. Remove the lemon and thyme from the cavity, then slice the chicken meat. Serve with the vegetables.

PENEQUES
BATTERED STUFFED TORTILLAS

Peneques are puffy corn tortilla parcels sold by the bagful by women at the markets or tianguis. They seem so unusual – you don't see them on menus anywhere, or at least I haven't – that I actually pondered for a while whether to even include them in this book. But then, on different visits to Mexico City, they seemed to be following me, popping up at market stalls I'd never seen before.

Of course the vendors offered me a recipe: slice them open, stuff them with beans and cheese and then dunk them in a light egg batter known in Spanish as the capeado. *This is the same batter used for* chiles rellenos, *and vegetable or meat fritters known as* tortitas. *Interestingly, the tortilla acts as a chilli in this case, nestling beans and cheese in its eggy coat.*

My version includes vegetables, which add a bit of snap amid the oozy cheese. The result, drenched in spicy tomato sauce, makes for an extremely dignified meal, made more ingenious considering peneques *can use up any leftover scraps in the fridge. I like serving these with Basic Cooked Beans (page 107).*

1 batch Ranchera Sauce
(page 105)
2 teaspoons plus 120ml
rapeseed oil
3 tablespoons chopped onion
1 small garlic clove, very finely
chopped
175g green beans, cut into
4cm pieces
2 small Mexican squash or
courgettes, sliced into
5mm-thick half-moons
6 corn tortillas
115g Monterey Jack cheese,
grated
1 teaspoon plain flour, plus more
for dredging
5 medium eggs, separated
salt

1   Make the ranchera sauce and set aside. The sauce can be made up to 1 day in advance and stored in the fridge.

2   Heat the 2 teaspoons rapeseed oil over a medium heat in a medium frying pan. When hot, add the onion and garlic and cook, stirring often, for 2 minutes until the onion is translucent and aromatic.

3   Add the green beans and a few pinches of salt. Stir well to coat in the onion-garlic mixture, then add a few tablespoons of water. Reduce the heat to low, cover and cook for 3 minutes until the green beans are just tender.

4   Add the squash and another pinch of salt, and stir well. Return the heat to medium and cook, uncovered and stirring often, for 4 minutes until tender. Taste and add more salt if necessary. (You want the filling slightly saltier than you might think, in order for it to stand out inside the tortilla parcel.) Remove from the heat, cover and set aside.

5   Warm the tortillas on a *comal* or non-stick frying pan, crisping them slightly. Place in a tea towel to keep warm.

6   Create a work space with the cheese, filling, a small plate with flour for dredging and the warm tortillas. Place a wire rack on a rimmed baking tray in a warm oven.

7   Grab a tortilla and fill it with a few pinches of vegetables and one pinch of grated cheese. Fold the tortilla into a half-moon shape (the filling should not spill out; if it does, you have too much). Dredge both sides lightly in the flour and place on a plate. Repeat with the remaining tortillas.

8   In a medium bowl, whisk the egg whites by hand or with an electric whisk until stiff peaks form. Using a rubber spatula, fold in the egg yolks one by one, and then gently stir in the flour and ½ teaspoon salt.

9   Warm the remaining 120ml oil in a large frying pan over a medium-high to high heat. To test when it's ready for frying, add a little of the egg batter to the pan. If it bubbles and turns golden brown at the edges within 5–10 seconds, it's ready. If the batter immediately turns dark brown, the oil is too hot.

10   Once the oil is almost ready, begin warming up your ranchera sauce in a saucepan over a low heat and leave, covered, while you fry the *peneques*.

11   Give the egg batter one more stir. Then, using both thumbs to pinch the tortilla closed, scoop a *peneque* deeply through the egg batter and place in the hot oil. It should sizzle and puff up into a cloud. Place a dollop of egg batter on the bare space where your thumbs were. Using a spoon, bathe the *peneque* in the hot oil – this will make it easier to flip later. Cook for 20–30 seconds, then flip, taking care not to slosh around the hot oil. (If it's easier for you to flip using two spatulas, do it.) Cook for a further 30 seconds, bathing any uncooked sides of the *peneque* in oil, until golden brown. Transfer to the wire rack in the oven to drain. (The egg may deflate a little upon serving, but that's okay.) Repeat with the remaining *peneques*. Alternatively, serve the hot *peneque* immediately.

12   To serve, place one *peneque* on a plate and ladle enough ranchera sauce on top to completely cover it.

COOKING TIPS: *Puffy tortilla parcels are next to impossible to find outside Mexico, so I use ordinary corn tortillas here. Mastering the correct way to dunk an item in the* capeado *takes practice if you've never done it before. The egg whites should be fluffy and frothy, and the yolks completely integrated. Make space for your batter bowl near the hob so that you don't drip batter across the kitchen floor.*

HUEVOS A LA MEXICANA
MEXICAN-STYLE EGGS

Many Mexican market stalls that serve breakfast don't have menus, so when you arrive, after the obligatory 'Buenos días' greeting, it's customary to plop yourself down on a stool and ask, 'Qué hay?' (What is there?). The reply is usually a recitation of delicious-sounding items: 'Mire, tenemos riquísimas enchiladas verdes. Tenemos sopes preparados, y huevos al gusto. Lo que usted desea.' Translation: 'Look, we have delicious green enchiladas. We have sopes with all the toppings, and eggs any way you like. Whatever you wish.'

Huevos a la Mexicana – usually lumped under the heading al gusto, or the customer's preference – was the first breakfast dish I learnt to order at a market on my own, and it quickly became a favourite for its simple mix of egg, tomato, chilli and onion. (Sometimes my stomach can't handle enchilada sauce at ten in the morning.)

1 tablespoon rapeseed oil
75g onion, chopped
1 garlic clove, very finely chopped
1 serrano chilli, deseeded and very finely
    chopped (or keep seeds in for more heat)
2 ripe plum tomatoes, chopped
8 medium eggs, beaten lightly with
    ¼ teaspoon salt
corn tortillas
salsa of choice, optional
salt

1   Heat the oil in a medium frying pan over a medium heat.

2   When hot, add the onion, garlic, chilli and a pinch of salt. Cook for about 3 minutes until the onion is translucent.

3   Add the tomatoes and ¼ teaspoon salt. Cook for about 3 minutes until the tomatoes are tender but not yet breaking down into a paste.

4   Reduce the heat and stir in the eggs. Stir constantly, gently folding the eggs over themselves, until they scramble. If the eggs turn brown, reduce the heat or remove the pan from the heat. Cook until the eggs are fluffy and no longer wet.

5   Serve with warm corn tortillas and salsa, if desired.

TAMALES DE ELOTE
SWEETCORN TAMALES

Sweetcorn tamales are a mainstay at the weekly tianguis, *sold at the same stalls that offer fresh corn tortillas, tlacoyos and sopes. They're smaller than the big, dense tamales sold on the street, so they're perfect as a snack or light breakfast. The corn flavour should shine, so it's best to use both fresh sweetcorn and fresh masa for tamales, if you can. Otherwise, frozen sweetcorn and masa harina are acceptable substitutes. Serve these with a little crema on the side, or Chilli Pasilla Salsa (page 73) if you like sweet and savoury things. For steaming instructions, see page 37.*

1   To make the masa, in a small saucepan, gently warm the milk – either 1.2 litres or 120ml – until it's just above lukewarm. Turn off the heat.

2   If using masa harina, in a large, deep bowl, whisk together the masa harina, baking powder and salt. Slowly add the 1.2 litres warmed milk, incorporating the liquid thoroughly. You should end up with a moist, cohesive dough. Set aside for 10 minutes. Alternatively, if using fresh masa, pour the 120ml warmed milk over the dough and knead lightly until moist and soft. Cover with a damp tea towel.

3   Using a stand mixer, cream the butter and sugar (amounts dependent on the type of masa you're using) for about 5 minutes until fluffy and lighter in colour. With the mixer running on high, add the masa mixture, a little at a time. Mix well after each addition, scraping down the sides of the bowl to ensure that the masa incorporates thoroughly. Keep mixing until a sticky, cohesive dough forms, similar to a thick muffin batter. Don't worry about the dough seeming too wet or sticky – it will steam up later in the pan.

4   If using fresh masa, add the baking powder and salt now, mixing well. Taste and see if the dough needs more salt, keeping in mind that steaming will mute the saltiness factor just a bit.

5   The masa should be kept at room temperature until ready to use. If it's very hot in the kitchen, chill it in the fridge. Masa made with masa harina can be stored for up to 24 hours in the fridge. Fresh masa must be used the same day, or it will turn sour.

6   Soak the corn husks in a large pan of hot water for at least 30 minutes.

7   Add the sweetcorn to a food processor and pulse a few times until thick and chunky. Transfer to a bowl and stir in the sugar and salt. Little by little, stir the corn mixture into the masa. Taste for salt and add more if necessary.

8   Assemble and steam the tamales as per the instructions in steps 5–12 on pages 36–37.

For masa made with masa harina:

1.2 litres full-fat milk, at room temperature

690g masa harina for tamales

3 teaspoons baking powder

1¼ teaspoons salt

340g unsalted butter,
    at room temperature

100g unrefined cane sugar or dark soft
    brown sugar

For fresh masa:

120ml full-fat milk, at room temperature

1.8kg fresh masa for tamales

400g unsalted butter, at room temperature

150g unrefined cane sugar or dark soft
    brown sugar

3 teaspoons baking powder

1¼ teaspoons salt

at least 36 corn husks

660g fresh or frozen sweetcorn, defrosted
    (fresh sweetcorn may be much sweeter
    than frozen and require less sugar)

200g unrefined cane sugar or dark soft
    brown sugar

1¼ teaspoons salt

Homemade Crema (page 139) or
    salsa of choice, for serving

Chocolate
$9

NUEZ
$10

Pistache
$9⁰⁰ :)

crema
mango
$9

FRESA
$6

ANIS
$6

GELATINA DE NARANJA CON MEZCAL
CREAMY ORANGE JELLY WITH MEZCAL

Plump single-size jellies – both milk- and water-based – are often sold on the streets, from small glass cases that vendors carry or tote on their backs, or in markets. They come in tropical fruit flavours (mamey, guava, coconut) or they're mixed with nuts or even sherry. Often they're eaten on the go, wrapped in a square of greaseproof paper. The base of this recipe comes from my friend Graciela Montaño, a Mexico City native who teaches cooking classes and makes jellies in her spare time. I particularly like serving this jelly after a spicy main course. An orange sauce or syrup would work nicely drizzled on top, although it's not necessary.

1 The day before you'd like to eat the jellies, pour 120ml cold water into a bowl and sprinkle the gelatine on top. Leave to stand while you continue with the next steps.

2 Pour the cream and milk into a small saucepan and heat to medium-low. Stir in the sugar until dissolved, and then add the orange zest.

3 When the mixture just starts to boil, add the mezcal or tequila and cook for 3 minutes to allow the flavours to combine.

4 Remove the pan from the heat and then whisk in the gelatine solution until it's no longer lumpy.

5 Place the jelly moulds or silicone tray (see Tip) on top of a baking tray, and whisk the gelatine mixture once more to ensure that the zest is evenly distributed. Using a ladle, pour the hot gelatine mixture gently into each mould. Leave to cool for 20 minutes, then refrigerate overnight.

6 When ready to serve, remove the moulds from the fridge and leave them for about 15 minutes to bring slightly up to room temperature. Use a butter knife to delicately release the sides of each jelly. Place a baking tray on top of your moulds, and flip. Allow the jellies to be released from the moulds on their own, or if using silicone, you can gently push them out.

7 Scoop the jellies onto small serving dishes and serve cold. Extra jellies will keep wrapped in clingfilm or in an airtight container for up to a week.

1 scant tablespoon powdered
  gelatine
360g double cream
120ml full-fat milk
65g caster sugar
1 teaspoon grated orange zest
2 teaspoons mezcal or tequila,
  or more to taste

COOKING TIP: *You can use either individual metal moulds for this dish or a silicone tray with six separate cups. I like silicone because it's naturally non-stick. If you use metal moulds, rinse them in cold water beforehand and store them in the fridge while you cook – this step will make the jellies easier to unmould.*

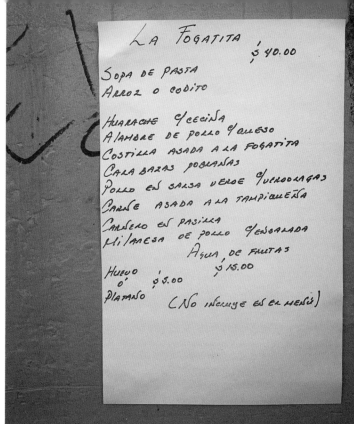

La Fogatita $40.00

Sopa de pasta
Arroz o codito

Huarache c/cecina
Alambre de pollo y queso
Costilla asada a la fogatita
Calabazas poblanas
Pollo en salsa verde c/chochoyotas
Carne asada a la tampiqueña
Carnero en pasilla
Milanesa de pollo c/ensalada
          Agua de frutas
                    $15.00
Huevo
  o' $5.00
Platano   (No incluye en el menú)

CHAPTER 3

IN
THE
FONDAS

In Mexico City on any given day, you'll find a written record of what many people eat for lunch, taped onto stoplights and telephone poles. The papers neatly list three courses from nearby *fondas*, or small homestyle restaurants: a vegetable or chicken soup to start; a 'dry' soup (*sopa seca*), such as rice or noodles to follow; then a heavy main course – green enchiladas, liver and onions, a spicy beef *mole de olla* or *chiles rellenos*, for instance. This meal, sold at an economical price with a warm basket of tortillas, is called *comida corrida*, and it's designed to keep you full until dinnertime. The only required condiments are table salsas (*salsas de mesa),* which are plonked on the table shortly after you sit down and designed to be spooned on top of your meal.

For a long time I didn't like *comida corrida*, simply because I thought it was too much food. Who eats three courses for lunch? But eventually I warmed to the tradition, and the fleeting daily menu that tomorrow would be ripped down, replaced and forgotten. (*Fondas* rotate their menus, but they do not repeat them two days in a row.) Seeing these *comida corrida* menus as living historical documents, I started snapping pictures of them. As my photo collection grew, I got over my fear and wandered inside, where I found several more things to love.

A MEAL TO LINGER OVER

Comida corrida – and, generally, lunch in Mexico – is lingered over. No one rushes anybody. A jug of *aguas frescas* is brought to the table so that you can refill your glass yourself. One hour can stretch into two, or even three. The tortilla basket is continually filled, the salsas sit on the table throughout the afternoon and still taste freshly made.

Many of these dishes have been eaten in Mexico for at least a hundred years, a fact I learnt after researching in the local gastronomy library. They may not taste as they once did, but to this American, the food is still soul-nourishing. Pork ribs dunked in a dish of *verdolagas en salsa verde* slip off the bone. *Mole verde* demands multiple tortillas to soak up the cuminy, herbal sauce. *Bistec en salsa pasilla* soothes you with its thick, brick-coloured bitterness. Dessert at the *fondas*, generally flan or rice pudding, sometimes feels like an afterthought, but most people don't go there for dessert anyway. It's the tradition of the three-course meal, the low price and the familiarity that draws customers, starting with the little paper menu fluttering on a telephone pole.

AGUA DE JAMAICA
HIBISCUS FLOWER TEA

Purplish-red dried hibiscus flowers, called flores de jamaica *in Spanish, can be bought cheaply and abundantly year-round in Mexico. They're steeped in a tea and served cold or at room temperature at nearly every* fonda *in Mexico City. The taste is sweet and floral and slightly acidic.*

55g dried hibiscus flowers
125g sugar, or other sweetener,
   such as agave syrup, to taste
fresh lime juice, optional

1   Pick out any twigs from your hibiscus flowers and rinse briefly in cold water to remove any dust or grit.

2   Bring 1.9 litres water to the boil. Add the hibiscus flowers and cook for 5 minutes, stirring occasionally.

3   Stir in the sugar and cook for a few minutes until dissolved. Turn off the heat. Leave to cool to room temperature, then strain the tea into a jug and add lime juice, if using. Refrigerate or serve over ice.

COOKING TIP: *Outside of Mexico, the quality of hibiscus can vary – some may not taste like anything at all, and others may be slightly gritty. You can find dried hibiscus flowers online from specialist or health food suppliers or from Mexican grocery stores.*

SALSA DE JALAPEÑO
CREAMY JALAPEÑO SALSA

This green, creamy table salsa is so good, I have to restrain myself from eating it like pudding. The recipe comes from a fonda in the Roma neighbourhood called Con Sabor a Tixtla, run by a family from Tixtla, Guerrero. The only ingredients are olive oil, onions and jalapeños, but the sauce tastes much more complex. There are two small tricks: you should blend it for several minutes and you can't, under any circumstances, have a spot of water in your blender – if you do, the folks at Con Sabor a Tixtla insist that the sauce won't come together. I've never tested the theory. The smell of jalapeños, onions and garlic browning in olive oil is enough to send me wiping down my blender jug with tea towels.

130ml olive oil
4 jalapeño chillies, stems
   removed
2 medium or large garlic cloves,
   peeled
2 × 1cm-thick slices of onion
¼ teaspoon salt, or more to taste

1   Heat the oil in a large saucepan over a medium or medium-low heat. When hot, add the jalapeños, garlic and onion – they should sizzle in the pan; if not, turn up the heat. Cook, turning everything frequently with tongs, for 5–7 minutes until the jalapeño skins loosen, whiten slightly and char a bit, and the garlic and olive oil turn a splotchy caramel colour. (Don't wear your best clothes, as this can splatter.)

2   Cool for 20 minutes, then pour into a blender and add the salt. Blend on high for about 4 minutes until the salsa looks creamy and no longer mottled. Serve immediately.

SOPA SECA DE ARROZ
MEXICAN-STYLE RED RICE

Mexican rice, deepened to a red colour by a fresh tomato purée, is the classic second course at fondas,
served after soup and before the main meal. In Mexico City, it's often called sopa seca, or dry soup.
Like most Mexican rice preparations, the rice is fried first in oil, and it's customary to add a few
vegetables. I serve this with almost anything, including Runner Beans with Cactus (page 146),
Beer-braised Rabbit (page 153), and Rajas con Crema (page 78). It's also very common in Mexico to
simply spoon the rice into a warm tortilla with slices of hard-boiled egg and salsa, a presentation
known as a taco placero. The rice keeps in an airtight container in the fridge for about a week.

1   Fill a medium saucepan two-thirds full with water and add the tomatoes. Bring to a gentle simmer over a medium heat. Cook for 7–10 minutes until the tomatoes have softened. Transfer the tomatoes to a blender, reserving the cooking water for the rice. (Drain the water if you plan to use stock.)

2   Blend the tomatoes until very smooth, making about 240ml puréed tomatoes.

3   Heat the oil over a medium heat in a large saucepan or medium-sized clay pot, if you have one. When hot, add the rice and stir, coating it in the oil. (It may stick a little.) Add the onion and fry, stirring often, for about 10 minutes until the rice grains start to sound almost raspy, like pebbles shaking in the pan.

4   Add the puréed tomato, 720ml of the reserved tomato water or the stock and the peas and carrots. Stir in the salt, taste and add more if necessary. Top with the chilli.

5   Bring to the boil, then reduce the heat to the lowest it will go and cover. Cook for 12–15 minutes until all the liquid has been absorbed – the puréed tomato should have formed a layer on top of the rice. Stir well and serve immediately.

2 plum tomatoes, or other ripe,
    fresh tomato
60ml rapeseed oil
370g long-grain or
    extra-long-grain white rice
⅛ medium onion, chopped
720ml Basic Homemade Chicken
    Stock (page 98) or water
65g fresh or frozen peas
1 carrot, finely chopped
1½ teaspoons salt
1 serrano chilli, finely chopped

TO SOAK OR NOT TO SOAK?

In Mexico City, many cooks swear by soaking their rice in hot water before
cooking, insisting it's the key step to fluffy, well-cooked rice. Elsewhere, this step
is not necessary – if you soak the rice in hot water beforehand, it will overcook
in the pan and turn sticky.

CALDO DE POLLO
BASIC HOMEMADE CHICKEN STOCK

Many traditional Mexican dishes rely on homemade chicken stock for extra depth of flavour. It's essential in moles, as a base in soups, to thin down chilli sauces in guisados and when cooking rice or noodles. This is not a heavy, rich stock like you'd find in a European kitchen, and you don't need carrots, celery or parsley – just a little onion and garlic. Some Mexican cooks use chicken carcasses and feet to develop a gelatinous texture in the broth, and I'm a fan, too. You can generally find these sold cheaply at Chinese or Asian supermarkets, but feel free to use necks, legs and thighs. This stock freezes beautifully in airtight containers or in ice cube trays.

1.3kg chicken pieces, excess fat
   trimmed
225g chicken feet
½ medium onion, quartered,
   unpeeled
2 garlic cloves, peeled

1   Place the chicken pieces and feet in a large deep saucepan with enough water to cover. Add the onion and garlic. Bring to the boil.

2   Skim off any foam or scum that rises to the surface, then reduce the heat to medium-low and gently simmer, uncovered. Remove the thighs and drumsticks when the meat is tender, after about 25 minutes. When cool enough to handle, shred the meat and return the bones to the pan. Save the meat for another use.

3   Simmer the stock for a further 2½ hours, uncovered, adding more water if necessary. Leave to cool.

4   Refrigerate the stock overnight. In the morning, scoop off any fat that has accumulated on the surface. Warm the stock, strain and leave to cool. At this point the stock is ready to use or freeze.

COOKING TIP: *If you don't have time to make this stock, you can make a very light chicken broth by poaching chicken pieces in water with 1 small garlic clove and a small wedge of onion, plus a small bay leaf and a few black peppercorns. Place the ingredients in a saucepan and cover with 1.9 litres cold water. Bring to the boil, then cook over a very low heat, covered, for about 30 minutes for 1.1kg of chicken. Leave to cool, then shred the meat. At that point the broth can be strained and used.*

Low-salt chicken stock cubes will work in Mexican cooking most of the time, but I've found them too aggressive and rich for mole, which relies on a delicate balance of flavours, and white rice. In these cases, it's best to use homemade chicken stock.

CREMA DE ELOTE
CREAMY CORN SOUP

Creamy soups are served before the rice or as an alternative to consommé on fonda *menus. They're a bit heavier than their brothy counterparts, although many don't contain cream – just puréed vegetables and stock. This version is a modification of a corn soup found in Josefina Velázquez de León's excellent bilingual cookbook,* Mexican Cook Book Devoted to American Homes, *published in 1947. Because corn elsewhere is so sweet, it doesn't exactly mirror the corn soups served in Mexico, which are starchier and heartier. But it's still flavourful, not too rich and best served in late summer, when sweetcorn is at its peak. See page 100 for a photo, with Creamy Beet Soup (page 101).*

1   Melt the butter in a large, heavy-based saucepan over a medium-low heat. Add the onion and garlic. Cook, stirring often, for 3–4 minutes until the onion is translucent. Add the sweetcorn, stock, salt and white pepper.

2   Bring to the boil, then reduce the heat and simmer, covered, for about 20 minutes or until the flavours meld and the corn cooks through. Transfer the soup to a blender and blend until smooth, then pour it back into the pan (or use a stick blender). The soup should still be hot.

3   Stir in the cream, then taste and adjust the seasonings. Serve the soup immediately, topped with the cheese and a sprinkle of chopped fresh coriander.

COOKING TIP: *Crumbled queso añejo would be a typical garnish here, but good-quality queso añejo can be hard to find outside Mexico. As a substitute, queso de mano is available from online suppliers.*

60g unsalted butter

1 small onion, very finely chopped

2 medium garlic cloves, very finely chopped

6 fresh sweetcorn cobs, shucked, kernels cut from the cobs

1 litre Basic Homemade Chicken Stock (see opposite)

1½ teaspoons salt, or more to taste

⅛ teaspoon ground white pepper

120g double cream

60g queso de mano or queso añejo, grated or cubed

chopped fresh coriander

CREMA DE BETABEL
CREAMY BEETROOT SOUP

I spied this soup on a creative comida corrida *menu a few years back, and I took a picture to remind myself to try it. When I did, the soup was no longer on the menu. This version reflects how I imagine it might have tasted: full and earthy, with a contrasting texture from toasted pumpkin seeds. The colour is also gorgeous – a deep, intense pink like you'd see painted on a house in Mexico City. The soup works well as a starter to a heavier main course, such as Purslane in Tomatillo Sauce (page 110), or as a light dinner with a vegetable-forward* guisado, *such as Stewed Swiss Chard (page 111). This soup is photographed with the Creamy Corn Soup on page 99.*

1   Preheat the oven to 200°C/gas mark 6. If necessary, slice off and reserve the beetroot greens for another use. (They're great in *guisados* – see 'Sweated' Mexican Greens, page 79, or Stewed Swiss Chard, page 111, for inspiration.) Wrap the beetroots, garlic clove and onion tightly in foil and bake for 1 hour and 20 minutes, depending on their size, until very tender when pierced with a fork. (Unwrap every 30 minutes or so to make sure the beets are moist; if they look dry, add a tablespoon or so of water and wrap again tightly.) Leave to cool.

2   Reduce the oven temperature to 100°C or lowest gas setting and roast the pumpkin seeds on a baking tray for 8–10 minutes until slightly golden brown. (You can also do this on the hob in a dry frying pan.)

3   Meanwhile, place a piece of kitchen paper over your hand so that it doesn't stain, and then peel the beetroots. Cut off and discard the tops. Reserve 1 beetroot for garnish, if desired, dicing it into 5mm cubes; set aside. Chop the remaining beets roughly and set aside.

4   Working in batches if necessary, add the roughly chopped beetroot, roasted onion and garlic to a blender with the milk and chicken stock, blending on high for a few minutes until smooth. Add the crema and 65g of the pumpkin seeds and blend again until smooth.

5   Gently heat the oil in a large saucepan or casserole dish over a medium-low heat. When hot, add the beetroot purée, salt and pepper. Cook the soup for 5–8 minutes only until it is warmed through, being careful not to scald it. Taste and adjust the seasonings.

6   Serve immediately, topping each bowl with the remaining toasted pumpkin seeds, beetroot cubes and chopped fresh coriander. (For a little more acidity, toss the beetroot cubes with a few teaspoons of crema before adding to the soup.)

900g beetroots, scrubbed free
   of any dirt
1 garlic clove, unpeeled
¼ medium onion
100g pumpkin seeds
600ml full-fat milk
480ml Basic Homemade
   Chicken Stock (page 98)
120g Homemade Crema, plus
   more for serving (page 139)
1 tablespoon olive oil
¾ teaspoon salt, or more to taste
⅛ teaspoon white pepper
chopped fresh coriander

FIDEO NOODLES IN CHIPOTLE-TOMATO SAUCE

Another 'dry soup' served before the main meal, sopa seca de fideo is one of my favourite dishes in Mexico. Thin fried noodles mingle in a (sometimes spicy) tomato sauce, garnished with crema, avocado slices and, once when I was lucky, big pieces of chicharrón – it added a crunch and meatiness I didn't even know I was missing. Not everyone adds chipotles in adobo sauce; I like the heat and slight fruitiness it gives the sauce. This is usually served as a side dish, but can also stand up as a meal on its own. Leftovers will keep in the fridge for about a week.

6 ripe plum tomatoes

2 tablespoons very finely chopped canned chipotles in adobo sauce, plus 1 teaspoon adobo sauce

½ teaspoon brown sugar or grated *piloncillo* (see page 61)

2 garlic cloves, peeled

¼ medium onion

3 tablespoons rapeseed oil

350g *fideo* noodles

½ teaspoon salt, plus more to taste

120g Homemade Crema (page 139)

½ ripe Haas avocado, peeled, stoned and thinly sliced

100g queso fresco, crumbled

pieces of *chicharrón* (pork cracklings or scratchings), optional

1 Fill a medium saucepan two-thirds full with water and add the tomatoes. Bring to a gentle simmer over a medium heat and cook for 7–10 minutes until softened. (If the tomatoes start to split before they've softened, reduce the heat.) Transfer to a small bowl and reserve 240ml of the cooking water.

2 In a small bowl, mix together the chipotles, adobo sauce and sugar. Set aside.

3 Slip the skins off of the tomatoes and add them, with any juices left in the bowl, to a blender with the garlic, onion and 120ml of the reserved cooking water. Blend on high until very smooth.

4 Add 1 tablespoon of the oil to a large frying pan set over a medium heat. When hot, fry half the noodles, stirring often so that they don't burn, until they're a deep golden brown. Transfer to kitchen paper to drain. Wipe the pan and repeat with 1 tablespoon oil and the second batch of noodles.

5 Wipe the pan clean once more and heat the remaining tablespoon oil. When hot, pour in the puréed tomato (careful, it may splatter) and fry over a medium to medium-low heat, sprinkling on the salt. Cook, stirring occasionally, for 4–5 minutes until the sauce no longer tastes of raw onion and garlic. Mix in the chipotle paste and taste for seasoning.

6 Add the fried noodles and cook over a medium-low heat for about 5 minutes until they absorb nearly all the sauce. Taste the noodles – if they're still too chewy, add the remaining 120ml reserved cooking water and cook until all the sauce is just absorbed and the noodles are al dente.

7 Serve on individual plates, topped with the crema, avocado slices and crumbled cheese. Place *chicharrón* pieces on the side, if you like.

COOKING TIPS: *Fideo noodles are thin like angel hair pasta, and in Mexico City they come in various sizes; the most common is about 2.5cm long. Some sold at Mexican grocery stores come in bundles that can be broken into pieces. Canned chipotles in adobo sauce can vary in acidity, depending on the brand. Ensure that you taste and adjust the sugar or heat in the sauce as necessary.*

HUEVOS MONTULEÑOS
MONTULEÑO-STYLE EGGS

1 batch Ranchera Sauce (see opposite)
1 batch Quick Refried Beans (page 45)
8 corn tortillas
25g lard or 2 tablespoons rapeseed oil
200g fresh or frozen peas, defrosted
125g thick-cut ham, diced
4 medium eggs
100g queso fresco or queso añejo, crumbled
fried plantain slices, optional
salt and freshly ground black pepper

Originated in Yucatán, this snazzier version of huevos rancheros *(as I think of it) is served for breakfast in many Mexico City* fondas. *Corn tortillas are sandwiched together with refried beans, topped with fried eggs, a sprinkling of diced ham, cooked peas and a heavy ladleful of spicy tomato sauce. While the Yucatecan sauce may be somewhat chunky, at home I like to make this with a smooth, thick ranchera sauce. The traditional serving size is two eggs per person, but I think one is plenty, combined with all the other elements on the plate. Like a lot of Mexican breakfast dishes, this tastes best if served immediately, while the egg yolks are still runny.*

1   Prepare the ranchera sauce and the refried beans and set aside on the hob to keep warm.

2   In a large frying pan, fry two tortillas lightly in 2 teaspoons of the lard or oil until lightly toasted. (You don't want them too crispy.) Drain on a layer of kitchen paper or a wire rack set over a rimmed baking tray. Repeat until all the tortillas have been fried. Keep warm in a gently heated oven.

3   Add ½ teaspoon lard or oil to the same pan. When hot, add the peas and ham and season with salt and pepper to taste. Cook for about 2 minutes until just warmed through. Cover and keep warm.

4   Crack one egg into a small bowl. Coat the base of a small frying pan in lard or oil and warm over a medium heat. When hot, pour in the egg, cover the pan, reduce the heat slightly and cook for 2–3 minutes just until the whites have set.

5   Meanwhile, place two tortillas on a plate. Smear one with a layer of refried beans, then top with the other. Carefully slide the fried egg on top. Add a generous ladle of ranchera sauce and sprinkle with peas, ham and cheese. Nestle fried plantain slices on the side, if using. Serve immediately.

6   Repeat steps 4 and 5 with the remaining eggs, tortillas, refried beans and garnishes.

RANCHERA SAUCE

I serve this spicy, puréed tomato sauce with huevos rancheros, *Fried Huauzontle Patties (page 120) or even spooned onto scrambled eggs. You can make it as thin or as thick as you like, but I like mine slightly thicker than spaghetti sauce.*

1   Place the tomatoes, chillies, garlic and onion in a casserole dish and cover with cold water. (The tomatoes will float.) Bring to a medium heat and simmer gently for about 8 minutes until the tomato flesh softens. The chilli and onion may take a few minutes longer – the chilli is done when the skin darkens and becomes slightly matt, while the onion should be translucent.

2   Drain and transfer the tomato mixture to a bowl, reserving 60ml of the cooking water. Leave to cool to room temperature.

3   Stem the chillies and chop roughly. Place them in a blender with the onion and garlic. Slip off and discard the tomato skins, add the tomatoes to the blender and blend until smooth. (You may need to do this in batches, depending on the power of your blender). If the sauce seems very thick, add the reserved cooking water and blend again until smooth.

4   Heat the lard or oil in a large frying pan over a medium heat. When it melts or is hot, add the sauce in one quick pour. (Be careful – it might splatter.) Season with the salt, or more to taste. Bring to the boil, then reduce the heat and simmer gently, stirring occasionally, for about 5 minutes until the flavours meld. Keep warm if using immediately.

900g plum tomatoes
2 medium serrano chillies
1 large garlic clove, peeled
¼ medium onion
15g lard or 1 tablespoon
   rapeseed oil
¾ teaspoon salt

HUEVO CON FRIJOL
BEANS AND EGGS

Eating beans and eggs together is nothing new in Mexican cooking, but serving them in a fluffy, cylindrical shape is something I'd never seen before until I sat down for breakfast at Fonda La Indita in the Centro. The tiny, windowless spot looks like it hasn't changed in at least a hundred years – exposed wooden beams still line the tall ceilings, and a woman near the door still makes homemade corn tortillas from an old-fashioned conveyor-belt tortilla press.

A few months later, curious about this presentation, I went back and owner Amparo Reina Rendón kindly invited me into the kitchen. There, a cook mashed together beans and eggs, placed them in an oiled frying pan and jerked the pan forward and back. The mix slid up the side of the pan and flipped over into a perfect cylindrical roll. To eat, tear off a piece of warm corn tortilla, pinch off a bit of beans and eggs and spoon salsa on top.

700g Basic Cooked Beans
    (see opposite), with 60ml
    bean liquid
8 teaspoons rapeseed oil
8 medium eggs
8 corn tortillas
salsa of choice
salt

COOKING TIP: *You need a small, well-oiled (or non-stick) frying pan to ensure that the flip works correctly. The cylindrical shape doesn't affect the flavour, though, so if you can't get the hang of it, just serve them normally. For smaller portions, try 85g beans, 1 teaspoon bean liquid and 1 egg per person.*

1 Measure out 175g of the beans and 1 tablespoon of the cooking liquid into a small bowl. Mash lightly until coarsely textured. There should be some half-mashed beans and some beans left whole. Set aside.

2 Warm 1 teaspoon of the oil in a medium frying pan over a medium-high heat. Crack 2 eggs into a small bowl and beat them lightly.

3 Once the pan is hot, add the eggs and stir quickly, sprinkling on a pinch of salt. Keep stirring for about 30 seconds until the eggs are just cooked through.

4 Add the cooked eggs to the mashed beans and mash together with a flat instrument – I like using the base of a heatproof cup – until the mixture becomes a thick, evenly combined mass. Taste and season with more salt if needed.

5 Wipe out the frying pan and heat again to medium-high heat. Add another teaspoon of oil. When hot, add the bean and egg mixture, shaking the pan slightly to even out the mass. Cook for 15–20 seconds, stir and shake to even out again. Cook for a further 20–30 seconds until warmed through.

6 To flip, pick up the frying pan by the handle and gently but quickly flick it back, slightly up and then towards you. The mixture should slide to the back of the pan, inch up the side with the momentum and then flip over into a torpedo shape. (If you've made a French-style omelette before, it's a similar motion.)

7 Remove carefully to an ovenproof plate and place in a gently heated oven. Repeat steps 1–6 three times. Serve immediately with warm corn tortillas and salsa.

FRIJOLES BÁSICOS
BASIC COOKED BEANS

For years I wondered how to make stewed beans like the ones I'd enjoyed in the fondas. *They were so simple and perfect, I didn't think an unskilled hand could succeed. It turns out two factors make the biggest difference: the quality of the beans and the amount of liquid you cook them in. Soaking them, a practice roundly embraced in Mexico City, isn't always necessary, although they will take longer to cook if not. These go with almost anything: eggs, spooned into a tortilla, as a side dish for nearly any* guisado, *mashed and smeared onto a tostada or served warm and sprinkled with your favourite cheese.*

1   The day before you wish to eat them, pick over the beans and remove any stones or foreign matter. Place in a large bowl, cover with cold water and leave to soak overnight. (Alternatively, skip the soaking if you prefer.)

2   Drain the beans and cover with 5cm fresh cold water (7.5cm if unsoaked) and bring to the boil. Reduce the heat to medium, add the epazote, if using, and simmer for 45 minutes–1 hour, stirring occasionally, until the beans are tender and the innards creamy and smooth. (Unsoaked beans may take a further 45 minutes to cook.) About 5–10 minutes before the cooking time is up – when the beans are mostly soft, but not quite silky – add salt to taste. You can now eat the beans as is, or continue on.

3   Transfer the beans and cooking liquid to a bowl. Heat the lard in the same pan over a medium. When hot, add the garlic and onion and cook, stirring constantly, until blistered and dark golden.

4   Add the beans and cooking liquid in one swift pour (careful, it may splatter). Bring to the boil, taste and adjust the seasonings. Serve immediately.

450g dried beans, such as pinto or black
3–5 sprigs of epazote, optional
2 tablespoons lard or rapeseed oil
1 medium garlic clove, peeled
¼ medium onion, chopped
salt

VARIATION: *To create a richer, thicker bean cooking liquid, remove 175g beans and 240ml cooking liquid to a separate bowl once the beans have finished cooking. Mash together, just enough to release the bean starches into the broth (the beans should have a rustic texture). Strain and add the starchy broth back to the pan, or, if you don't mind small bits of mashed bean in your pan, add the whole thing. Continue cooking until warmed through.*

COOKING TIP: *Don't drown the beans in water at the beginning – the concentrated cooking liquid left at the end is almost as important as the beans themselves. Unsoaked beans might need perhaps 7.5cm water to cover; soaked beans a little less. At higher altitudes, you'll need a pressure cooker or a kettle filled with warm water, to replenish as necessary. (Don't use cold water, otherwise the beans may come out half-cooked.)*

I stew – 'guisar' – these beans after cooking them, meaning I fry them in a little lard, onion and garlic. This step adds a lot of flavour, but you can skip it or do it later if you're running short on time. In Mexico City, most cooked beans typically include epazote, which adds a subtle herbal bitterness. If you can't find it, leave it out.

Bean cooking times can vary, depending on altitude and how old the beans are. Aim for creamy, silky innards.

MOLE DE OLLA
MOLE FROM THE POT

Not all Mexican moles are thick sauces ladled over meat. This one, popular in fondas *and at homes across Central Mexico, is a soup. The dish starts with a full-bodied, chilli-accented beef stock, combined with chunks of stewed beef, corn on the cob, squash and green beans, traditionally eaten as a midday meal. The base of my version comes from my friend Janneth López, whom I met in cooking school. It calls for a bit more time and labour than other* mole de olla *recipes, but the result is a warm, rich broth that's so good you'll want to drink it plain, assuming you can handle the kick. It freezes beautifully.*

For the meat:

900g beef chuck steak or short
    ribs, cut into large pieces
450g veal or marrow bones
¼ large onion
2 garlic cloves, peeled
2 sprigs of fresh thyme
5 black peppercorns
1 celery stick, roughly chopped
1 carrot, roughly chopped

For the sauce:

8 costeño chillies (see Tip)
2 guajillo chillies
2 pasilla chillies
1 tablespoon rapeseed oil, plus
    more for frying
4 black peppercorns
2 cloves
½ teaspoon aniseed
½ teaspoon dried Mexican oregano
2 heaped teaspoons finely
    chopped fresh ginger
scant ½ teaspoon ground nutmeg
2 plum tomatoes, quartered
4 small garlic cloves, peeled
⅛ medium onion
2 teaspoons lard or rapeseed oil
2 corn cobs, husked and cut into
    four pieces each
110g green beans, cut into
    5cm lengths
1 chayote, unpeeled, sliced pole to
    pole and thinly sliced
1 large Mexican squash/courgette,

cut into 1cm-thick half-moons
5–8 sprigs of epazote, or to taste
12 corn tortillas
4 limes, cut into wedges
salt

COOKING TIP: *In Mexico, dried* costeño *chillies are short, red or yellow and quite hot. In the USA, they are squat, plump and not as hot. If you find the real ones, start with five, or use chilli puya, a type of hotter guajillo, or ordinary chilli guajillos.*

1   To prepare the meat, place all the ingredients in a large, deep saucepan and cover with cold water. Bring to the boil and skim off any scum that floats to the surface. Reduce the heat to low and simmer gently, partially covered, for about 1 hour 45 minutes until tender. Transfer the meat to a bowl and strain the stock, discarding the aromatics. Skim off any large pools of fat. Reserve 120ml of the stock for the sauce. At this point you can refrigerate the meat and remaining stock for up to 2 days.

2   To make the sauce, snip the stems off the dried chillies and shake out the seeds. (If they're too brittle, toast them first on a *comal* or non-stick frying pan to soften.) Coat a small frying pan with the oil and warm to medium heat. Add the chillies in batches, frying one variety at a time and stirring constantly, for about 10 seconds until they change colour and emit a spicy aroma. Be careful not to burn them. Set aside.

3   Grind the peppercorns, cloves and aniseed in a mortar. Transfer to a blender with the oregano, ginger, nutmeg, tomatoes, the reserved stock, garlic, onion, fried chillies and a pinch of salt. Blend on high until smooth.

4   Heat the lard (or oil) in a medium frying pan over a medium heat. Add the chilli sauce in one quick pour (stand back, as it may splatter). Cook for 8–10 minutes until it darkens, stirring often so that it doesn't stick on the base of the pan.

5   Bring the stock and meat to a gentle simmer in a large, deep saucepan. Pour in the chilli sauce and add the corn, green beans and 1 tablespoon salt. Bring to the boil, then reduce the heat to low and simmer for 15–20 minutes until the beans are almost tender. Add the chayote, squash and epazote and cook for 10 minutes or until the squash is tender. Taste and add more salt or epazote if desired – the herb should taste noticeable.

6   Serve the soup in large, deep bowls. Warm the tortillas and pass them round at the table in a basket or wrapped in a tea towel, along with the lime wedges.

VERDOLAGAS EN SALSA VERDE
PURSLANE IN TOMATILLO SAUCE

Purslane, known as verdolagas *in Spanish, is usually served cooked in Mexico City, although some upmarket restaurants have recently started to embrace its use in salads. Stewing the greens in tomatillo sauce – often in a clay pot – is a classic preparation: earthy and lightly acidic, with a pleasing al dente texture. Corn tortillas and beans are usually the only accompaniments.*

1   Rinse the pork and place in a large pan. Cover with cold water and add the onion and garlic. Bring to the boil with a few hefty pinches of salt. Skim off any scum that accumulates on the surface. Reduce the heat to medium-low, cover and simmer gently for about 2 hours until the meat is extremely tender when pierced with a fork. Remove 480ml of the liquid from the pan and set aside. Leave the meat to sit in the pan while you make the sauce.

2   Fill a medium saucepan two-thirds full with water and bring to a slow, rolling boil. Add the tomatillos, serranos, garlic and onion and boil for 8–10 minutes until the tomatillos and chillies have softened and turned a dull green colour. Strain and transfer to a blender with 240ml of the reserved pork cooking liquid. Blend on a high speed until smooth.

1.1kg pork back bones (pork spine) or pork
   ribs (see Tip), cut into large pieces
¼ medium onion
1 large garlic clove
salt

For the sauce:
900g tomatillos, husked and rinsed
2 large serrano chillies
2 medium garlic cloves, peeled
1 small onion, cut in half
2 teaspoons lard or rapeseed oil
900g purslane, ends trimmed
2 heaped tablespoons roughly chopped
   fresh coriander, or more to taste
1 batch Basic Cooked Beans (page 107)
8–12 corn tortillas, warmed
salt

3   Heat the lard or oil over a medium heat in a large. deep pan or casserole dish. When hot, add the tomatillo sauce in one quick pour and fry for a few minutes, seasoning with salt. Add the meat and bring to the boil. (Add the remaining 240ml of the reserved pork cooking liquid if you want a thinner texture.) Reduce the heat to medium and cook for 5–8 minutes until the flavours meld. Add the purslane and cook for a further 5 minutes, partially covered, until limp and tender. Stir in the coriander.

4   To serve, spoon the pork, greens and sauce onto individual plates, giving each a side of beans. Pass round warm corn tortillas at the table.

COOKING TIP: *Tomatillos vary in acidity. The sauce should be acidic, but not mouth-puckeringly so. If yours are too tart, add more onion to the blender.*
   If you can't find pork back bones, the spine cut crossways with two sections of tenderloin attached – a cheaper cut known as espinazo *in Spanish – try pork ribs. Vegetarians can leave out the meat and lard and increase the veggies, and use the tomatillo cooking water or vegetable stock in lieu of the pork broth.*

GUISADO DE ACELGAS
STEWED SWISS CHARD

Chard is available year-round in Mexico City, and it's most commonly consumed stewed in a mix of chilli, onion, garlic and perhaps tomatoes. There's no exact ratio that works best – the ideal dish should be simple and comforting. I've added chickpeas here after seeing the idea in an out-of-print Mexican cookbook; they add a creaminess to the dish that I like. You can add a very finely chopped serrano chilli, too, for a touch of heat. Nothing else is needed but corn tortillas, salsa and a little avocado.

1   Heat the oil in a casserole dish over a medium-high heat. Add the onion and garlic and cook for about 3 minutes until the onion is softened and translucent.

2   Reduce the heat to medium. Add the tomatoes and chard stems and sprinkle with salt. Cook for 3–4 minutes until the tomatoes start to break down and soften.

3   Stir in the chickpeas and chicken stock. Then add the chard leaves in batches, tossing together with tongs until wilted. Sprinkle with more salt, reduce the heat, cover and cook for 5–8 minutes until the leaves soften and the stems are tender. Taste and adjust seasonings, then transfer to a serving bowl.

4   Serve with warm corn tortillas, sliced avocado, lime wedges and salsa so that guests can make their own tacos.

3 teaspoons rapeseed oil

75g onion, chopped

2 garlic cloves, very finely chopped

2 plum tomatoes, chopped

2 large bunches of Swiss chard, stems diced and leaves torn into small pieces

170g cooked chickpeas, or 400g can, drained and rinsed

60ml Basic Homemade Chicken Stock (page 98), vegetable stock or water

12 corn tortillas, warmed

1 ripe Haas avocado, peeled, stoned and thinly sliced

3 limes, cut into wedges

salsa of choice

salt

BISTEC EN SALSA DE CHILE PASILLA
STEAK IN CHILLI PASILLA SAUCE

This guisado is popular across Central Mexico, and you'll often see it in fondas, simmering away in a clay pot. Thin pieces of steak, cooked until tender, are added to a seasoned chilli pasilla sauce that is so good it's nearly impossible not to sop up every bit with a rolled-up tortilla. Lightly fried potatoes on the side add a good, starchy counterpoint. (And another reason to slather your plate with sauce.)

3 large waxy potatoes, scrubbed

7 pasilla chillies, seeds and veins removed, and toasted briefly on a *comal* or non-stick frying pan

275g tomatillos

1 small onion, cut into quarters or thickly sliced

1 garlic clove, unpeeled

360ml Basic Homemade Chicken Stock (page 98), beef stock or both mixed with a little chilli water

900g beef steaks, sliced very thinly and cut into 5cm pieces

25g plus 2 teaspoons lard or 2 tablespoons plus 2 teaspoons rapeseed oil

12 corn tortillas, warmed on a *comal* or a large griddle or frying pan

salt and freshly ground black pepper

1 Place the potatoes in a large saucepan and cover with cold water. Bring to the boil, then reduce the heat to medium-high and simmer for about 20 minutes until just tender when pierced with a fork. Place the chillies in a bowl of warm water and leave to soak for 15–20 minutes until their skins soften. (Reserve the soaking water if you'd like to use it as flavouring later.)

2 Meanwhile, place the tomatillos, onion and garlic on a *comal* or non-stick frying pan over a medium heat. Cook, turning occasionally, for 10–12 minutes until blackened in spots and the garlic turns a bit squishy. Peel the garlic and place in a blender with the tomatillos, onion, softened chillies and 240ml of the chicken or beef stock. Blend on high until very smooth and set aside. Strain the potatoes, then cut into any shape you want (I like half-moons) and set aside.

3 Season the steaks well with salt and pepper. In a large saucepan or casserole dish, warm the 25g lard or 2 tablespoons oil over a high heat. Add the steaks and cook, flipping once, for 6–8 minutes until the meat turns juicy and darkens in colour and the fat foams and then subsides.

4 Add the sauce in one quick pour, plus 120ml of the reserved chilli water or the remaining chicken or beef stock. Stir well, then turn to a very low heat, cover and simmer for about 20 minutes until the flavours meld and the meat softens a bit. Season with more salt.

5 Meanwhile, heat the remaining 2 teaspoons lard or oil in a large frying pan over a medium-high heat. Add the potatoes in an even layer and sprinkle with a hefty pinch of salt. Leave undisturbed for 4–5 minutes, then turn over and cook the other side – they should have a nice golden-brown crust. Sprinkle with more salt, reduce the heat and cover, stirring occasionally, for 15–20 minutes until crispy on the outside and soft in the middle. Serve immediately, transferring the meat to a large bowl in the middle of the table and letting guests help themselves. Pass the potatoes and warm corn tortillas.

COOKING TIP: *In Mexico, you can ask the butcher for 'steak for making* bistec en salsa de pasilla' *and he'll know exactly what you mean. Elsewhere, look for a cut without too much connective tissue – the meat simmers for less than half an hour in the sauce, so it doesn't have a lot of time to break down and soften. Ideally a butcher will slice the steaks for you; the thinner the slices, the faster they will cook in the sauce.*

ALBONDIGAS AL CHIPOTLE
MEATBALLS IN CHIPOTLE SAUCE

In Central Mexico, meatballs in chipotle sauce are a thick, nourishing dish, served as the main midday meal. Inside the large meatballs you often get a little surprise: a piece of cooked egg. This recipe comes from my friend Nick Zukin, a cook and author who owns the Mi Mero Mole taquerias in Portland, Oregon, which specialise in guisados *from Mexico City. While* fondas *in Mexico would generally serve two or three of these large meatballs on a plate, smothered in sauce, Nick's favourite way to eat them is in a torta with stringy, melted quesillo cheese. The only accompaniments you need here are warm corn tortillas, beans and rice – or a roll and cheese if you go Nick's route.*

1 To make the meatballs, mix together the beef, pork, ham, breadcrumbs, salt and pepper. (This works best with your hands.) Mix in the milk and beaten egg until thoroughly combined. Divide into 24 (2-tablespoon) portions. Form each into a patty and place a piece of chopped boiled egg in the centre, then wrap the patty around the egg and ensure that you close any seams tightly. Roll into a ball. Set aside.

2 To make the sauce, heat the 15g lard or 1 tablespoon oil in a casserole dish or large saucepan over a medium heat. When hot, add the onion and garlic and cook for 3 minutes until translucent and soft. Transfer to a blender jug with the tomatoes, chipotles and chicken stock and blend on high until very smooth. Add the salt and refrigerate the sauce for up to 24 hours if you're not ready to use it. To reheat, add 2 teaspoons lard or oil to the same pan, and when hot, add the sauce.

3 Bring the sauce to the boil and add the meatballs, ensuring not to break them. Shake the pan a bit to settle the meatballs fully into the sauce. Return to the boil, then reduce the heat to medium or medium-low, simmering gently, covered, for 1 hour or until fully cooked.

4 To serve, warm the corn tortillas on a *comal* or a large griddle or frying pan and place them in a basket or tea towel. Ladle the meatballs and heavy spoonfuls of the sauce onto individual plates, ensuring that the meatballs are completely covered with sauce. Spoon a side of rice and beans onto each plate. Pass round the warm tortillas at the table.

COOKING TIP: *Unless you can find excellent fresh ripe tomatoes, I'd recommend using canned tomatoes for this dish, which are actually more flavourful than many of the bland fresh tomatoes on sale, especially out of season. The sauce can be prepared ahead of time, and any extra sauce works well drizzled over eggs or pasta.*

For the meatballs:

225g beef mince

225g pork mince

100g ham steak, finely chopped

1 slice of white bread, toasted and pulsed in a food processor

1 teaspoon salt

¼ teaspoon ground black pepper

60ml full-fat milk

1 medium egg, lightly beaten

2 medium eggs, hard-boiled, each chopped into 12 pieces

For the sauce:

15g lard or 1 tablespoon rapeseed oil, plus more for frying

½ large onion, chopped

1 garlic clove, roughly chopped

3 × 410g cans fire-roasted tomatoes, or 3 × 400g cans good-quality tomatoes, drained

3 canned chipotles in adobo sauce (or less for less heat)

120ml Basic Homemade Chicken Stock (page 98)

1½ teaspoons salt, or to taste

18 corn tortillas

1 batch Mexican-style Red Rice (page 97)

1 batch Basic Cooked Beans (page 107)

TACOS DORADOS DE ZANAHORIA
CRISPY CARROT TACOS

Tacos dorados in Mexico City are what I grew up knowing as taquitos: *rolled tubes of corn tortillas, stuffed with some sort of meat and fried until crisp. At* fondas *in the capital, they're generally served three or four to a plate and covered in crema, crumbly cheese and lettuce. Most* fondas *will prepare at least one vegetarian dish on their* comida corrida *menu, but it still surprised me to see carrot tacos at my friend Miguel Garduño's tiny eatery in Azcapotzalco. One bite revealed a crispy exterior and steamy, salty grated carrot innards, so plain and pretty that I couldn't help wanting to make them at home. They're deceptively easy and don't need much beyond raw carrots and salt. I pan-fry these instead of deep-frying, and I like lots of acid (lime juice and tomatillo salsa) and beans on the side. You'll also need wooden cocktail sticks to secure them closed while cooking.*

1 Heat the oven to 100°C or lowest gas setting and line a baking tray with a wire rack, or several layers of kitchen paper.

2 In a mixing bowl, toss the grated carrot with the salt.

3 Warm the corn tortillas on a *comal* or a large griddle or frying pan and place in a tea towel to keep warm.

4 Place one tortilla on a work surface. Using your hands or tongs, place a small handful of carrot in the centre, taking care not to spread the filling all the way to the edge. Roll the tortilla tightly around the filling and secure closed with a wooden cocktail stick. Repeat until you've got 12 tacos.

5 Heat the oil in a large frying pan over a medium heat. Add a batch of the tacos, seam-side down, and cook for 2–3 minutes until they start to smell toasty. Turn over and fry on the other side until golden. (If you're a perfectionist like me, you can also roll them around a bit with tongs to ensure that they're fried evenly on all sides.) Transfer to the prepared baking tray, then keep warm in the oven. Repeat until all the tacos have been fried.

6 To serve, place three tacos on a plate, slather with a layer of crema and top with crumbled cheese. Pass round lime wedges and tomatillo salsa at the table.

3 large carrots, grated
½ teaspoon salt
12 corn tortillas
60ml rapeseed oil, plus more if needed
450g Homemade Crema (page 139)
400g queso fresco, or any other creamy cheese, crumbled
3–4 limes, cut into wedges
1 batch Raw Tomatillo Salsa (page 26)

ENCHILADAS POTOSINAS
CHEESY ENCHILADA PARCELS

These enchiladas, made from tortillas infused with guajillo chilli sauce, are native to San Luis Potosí, a capital city located about five hours north of the Federal District by bus. While they're not extremely common in Mexico City, you can find them at the occasional fonda or market food stall, lightly fried and topped with spoonfuls of crema and salsa. To me they resemble quesadillas more than enchiladas. In either case, they're firecrackers: a bold tortilla parcel wrapped around a crumbly, spicy filling.

You'll need a tortilla press for this, and plastic sheets (such as those cut from a plain shopping bag) for lining the plates. It's also helpful to have a friend assisting with the stuffing or cooking, to help things move faster. You can freeze these after cooking, then defrost and fry to reheat.

3 guajillo chillies, toasted lightly on a *comal* or non-stick frying pan, de-stemmed and deseeded
1 garlic clove, unpeeled, toasted on a *comal* or non-stick frying pan until soft
450g fresh tortilla masa
2 teaspoons lard or rapeseed oil, plus 15–25g lard or 1–2 tablespoons oil for frying
3 plum tomatoes, cored, deseeded and diced
1 large jalapeño chilli, deseeded and very finely chopped
130g queso fresco, crumbled
450g Homemade Crema (page 139)
salsa of choice
salt

1   Place the chillies in a bowl of warm water and leave to soak for about 20 minutes until the skins soften. Strain and reserve the soaking liquid.

2   Peel the garlic clove and place in a blender with the softened chillies and about 3 tablespoons of the reserved chilli water (just enough so that the blades move easily). Blend until very smooth – the sauce should not be too thin. Add ½ teaspoon salt and blend again. Taste and adjust the seasonings. Set aside.

3   Knead the masa for about 1 minute if it looks dry and cracked. Add the chilli sauce and knead until the sauce is completely integrated and the masa has an even orangey red colour. It will be sticky (if it's a humid day, it could be even stickier). Leave to rest, uncovered, for 10 minutes.

4   Heat the 2 teaspoons lard or oil in a medium frying pan over a medium heat. Add the tomatoes and jalapeño and cook for about 2 minutes just until the tomatoes soften. (Don't overcook them, or they'll become too watery, making the tortillas soggy later.) Remove the pan from the heat. Stir in the cheese, season with salt and stir again.

5   Heat a *comal* or non-stick frying pan to medium or slightly medium-low heat. Form the tortilla dough into 16 balls, roughly the size of golf balls.

6   Open the tortilla press and line both plates with plastic sheets. Place one tortilla ball on the bottom half of the press and flatten it slightly with your hand. Lower the top plate and push on the lever.

7   With lightly dampened hands, open the press, carefully peel off the top plastic sheet and flip the tortilla onto your open palm. Gently peel back the second layer of plastic and, sweeping your hand from left to right, or right to left, drape the tortilla across the hot *comal*. (See 'Making Corn Tortillas' on page 23 for detailed instructions.)

8   Cook the tortilla for about 25 seconds or until the outer edges start to darken and crisp. Flip and cook about a further 10 seconds – the tortilla should have some brown freckles, as well as a few patches that look shiny-red and raw. If it's not browned at all, turn up the heat a little and keep cooking.

9   Transfer the half-cooked tortilla to your work surface. Add about 1 tablespoon filling to one half of the tortilla, fold over and press the sides closed with your fingertips – they should squeeze together easily. If the tortilla cracks along the seam when you fold it, it hasn't been cooked long enough. (It's still edible, but make a note for the next one.) Conversely, if the edges aren't doughy enough to pinch closed, you've cooked it too long.

10   Return the enchilada to the *comal*, turning occasionally and moving to the outer edges of the pan, away from direct heat as it cooks, for about 45 seconds on each side until no longer raw in the middle. You may want to cut this first one open to test if it's fully cooked in the middle. Finish forming and cooking the remaining enchiladas.

11   Heat 15g lard or 1 tablespoon oil in a large frying pan over a medium heat. Add four enchiladas (or fewer, depending on how large your pan is) and fry, cooking for about 2 minutes per side until golden brown. They taste best served immediately. Repeat, frying the remaining enchiladas, adding more lard or oil to the pan as needed. Pass round the crema and salsa at the table, for guests to spoon on top.

COOKING TIPS: *If you're new to making tortillas from scratch, or even new to working with stickier masa, it may take you a few tries to get this right. Watch the tortilla carefully as it cooks – if you overcook it, or overstuff it, the seams won't pinch closed. (This is not the end of the world, as they'll still taste good.)*

I don't recommend substituting masa harina for fresh tortilla masa here. The flour will not absorb the liquid correctly, and the masa will taste crumbly and weird. Take off your rings and don't wear your best clothes, as the guajillo paste stains.

CHILES RELLENOS DE FRIJOL Y QUESO
ANCHO CHILLIES STUFFED WITH BEANS AND CHEESE

Stuffed chillies, their stems peeking out from a layer of crisp, fried egg batter, are an iconic main course served at almost every fonda in the city, every day. There are countless ways to prepare them – with poblano chillies, with ancho chillies, with meaty picadillo filling or even stuffed with seafood – but the simplest and best preparation in my opinion are ancho chillies stuffed with a plain, spongy Mexican cheese, served with a thin tomato caldillo, or tomato broth, on top.

I've had trouble finding good-quality Mexican cheese outside Mexico, so here I've mixed refried black beans with fingers of queso fresco, which makes the chilli more plump and filling. I've morphed the traditional caldillo – which can taste bland if you don't have great tomatoes – into a roasted tomato sauce. Feel free to use fire-roasted or other superior canned tomatoes if you can't find ripe fresh. You still get all the effects of the fonda classic: a golden chilli sitting under a pool of sauce, ready to be mopped up with tortillas.

4 ancho chillies, briefly toasted on a *comal* or non-stick frying pan
6 plum tomatoes
¼ medium onion
1 garlic clove, unpeeled
2 teaspoons lard
2 sprigs of fresh coriander, chopped
1 batch Quick Refried Beans (page 45)
4 pieces of queso fresco, cut into long lengths roughly the size of your chillies
1 batch Basic Cooked Beans (page 107)
1 tablespoon plus 1 teaspoon plain flour
4 medium eggs, separated
75ml rapeseed oil, plus more as needed
8 corn tortillas, warmed
450g Homemade Crema (page 139)
salt

COOKING TIP: *If you're selecting chillies from a packaged bag, choose four that are more or less the same size.*

1   Place the chillies on a work surface and carefully make an incision into each, leaving 2.5cm of space at either end and slicing from pole to pole. As gently as possible, using a small spoon or your fingers, scrape out the seeds, ensuring that the chillies do not tear and that the stem stays intact. (The stem is for aesthetic purposes and nothing more, but it will look cool in the end.) Place the chillies in a bowl of warm water and leave to soak for 15–20 minutes until their skins soften, reserving the soaking water.

2   Meanwhile, heat a *comal* or non-stick frying pan over a medium heat. Add the tomatoes, onion and garlic. Cook, turning often, for 7–10 minutes until softened and blackened in spots. Set aside to cool.

3   Peel the garlic and place in a blender with the tomatoes, onion and any juices. Blend on high until smooth. Add 60ml of the chilli water and blend until combined.

4   Heat the lard in a medium saucepan over a medium heat. Add the sauce in one quick pour, plus salt to taste. If you like a thinner texture, add more chilli water, and more salt as needed. Add the coriander sprigs and bring the sauce to the boil, then reduce the heat to medium or medium-low and simmer for about 5 minutes until the flavours meld. Cover and keep warm.

5   Gently remove the chillies from their bath and pat dry with kitchen paper. Fill each chilli with about 4 tablespoons refried beans, depending on their size. They should look plump. Nestle a piece of cheese inside, add some of the cooked beans mixture and push the seams closed.

6   Line a baking tray with kitchen paper or a wire rack. Place 1 tablespoon flour on a plate. Roll the chillies in the flour and brush off excess. Set aside.

7   Beat the egg whites until stiff peaks form. Stir in the egg yolks one by one, mixing well after each addition. Stir in the remaining 1 teaspoon flour and ½ teaspoon salt.

8 Heat the oil in a large frying pan over a high heat. To test to see if the oil is ready (it must be hot enough, or else the chillies will turn soggy and taste greasy), drop a 2cm piece of batter in the oil – if it sizzles and turns golden brown within 20 seconds, it's done. Conversely, if the batter turns dark brown almost immediately, the oil is too hot and the heat must be reduced.

9 Place the bowl of batter near the hob. Holding a chilli by its stem, dunk it gently into the egg batter, slathering the batter lightly on all sides. Place the chilli carefully in the hot oil (the batter should puff up like a cloud). Using a spoon or spatula, bathe the chilli in the hot oil for 20–45 seconds until the edges start to brown. Carefully flip over and brown the other side. Transfer to the prepared baking tray and fry the remaining chillies. Keep the finished chillies warm in a gently heated oven.

10 To serve, place one chilli in the centre of a plate. Ladle the roasted tomato sauce on top and some cooked beans on the side. Pass round the warm corn tortillas and the crema at the table.

TORTITAS DE HUAUZONTLE
FRIED HUAUZONTLE PATTIES

The huauzontle, also called Aztec spinach, is a tall, bushy vegetable in the goosefoot family. They take a fairly long time to clean, but I think they're worth the effort – the fluffy, spongy texture is unlike any other vegetable, and the taste is intensely green, like a cross between broccoli and chard. In Central Mexico, the soft, unseeded buds are scraped off the stalk, boiled and shaped into fried patties known as tortitas. Fondas *serve the patties as a midday main course, doused in a pool of homemade tomato sauce with beans and warm tortillas on the side.*

salt and freshly ground black
    pepper
2 large bunches of huauzontles
    (Aztec spinach) (about 700g),
    cleaned (see page 171)
1 batch Ranchera Sauce (page
    105)
1 tablespoon plus 1 teaspoon
    plain flour
4 medium eggs, separated
60ml rapeseed oil, plus more for
    frying
12 corn tortillas
1 batch Basic Cooked Beans
    (page 107)

1 Fill a large saucepan two-thirds full with cold water. Bring to a vigorous boil and add a hefty pinch of salt. Add the huauzontles and reduce the heat to medium. Simmer for about 10 minutes until tender and soft, and darker in colour. Strain and set aside while you prepare the ranchera sauce. Cover the sauce and keep warm.

2 Gather the huauzontles together with your hands and squeeze together firmly, draining out any excess water. Keep squeezing until mostly dry and slightly crumbly. (This is important – if the huazontles are soggy, they will not come together and form a patty, and they'll taste rather limp.) Season with salt and pepper, tossing to combine.

3 Sprinkle 1 tablespoon flour onto a plate. Separate the huauzontles into four equal piles. Grab one and press tightly together, forming a patty. Repeat with the remaining huauzontles. Dust each patty lightly in flour and set aside.

4 Beat the egg whites until stiff peaks form, or when you turn the bowl upside down, the whites stay in place (in Spanish this is called *a punto de turrón*). Slowly integrate the egg yolks one by one, then add the remaining teaspoon flour and ½ teaspoon salt.

5 Pour at least 5mm oil into a large frying pan and heat over a high heat. The oil must be hot enough for the patties to fry correctly. To test it, place a 2cm circle of the batter in the pan. If it sizzles and turns golden brown within 20 seconds, it's ready. If it immediately turns dark brown or golden, the oil is too hot; reduce the heat.

6 Place the bowl of egg batter near the hob. Nearby, set a wire rack over a baking tray, or a plate covered with layers of kitchen paper.

7 Take one patty and scoop it into the egg batter, then place in the hot pan. Place a little of the egg batter on the patty to cover the bare spot where your fingers were. Use a small spoon to bathe the patty in the hot oil for about 30 seconds (this cooks the top side so that you can flip with ease), then flip and cook the other side. Once the patty is golden brown all over, transfer to the prepared tray or plate to drain.

8 These are best eaten immediately. To serve, warm the corn tortillas and place in a tea towel or basket. Place one patty on a plate and ladle on a heavy spoonful of ranchera sauce. Spoon a serving of beans on the side, and pass round the tortillas at the table.

COCHINITA PIBIL
SLOW-COOKED CITRUSY PORK

Cochinita pibil isn't native to Mexico City, but it's become part of the city's culinary cannon. A hefty pork roast is marinated in annatto seeds (achiote), aromatic spices and sour orange juice, then wrapped in banana leaves and baked. The pork, tender from so many hours of cooking, ends up citrusy, tangy and just the slightest bit sweet. In Yucatán, where the dish is native, the pork is traditionally smoked in a pib, or earth oven. Mexico City cooks often make a guisado, meaning the meat is cooked first without the marinade and then added to the citrusy sauce. I like it this way, because the sauce infuses the entire dish. The required toppings, as you make your taco, are pickled red onions and habanero salsa.

1   Preheat the oven to 150°C/gas mark 2. Season the pork well with salt and pepper.

2   To soften the banana leaves – an essential step so that they'll fold tightly over the joint and not tear – heat a gas burner to medium. Run the leaves lightly over the flame for 3–5 seconds until the skin darkens, softens and emits a lovely perfume. Make sure you move and angle the leaves so that the heat hits every part of the skin.

3   Lay a leaf on a work surface. Take another leaf and lay it on top, in a cross formation. (If your leaves have tears, lay them one on top of the other to make them longer.) Place the pork joint in the centre of the cross. Pick up the ends of the leaves and wrap the meat like a parcel. Place in a large casserole dish and cover tightly with a layer of foil. Cover and bake for 3½–4 hours until the meat is falling off the bone or the internal temperature reads 88°C. Leave to cool to room temperature, then cut into medium chunks.

4   Heat a *comal* or non-stick frying pan to medium or medium-low heat, and when hot, add the garlic cloves. Cook, turning occasionally, for 5–7 minutes until soft and slightly squishy. Transfer to a bowl and leave to cool. Peel the garlic once cool enough to handle.

5   Crumble the achiote paste into a blender. Add the Seville orange juice, garlic, cumin seeds, peppercorns, allspice berries and cinnamon and blend until smooth.

6   Heat the lard in a large, deep saucepan over a medium heat. (Don't burn it, or it will give the sauce an off flavour.) Add the sauce and fry for 2–3 minutes, stirring constantly so that it doesn't burn. Stir in 720ml stock and the orange juice, and season lightly with salt. Simmer for 35 minutes, uncovered, to allow the juice to reduce a bit.

7   Add the meat to the pan and stir to ensure that it's evenly coated in the sauce. Simmer for a further 20 minutes, uncovered, over a medium heat, stirring occasionally and adding more stock if it looks too dry. Stir in 1½ teaspoons salt or to taste.

8   Warm the tortillas on a *comal* or a large griddle or frying pan and place in a tea towel or basket. Serve the *cochinita pibil* in individual warm corn tortillas, or in a covered serving bowl at the table. Pass round the pickled onions and salsa so that everyone can make their own taco.

2.25kg bone-in pork shoulder joint, with fat and skin intact
2 long fresh banana leaves
1 garlic bulb, cloves separated but unpeeled
100g bar of achiote paste (I like El Yucateco or Marin brands)
240ml Seville orange juice (about 7 Seville oranges), or Sour Orange Substitute (page 123)
1 teaspoon cumin seeds, toasted
½ teaspoon black peppercorns
3 allspice berries
5cm piece of cinnamon stick, toasted
1 teaspoon lard or rapeseed oil
720–960ml pork stock or Basic Homemade Chicken Stock (page 98)
180ml freshly squeezed orange juice
24–30 corn tortillas
Pickled Red Onions (page 123)
Roasted Habanero Salsa (page 123)
salt and freshly ground black pepper

COOKING TIPS: *I've made this dish by grinding my own annatto seeds from scratch, but it doesn't taste like the Mexico City version. Most cooks there use ready-made achiote paste sold in rectangular bars at the markets. That's what I prefer, although the bars contain preservatives and technically aren't as pure as plain old achiote. You can find the bars online under the brands El Yucateco or Marin.*

Seville oranges, sold at supermarkets and greengrocers when in season (end of December to mid-February), taste less sour if they're too old. If they have brown spots inside, they're past their prime, in which case, and when out of season, you can use this Sour Orange Substitute, whose ratios I found in David Sterling's excellent Yucatán cookbook. Don't leave out the banana leaves, which add a depth of flavour to the meat. You can find them at Asian supermarkets or from online suppliers.

SOUR ORANGE SUBSTITUTE

This makes a decent approximation of a Seville orange's tart and bitter taste. Use it only if you can't find fresh Seville (sour) oranges.

120ml freshly squeezed lime juice
60ml freshly squeezed orange juice
60ml freshly squeezed grapefruit juice

Mix the juices together in a large measuring jug or bowl. Refrigerate until ready to use.

PICKLED RED ONIONS

These tangy, sour onions add colour and a burst of flavour to this citrusy slow-cooked pork. I also like them in salads, vegetable tacos or in quesadillas.

1 large red onion, thinly sliced
140ml freshly squeezed lime juice
165ml freshly squeezed orange juice
1 heaped teaspoon salt

Mix the onion, lime juice, orange juice and salt in a bowl. Refrigerate overnight or longer before serving. These will keep for a few months in an airtight container in the fridge.

ROASTED HABANERO SALSA

This fiery salsa was made for the tart, citrusy cochinita pibil, *but it's also excellent on eggs, beans or anywhere else you want a lot of heat. The salsa will keep for up to five days in an airtight container in the fridge.*

1   Heat a *comal* or non-stick frying pan to medium or medium-high heat, and when hot, add the chillies and tomatillos in an even layer. Place the garlic cloves near the edge of the pan so that they don't burn. Cook, turning occasionally, until soft and blackened in spots.

2   Peel the garlic cloves and roughly chop both the garlic and chillies. Add to a blender with the roasted tomatillos. Blend on a high speed, adding a little water if necessary to help the blender blades turn. (Or add more water if you want a thinner salsa.) Pour the salsa into a bowl and stir in salt to taste. Serve at room temperature.

5 habanero chillies
225g tomatillos
2 garlic cloves, unpeeled
salt

MOLE VERDE CON POLLO
GREEN MOLE WITH CHICKEN

At local fondas, *green mole is the second-most popular after* mole poblano, *served slathered over a chicken leg with a stack of warm corn tortillas. The ingredients depend on the cook – and the cook's home town – but my favourite versions are bright, herbal and lightly tangy, and not too soupy. Green mole is quicker to prepare than other* moles, *since the fresh items go into the blender raw. You can also tweak the ingredients, substituting other greens for radish leaves, for instance, or fewer tomatillos if you want less tang. Vegetarians can serve this with slices of cooked squash, green beans and broad beans.*

1 chicken, about 1.6kg, cut into 7 pieces
1 small wedge plus ½ medium onion
3 garlic cloves, peeled
3 poblano chillies
130g pumpkin seeds
2 tablespoons sesame seeds
1 teaspoon cumin seeds
800g tomatillos, husked, rinsed and roughly chopped
3 large serrano chillies
1 small bunch of radish leaves
4 cos (romaine) lettuce leaves
6 sprigs of fresh coriander
2 sprigs of epazote (about 10 leaves)
25g lard or 2 tablespoons rapeseed oil
2½ teaspoons salt, or more to taste
12–15 corn tortillas

1   Place the chicken in a large, deep saucepan and cover with cold water. Add the onion wedge and 1 garlic clove and bring to the boil. Cover, reduce the heat and simmer for 20 minutes. Remove the chicken, strain out 1.2 litres of the stock and set both aside.

2   Roast the poblano chillies over a gas flame until blackened in spots, and then wrap in a tea towel to sweat for 20 minutes until the skins soften. Peel off the skin with the pads of your fingers, then remove and discard the seeds, stems and veins (see page 37 for instructions). Chop the chillies roughly and set aside.

3   While the chillies sweat, toast the pumpkin seeds over a low heat in a small frying pan, stirring often, until they turn slightly golden and start to pop. Transfer immediately to a bowl so that they don't burn. Add the cumin seeds to the pan and toast until aromatic, then transfer to a separate bowl and set aside. Turn off the heat and pour the sesame seeds into the same pan, swirling them around the pan slowly, until they turn a light golden colour. Transfer to another small bowl.

4   Grind the pumpkin seeds in a coffee or spice grinder until light and powdery. Scrape into a small bowl, and then do the same with the sesame seeds. (Grinding the seeds separately helps ensure the smoothest texture possible – you can skip this step if you have a high-powered blender such as a Vitamix.)

5   In a blender, working in batches, blend the vegetables – tomatillos, serrano chillies, remaining 2 garlic cloves, poblano chillies, radish leaves, lettuce leaves, coriander and epazote – with 240ml of the reserved stock until smooth.

6   Add the ground pumpkin and sesame seeds along with the whole cumin seeds, and blend on a high speed until very smooth.

7   Heat the lard or oil in a large, deep, heavy-based saucepan over a medium heat. Add the contents of the blender in one quick pour. Add a little stock to the blender jug, swish the liquid around gently and pour the remnants into the pan as well. Bring to the boil, stirring constantly, and cook for 10 minutes until it thickens slightly.

8   Stir in an additional 480ml of the stock and season with the salt. Cook over a very low heat for about 45 minutes, simmering gently and stirring often with a wooden spoon, taking care to ensure that the *mole* doesn't stick or burn. Add the remaining stock gradually, once the *mole* thickens and the liquid starts to evaporate – the ideal texture should be slightly thicker than gravy. Add the chicken to the pan and cook for about 5 minutes until pools of fat form on the surface.

9 To serve, warm the tortillas and place in a tea towel or basket. Place one breast, or a leg and a thigh, on a plate. Ladle lots of sauce on top. Pass round the tortillas at the table.

COOKING TIP: *One of the mysteries of this* mole *is that sometimes the pumpkin seeds separate from the sauce, creating a half-chunky, half-watery mixture. Contrary to some advice I recently found in an older Mexican cookbook (translating from the Spanish): 'According to tradition, you must stir in only one direction with a wooden spoon, and not keep entering and removing the spoon, or else the sauce will separate' – I've found it's important to keep the heat low and stir very often. If the pumpkin seeds do separate from the rest of the sauce, pour the sauce into a blender, give it a whizz and then return to the pan.*

You may have some sauce left over, which you can use to feed a few more people (buy a couple of extra chicken legs and thighs), or for simple enmoladas, *tortillas dredged in warm* mole, *folded on a plate, topped with more* mole.

CHAPTER 4

IN
THE
COUNTRY

I started a street food tourism company in Mexico City in 2010, and when I first began giving the tours, I was surprised to find out how many of the street and market vendors lived outside the city limits. Their commutes were brutal: at least 90 minutes from the State of Mexico, a neighbouring state that wrapped around the capital like a cloche hat, and easily two hours one way from Milpa Alta, an area technically within Mexico City, but tucked at its southernmost edge. Or they lived in Xochimilco, about 45 minutes away depending on traffic, where some farmers grow produce and supply a few of the upmarket restaurants I like in Mexico City.

I made friends with a nice young guy who sold dried chillies at the Medellín Market in Roma, and one day he invited me to his house in San Pedro Atocpan, a quiet town with cobblestone streets in Milpa Alta. (The town is best known for its large number of families who make *mole* paste and sell it at the *tianguis*.) To get there, my husband and I took the subway to Tasqueña and then switched to a *pesero*, one of the small, rumbly buses that penetrate the deeper nooks of the capital. After about an hour of cruising wide avenues and then smaller back streets, we trudged up a four-lane road that wound up a steep hill, past fields of cactus and larger hills blanketed in grass and brush. The sky stared a shade of blue rarely seen in the city centre.

We were still in Mexico City, but technically closer to the Mexican state of Morelos when we walked into his family's large patio, planted with fruit trees. The air smelled like spices and dried chillies, and butter and yeast – his family also baked bread to sell in the neighbourhood.

JUST FOR A TASTE

Over the next few years, I'd make several more trips to San Pedro and a few to the neighbouring city of Milpa Alta, to eat and shop at the markets and visit. I bought sweet, canary-yellow tomatillos grown in nearby Morelos, and tried *atole de novia*, a warm beverage made from ground corn, chocolate and ground hazelnuts. At the Milpa Alta *tianguis,* I walked down the pavement open-mouthed, dumbstruck at how gorgeous everything was: squash flowers as big as my hand; blackened, charred tamales with whole fish inside; freshly killed rabbits with their fur still on. Piles of fresh mushrooms, grown nearby, lay next to fresh water-coloured corn with purplish-red splotches, a shade I'd never seen before. We ate mushroom tamales drenched in green sauce, and caramel-coloured, crunchy homemade *chicharrón*.

I don't want to romanticise the city's rural areas, many of which tend to be poor. Life there – and everywhere in the city – is not easy. But it's interesting to think that, even in one of the most urban places in the world, the food can change, transform from something good and enjoyable to something electric and essential, capable of luring you onto a bumpy bus for two hours, just for a taste.

AGUA DE PIÑA CON PEREJIL
PINEAPPLE-PARSLEY COOLER

Every market in Mexico City, both in the city and the outskirts, sells aguas frescas, *a drink of puréed fruit, sugar and water. Pairing parsley with pineapple is popular – the bitter, grassy stalks balance out the sweetness, leaving you with a drink that actually tastes healthy. Pineapple can vary in acidity, so it's best to taste and decide for yourself whether you want sugar. This* agua fresca *is best served within one or two days.*

1   Combine the pineapple, water and parsley in a blender and blend until very smooth. Taste, and if you think it needs sweetener, add 1 tablespoon sugar and continue blending, tasting and adding more if desired.

2   Pour into a jug and serve cold, either refrigerated or over ice. You can also strain it, if you don't like the little parsley pieces. (I do.)

330g very ripe fresh pineapple
 flesh, roughly chopped
1 litre cold water
10g fresh flat-leaf parsley leaves
sugar, to taste

AGUA DE LIMÓN
LIME AND BROWN SUGAR COOLER

Most lime aguas frescas in Mexico City taste like a tangier version of lemonade. My recipe is slightly different, as it uses brown sugar instead of white, giving the beverage a warm, molasses-y undertone. A pinch of lime zest amps up the lime flavour. The only slightly strange thing is the colour – brown sugar turns the drink brown instead of light green. This quantity works well for large groups, or divide the recipe in half if there are only two of you.

Working in batches if necessary, place all ingredients in the blender and blend until very smooth. Serve chilled or at room temperature.

COOKING TIP: *Smaller key limes tend to be more flavourful than larger standard limes, so try them if you can find them. For a slightly sweeter taste, you can use* piloncillo, *an unrefined Mexican cane sugar sold in cone-shaped packages by Mexican grocery stores or online suppliers (see page 61 to learn how to grate or chop it), or dark soft brown sugar.*

2.8 litres cold water
½ teaspoon grated lime zest
120ml freshly squeezed lime
 juice
75g unrefined cane sugar

ATOLE DE PINOLE
PINOLE ATOLE

Atole is a thick, warm, sweetened beverage traditionally served with tamales, and in the urban part of Mexico City, vendors usually sell the same two or three varieties – often Champurrado *(page 55) and* Atole de Arroz. *Moving further south, however, that changes. In Xochimilco and Milpa Alta, vendors sell* atoles *with fresh seasonal fruit mixed in. And they also sell* atole de pinole *(pea-NO-lay), a mix of milk or water and a powder made from toasted, ground corn – usually red corn – and cinnamon and sugar. If you did not grow up drinking* atole, *it can be difficult to imagine pairing this hearty beverage with food. I think it works well as a snack on a cold day, or at a party served with lots of tamales.*

480ml full-fat milk
55g *pinole* (see Tip)
2 tablespoons masa harina,
    or 1 teaspoon cornflour
2–3 tablespoons sugar, or
    to taste

1   Pour 240ml of the milk into a medium bowl and add the *pinole* a little at a time, whisking after each addition. Once the *pinole* has dissolved, set aside.

2   Sprinkle the masa harina or cornflour over 60ml water and whisk well.

3   Heat the remaining 240ml milk with 300ml water over a medium heat in a medium saucepan. When hot, stir in the masa or cornflour mixture, whisking constantly so that the masa doesn't seize and cause lumps. When fully dissolved, stir in the *pinole*, milk and sugar. Simmer, stirring constantly and scraping the base of the pan so that the *atole* doesn't stick and burn, for about 15 minutes or until the beverage has thickened and no longer tastes powdery. If you're using cornflour, which thickens more heavily than masa harina, you may need a bit more water to reach the desired consistency.

4   Serve warm, ladled into mugs or heatproof glasses.

COOKING TIP: *You can find* pinole *at some Mexican grocery stores or online. I like the Rancho Gordo brand. The amount of sugar can vary, so you may need more or less sweetener than what's called for in this recipe. Leftover* pinole *can be whisked into water or milk and sipped cold, as a traditional Mexican energy drink. It also makes a wonderful ingredient in ice cream.*

    The use of cornflour in atole *is authentic to Mexico City.* Atole *made with masa harina will produce a slightly grainier texture.*

SALSA MACHA
TOASTED ÁRBOL CHILLI SALSA

On a recent trip to Mexico City, I saw this deep red, sediment-like salsa at the long row of tortillerías *inside the Xochimilco Market. I had tried* salsa macha *before – the name roughly translates to 'extremely bold, hot salsa' – but never with so many nuts and seeds. My friends and I bought some, along with tortillas and* tlacoyos, *and over the course of a few hours we wound through Xochimilco's canals and spooned the oily salsa on everything. Even on a plain tortilla, it was powerful: toasty, smoky, garlicky. The salsa is simple to make at home. The only trick is to keep the chillies from burning, otherwise the sauce will taste bitter. A warning: this stuff is hot.*

1   Heat the oil in a medium saucepan over a medium heat. Add the garlic clove and cook for about 2 minutes until dark golden brown and blistered. Transfer to a small bowl and set aside.

2   Add the chillies and cook briefly, about 10 seconds, stirring constantly with tongs until they release a spicy aroma. Be careful not to burn them. Transfer the chillies to a bowl using a slotted spoon and reserve the cooking oil.

3   Cut the chillies into pieces using kitchen scissors or a sharp knife, and roughly chop the garlic. Place both, with any chilli seeds, in a blender. Blend into a dry, crumbly mixture. It should be fairly fine – if the mixture is quite coarse, scrape down the sides of the blender jug and blend again. It may take several tries to get the desired consistency.

4   Transfer the chilli-garlic mix to a bowl and pour at least 60ml of the reserved chilli oil on top. (The amount of oil is really up to you, but it should definitely come up at least 1cm over the chilli mixture.) Stir in the sunflower seeds and peanuts, and add salt to taste. Stir again until thoroughly combined. Serve at room temperature.

5   Store the salsa in an airtight container in a cool place for up to a week.

120ml rapeseed oil

1 large garlic clove, peeled

25 dried árbol chillies, stems snipped if they're very long

1 tablespoon raw unsalted sunflower seeds, toasted

1 tablespoon raw unsalted peanuts, toasted

salt

HOW TO PEEL XOCONOSTLES

The xoconostles must be mostly charred and soft before peeling. Cut them in half and scoop out the black- and magenta-coloured seed sack in the centre. Then gently peel off the tough outer skin and any rough patches at the top of the fruit. A small spoon may also help scoop out the flesh from the skin. The edible part of the fruit should be a moist, pale pink.

SALSA DE XOCONOSTLE
SOUR CACTUS FRUIT SALSA

Xoconostles are sour cactus fruits native to Central Mexico. They look like small prickly pears – reddish-green or pink when ripe – but the taste is more mouth-puckering than your average tuna or cactus fruit. (The name of the fruit is pronounced 'show-coh-NO-stlay'; it's a Nahuatl word.) When roasted, they smell like no other fruit I know of: a mix of sweet apricot and peach, with a hint of earth and smoke and char. In Mexico City, xoconostles are most commonly used in salsas or as a condiment in Mole de Olla (page 108); they're also common in the State of Mexico, Hildago, and Tlaxcala. Due to its sourness, this salsa works best when you want more acidity and punch (more than, say, an ordinary green salsa). I like it with Barbacoa (page 154) or salty tortilla chips.

1   Warm a *comal* or non-stick frying pan over a medium heat. When hot, add the xoconostles and tomatillos, along with the garlic clove near the edge, away from direct heat. Cook, turning occasionally with tongs, for about 12 minutes until the tomatillos and garlic are blackened in spots and soft. Set aside. Increase the heat and keep cooking the xoconostles for about 30 minutes until very soft and black nearly all over – this will make them easier to peel. Peel the garlic when cool enough to handle.

2   Heat the oil in a small frying pan over a medium or medium-low heat. (This shouldn't be too hot, otherwise the chillies will burn.) When preheated, add the chillies and fry, turning constantly with tongs, for 10–15 seconds just until they begin to emit a spicy aroma. Transfer to a bowl or plate.

3   Cut the xoconostles and remove the seeds and skin (see opposite.) Place with the tomatillos, garlic clove and chilllies in a blender and blend into a coarse, chunky mixture, adding up to 2 tablespoons water if desired to thin it down. Pour into a serving bowl and stir in the salt. Serve at room temperature.

3 xoconostles (sour cactus fruits)
6 small tomatillos, husked and rinsed
1 medium garlic clove, unpeeled
2 teaspoons rapeseed oil
4 dried árbol chillies, stems removed
½ teaspoon plus a pinch of salt

COOKING TIP: *Look for xoconostles in select Mexican grocery stores or market stalls.*

CHICHARRÓN CASERA
HOMEMADE CHICHARRÓN

Large jagged sheets of chicharrón, or pork crackling, can be found at any Mexico City market. It's most often eaten as a snack – as a crunchy vehicle for guacamole and salsas – or in a guisado, when it's drenched in salsa and cooked until soggy, then spooned into a tortilla. Most vendors sell two varieties: light and puffy with no fat or meat clinging to the skin, and a meaty, fatty version. Only in the outskirts of the city have I seen homemade chicharrón and it turns out it's not too difficult to make. Homemade chicharrón is wonderful with pico de gallo, any salsa, guacamole, or cooked in green sauce (like the Enchiladas Verdes sauce, page 50) and served in a taco when soft. I've kept the pieces large on purpose here, as it's customary in Mexico to break off a piece with your hands, then dip it in a salsa or guacamole.

700–900g pork skin
480ml rapeseed oil
salsa of choice or guacamole,
    optional
salt

1 Preheat the oven to 120°C/gas mark ½.

2 Cut the skin into large, wide pieces, about 15cm long by 10cm wide.

3 Lay the skin on a rack set over a baking tray and bake for 1 hour. Reduce the heat to 100°C or lowest gas setting and bake for a further 2–3 hours or a dark caramel brown and the top is no longer moist or sticky. (The bottom may still be slightly moist with fat.) Wash the rack and tray, return the rack to the tray and set next to the hob.

4 Heat the oil in a large casserole dish over a high heat. When very hot (at least 160°C), add a piece of pork skin. After about 30 seconds, it should bubble and puff up into a *chicharrón*. Flip if necessary to ensure that both sides are cooked. Once puffy and golden brown, transfer to your prepared baking tray and season with salt. Repeat with the remaining pieces of pork skin.

5 Serve as soon as the pieces have cooled, with salsa or guacamole if desired. Or store the pieces in an airtight container for snacking later. They will keep for up to 5 days.

COOKING TIP: *You'll need to find a butcher who sells pork skin, and if they won't slice off the fat for you, you'll need a very sharp knife and a lot of patience, unless you're particularly skilled at butchery. (I recommend buying the skin with the fat already scraped off, unless you prefer your chicharrón with a thin layer of fat or meat.)*

Deep-frying the chicharrón in lard, as cooks do in Mexico, boosts the pork flavour, but it's pungent and can be messy. For something slightly less porcine, try rapeseed oil or another neutral oil suitable for frying.

SOPES DE MAÍZ AZUL
BLUE CORN SOPES

450g fresh blue corn tortilla masa or
    230g masa harina
360ml warm water, if using masa harina
1 batch Quick Refried Beans (page 45)
salsa of choice, such as Raw Tomatillo Salsa
    (page 26)
Homemade Crema (see opposite)
crumbled queso fresco, goat's cheese or any
    other salty, tangy cheese

One summer day, I visited the farm of Abel Rodriguez and his wife, Emma Villanueva Buendía, who grow corn, beans and other crops in Tepetlixpa, a town about an hour and 20 minutes from Mexico City. Señora Villanueva made an almuerzo, or mid-morning meal, of blue corn sopes – small, toasted masa discs spread with a thin layer of cooked beans, green salsa and a dollop of what might've been the best Mexican crema I'd ever had. (Her neighbour makes it from scratch; for my version, see opposite.) The sopes were rustic and comforting, reminding me that even the simplest food in Mexico can taste as good as the most complex.

1   If using fresh masa, place in a deep bowl and knead, adding a few drops of water, until airy and soft. To test if it's ready, break off a knob, roll into a ball and flatten. If the ball cracks at the edges, you need more water.

2   Alternatively, if using masa harina, place the dry flour in a deep bowl and pour about half the water on top. Mix in with a rubber spatula or wooden spoon, and then add the remaining water a little at a time, kneading the masa with your fingers. Test to see if it's adequately hydrated the same way as above. Once the dough is sufficiently moist, cover it with a damp tea towel so that it doesn't dry out.

3   Heat a *comal* or non-stick frying pan to medium-low heat. Place a clean chopping board near the hob.

4   Line both plates of a tortilla press with plastic sheets. Break off a piece of masa the size of a golf ball and roll it into a smooth ball. Place on one side of the press, then close and push down on the lever. Don't press them too thin – the ideal shape should be slightly thicker than your average tortilla.

5   Open the press and peel off the top plastic sheet. Gently pick up and flip the tortilla over onto your palm, positioning it so half hangs off the side. (This is tricky, but you'll get it with practice.) Gently peel off the remaining plastic sheet. (If the dough breaks or sticks to the sheet, it's too wet – you can add a bit of masa harina to dry it out, but if you're using fresh masa, be aware that the taste will be affected.)

6   Making a sweeping motion with your hand, gently place the tortilla onto the hot *comal* or frying pan. Cook for about 30 seconds or until the tortilla darkens slightly and looks less moist, then flip. Cook for a further 20 seconds and then transfer to the chopping board. (The tortilla should still be half-raw at this point.) Leave to cool for 1 minute, then dig into the edges and pinch the raw masa slightly upwards, forming a raised border around the perimeter.

7   Place the *sope* back on the pan and continue cooking it for 4–5 minutes until the outer skin is crisp and the *sope* no longer feels soft or mushy. These may be cooked ahead of time, cooled and refrigerated in a sealed container for 1–2 days, or longer if frozen.

8   Warm the refried beans or other toppings, as necessary. Spoon a thin layer of beans onto the *sope* and top with a drizzle of salsa. Finish with a spoonful of crema and a sprinkling of cheese. Serve immediately.

9   To reheat *sopes* that have been frozen, defrost first and sprinkle with a little water if they look dry. Then reheat on the *comal* or frying pan.

COOKING TIPS: *My local* tortillería *in New York sells blue corn masa once a week, but if you can't find it where you live, feel free to use fresh yellow tortilla masa or masa harina. You can also top the* sopes *with whatever you want – I use beans, salsa and crema to mimic my original experience, but shredded poached chicken or fried potatoes and chorizo would work, too. Once cooked and filled, the* sopes *should be eaten immediately.*

HOW TO SHAPE SOPES

A sope is like a thicker version of a tortilla, with raised edges. In Mexico, women pinch the edges directly on the comal. *Unless you have extremely calloused fingers and you're an expert at working with masa, you'll want to remove the half-raw tortilla from the hob first and pinch the edges on a separate work surface. It may take you a few tries to master the technique. Don't give up if the first one doesn't come out perfectly.*

CREMA CASERA
HOMEMADE CREMA

The Mexican crema sold outside Mexico can vary widely in quality. Some are very thick, like soured cream; others are thin and soupy. Still others don't taste much like dairy at all. I think it's easiest just to make your own. My favourite Mexican cremas have a lactic tang, so I've used yogurt to try and mimic that. The result is a bit tangier than using buttermilk, which is often what's called for when making crème fraîche. You can use this for any recipe that calls for crema. You'll need a glass jar with a lid; the crema lasts for about five days in the fridge.

1   Two days before you'd like to eat the crema, warm the cream in a small saucepan over a medium-low heat. You should only heat it to take the chill off; be careful not to overheat. Stir in the yogurt and turn off the heat.

2   Pour into a small, clean jar and leave to cool. Place the lid loosely on top, without tightening, and leave to stand for 24 hours in a warm place.

3   Place the crema in the fridge for at least 6 hours to thicken. Stir and add salt to taste (I like just a pinch) before serving.

240g double cream
1 tablespoon natural yogurt
   (not Greek)
salt

SOPA MILPA
SQUASH FLOWER AND VEGETABLE SOUP

This delicate soup is served during the rainy season in Milpa Alta. That's when squash is most tender, and the squash flowers bloom to an exaggerated, lush size. This recipe comes from my friend Erick Valle, whose family lives in nearby San Pedro Atocpan. The stock is light on purpose, as an intense or rich chicken flavour would overwhelm the vegetables. For vegetarians, a flavourful vegetable stock would work equally well. You can serve this soup to accompany something else, but I think it works fine as a light meal, with warm tortillas on the side.

1   Place the chicken in a large saucepan. Cover with 2 litres cold water, add the spearmint, garlic and onion and season with salt. Bring to the boil, then reduce the heat, cover and simmer for 25 minutes. Strain the chicken stock and discard the bones, meat and aromatics. Set aside.

2   In a large saucepan, heat the oil over a medium-high heat. Add the squash, mushrooms and sweetcorn and fry, stirring occasionally, for 3–4 minutes until slightly softened. Pour in the chicken stock, add the epazote and season with salt. Bring the soup to the boil, then cover, reduce the heat to low and simmer for 5 minutes.

3   Add the courgette flowers, replace the lid and simmer for 20 minutes or until the flavours meld. Taste and adjust the seasonings.

4   To serve, heat the corn tortillas on a *comal* or non-stick frying pan until soft and pliable and place in a basket or tea towel to keep warm. Ladle the soup into bowls and pass round the corn tortillas at the table.

COOKING TIPS: *You can buy courgette flowers during the summer from specialist food suppliers and greengrocers, or look for them at farmers' markets and speciality food fairs.*

Most cooks in Mexico City tear their squash flowers by hand, instead of chopping them with a knife. I like the uneven texture that comes with tearing. To do so, break off the stem, and press on the base to gently open the flower into two pieces. Tear the petals into long strips, keeping the base intact if possible. Some people discard the stamen (the centre part of the flower), but I like it. You definitely want to keep the green base of the flower in the soup – it adds a nice, firm texture.

450g chicken pieces, such as a
    chicken carcass and 2 wings
1 sprig of spearmint
2 large garlic cloves
¼ medium onion
2 tablespoons rapeseed oil
450g round, tender young
    Mexican squash or other
    summer squash such as
    courgettes, cubed
225g white button or chestnut
    mushrooms, thinly sliced
250g sweetcorn kernels
1 sprig of epazote
2 large bunches of courgette
    flowers (about 275g), torn into
    strips
12–16 corn tortillas
salt

MEXTLAPIQUES
GRILLED FISH TAMALES

The word mextlapique *refers to a type of tamal made with freshwater fish, stuffed into a corn husk and grilled on a* comal. *Historians trace them to before the Spaniards' arrival in 1521, and they're still made this same way in some parts of Mexico City – you can spot the vendors by their piles of blackened corn husks. The corn husk, in this case, acts as a sort of parchment, steaming the fish and vegetables. I like finishing these with a touch of olive oil and lime juice, and Creamy Jalapeño Salsa.*

12–15 large dried corn husks,
   1 torn into strips
700–900g firm white fish fillets,
   such as cod or haddock, cut
   into 4 pieces
2 large cactus paddles, rinsed,
   spines removed and diced
   (see page 146)
¼ medium onion, cut into slivers
100g fresh tomato, diced
1 jalapeño or serrano chilli, cut
   into thin rounds
5 sprigs of epazote, leaves
   roughly chopped
olive oil, for serving
3–4 limes, cut into wedges
1 batch Creamy Jalapeño Salsa
   (page 96), or salsa of choice
salt and freshly ground black
   pepper

1   Place the corn husks in a large pan of hot water and leave to soften for 45 minutes.

2   Season the fish with salt and pepper. Grab a corn husk and shake it dry. Nestle a fish fillet inside and top with a quarter of the cactus, onion slivers, diced tomato and chilli. Add 1 tablespoon of the chopped epazote leaves and sprinkle on a little more salt.

3   Close the husk by bringing the edges together and folding down the narrower end. If there are any holes in the husk, wrap in another corn husk. Tie a few strips of corn husk around the width of the *tamal* to keep it closed. Repeat three times to make the rest of the tamales.

4   Heat a *comal* or griddle to medium heat. Add the tamales directly to the *comal* or pan and cook for 5–7 minutes on each side or until the fish and vegetables are tender. The husks will burn and blacken, but that's part of the flavour and presentation.

5   To serve, place on individual plates and let your guests unwrap. Pass round the olive oil, lime wedges and salsa at the table. The tamales should be eaten out of the husk.

COOKING TIP: *Depending on the size of your corn husks, you may need to cut the fish into smaller pieces, in order for them to fit comfortably inside.*

TAMALES DE HONGOS
MUSHROOM AND GREEN SALSA TAMALES

July is rainy season in Milpa Alta and mushrooms are everywhere in the market. Local farmers sell them in bunches on small tarpaulins: fat morels, smooth golden yemitas, fringy escobetilla (named as such because it looks like you could sweep the floor with it) and the long, thin mushroomy fingers of the clavito. On my first visit, I bought a mushroom tamal at a market stall with bits of clavito and dripping green salsa. It was a revelation: meaty and spicy and satisfying. These are particularly fantastic for breakfast, with a cup of Café de Olla (page 61). Any extra sauce can be served with the tamales, or stored and used for tacos, quesadillas, eggs or anything else.

at least 36 dried corn husks
450g tomatillos, husked and
    rinsed
1 medium garlic clove, peeled
2 serrano chillies
¼ medium white onion
60ml Basic Homemade Chicken
    Stock (page 98) or water
2 teaspoons lard or rapeseed oil
¼ teaspoon ground cumin
¾ teaspoon salt, or more to taste
275g buna shimeji (brown
    beech) mushrooms, roots
    trimmed and mushrooms
    separated into individual
    stems, or chestnut
    mushrooms, cut into quarters

For the masa:
460g masa harina, or 1.3kg fresh
    masa for tamales
2 teaspoons baking powder
1½ teaspoons salt
720ml room-temperature Basic
    Homemade Chicken Stock
    (page 98) for masa harina,
    300ml for fresh masa
300g lard for masa harina, or
    340g if using fresh masa

1   Place the corn husks in a large saucepan of hot water to soften for 45 minutes.

2   Place the tomatillos, garlic, chillies and onion in a large saucepan. Cover with cold water and bring to the boil, then reduce the heat to medium and simmer for about 12 minutes until the tomatillos turn pea green and soften.

3   Remove the stems from the chillies and roughly chop with the garlic. Add to a blender with the tomatillos, onion and stock. Blend until smooth.

4   Warm the lard or oil in a large frying pan over a medium heat. When melted, add the sauce in one quick pour. (Careful, it might splatter.) Stir in the cumin and salt and cook for about 5 minutes until the flavours meld. Transfer to a bowl and leave to cool.

5   Prepare the masa. If using masa harina, whisk together with the baking powder and salt in a large bowl. Working first with a spatula, and then with your hands, gradually add the 720ml stock, stirring and then kneading lightly until all the liquid has been absorbed. Set aside for 10 minutes to allow the liquid to fully soak into the flour. If using fresh masa, moisten with about 240ml stock, adding a little at a time. Knead well until soft, slightly sticky and pliable. (Depending on how dry the masa is, you may need the extra 60ml stock, or a little less.)

6   Meanwhile, in a stand mixer fitted with the paddle attachment, whip the lard on a medium speed for about 5 minutes until it's smooth and glossy. Increase the speed to high and integrate small, golf ball-sized bits of masa into the lard a little at a time, mixing well after each addition, until a cohesive, very sticky dough forms. It should look similar to a thick muffin batter. Add more liquid if the dough looks too dry and dense.

7   If using fresh masa, now sprinkle the baking powder and salt onto the dough. Mix well for several more minutes, and taste to see if the masa needs more salt. If so, add and keep mixing until well combined. Dough made with masa harina can be stored in the fridge, tightly covered, for up to 24 hours or until ready to use. (You may need to add more stock when you're ready to use it – masa harina sucks up liquid quickly.) Dough made with fresh masa must be used the very same day, or it will turn sour.

8   To form the tamales, lift some of the husks out of the pan and dry them lightly with kitchen paper. Place a husk vertically in your hand. Add 4 tablespoons masa and spread it, using the underside of the spoon, into a longish rectangle. Don't spread all the way to the edges, because the masa will expand in the pan, and you also need room to fold the husk over. Place three or four pieces of mushroom on top and cover with 1 tablespoon of the sauce.

9   Clutch both of the long edges of the husk and fold them over each other so that the masa covers the filling. The *tamal* should fold cleanly and securely, and the filling should not drip out. If it does, you've added too much. (You can open the husk and remove some, if so.)

10   Once closed, fold down the narrower end of the corn husk and press along the fold to seal. (With the thicker, more manicured corn husks, you may need to tie these closed with an extra strip of husk.) Look over the tamal carefully to make sure there aren't any holes where masa could seep out during cooking. If there are holes, wrap the tamal another leaf. The finished tamal should look elongated, like a slightly flattened sausage. Set aside on a baking tray and repeat to make about 24 tamales. (See page 143 for photos.)

11   Add water to the steamer pan and place a coin in the bottom; the coin will rattle when the water starts to boil. Very carefully, place the tamales in a loose vertical position in the steamer pan, with the folded sides touching the pan floor. Cover with more husks, then a layer of clingfilm, then the lid. If the pan has a side opening for the purpose of adding water, cover it with foil.

12   Steam for 50 minutes–1 hour over a high heat. (At higher altitudes, this may take longer.) Listen to the pan occasionally to make sure the coin keeps rattling; if not, add more water, taking extreme care not to dampen the tamales. To check for doneness, remove one *tamal* from the pan and open the husk. If it peels back cleanly, without sticking, the *tamal* is done.

13   Leave to cool for at least 15 minutes before serving. Serve in the husk, with plenty of salsa.

COOKING TIPS: *This recipe uses buna shimeji mushrooms, sometimes called brown beech mushrooms, which are available from select supermarkets and Asian supermarkets. If you can't find them, use chestnut or another flavourful mushroom (not button). Chicken stock cubes or powder can overwhelm the delicate mushroom flavour, so avoid those here if possible. Like any tamal recipe, this works much faster if you've got a friend to help you stuff them. You'll need a large steamer pan, but if you don't have one, see the Cooking Tip on page 37.*

AYOCOTES CON NOPALES
RUNNER BEANS WITH CACTUS

Large, starchy ayocote *beans are like the butter bean of Mexico. They've got a bit of a stronger flavour, but the creamy innards are just as seductive. I have eaten* ayocotes *– known in English as runner beans – many times, but I particularly love this combination, prepared at the home of Emma Villanueva Buendía, who, along with her husband Abel, farms corn in Tepetlixpa, in the State of Mexico just outside Mexico City. She seasons the beans only with a bit of onion and a Mexican bay leaf, which infuses its flavour into the broth. The cactus, meanwhile, thickens the bean broth with its viscous sap. It's delicious with a helping of Mexican rice on the side.*

4 cactus paddles (about 400g)

450g dried purple *ayocote* (runner) beans (see Tip), rinsed and soaked overnight

2 teaspoons lard or rapeseed oil

¼ medium onion, chopped

1 dried Mexican bay leaf

12–16 corn tortillas

1 batch Mexican-style Red Rice (page 97)

salt

COOKING TIP: *You should be able to find dried runner beans at Mexican grocery stores. They're usually black, purple or white. You can also grow and dry your own scarlet runner beans.*

1   Remove the spines from the cactus paddles and rinse (see below for photos), then cut them into 4cm by 5mm pieces. Set aside.

2   Drain the beans, place in a large saucepan and cover with 7.5–10cm fresh cold water. Bring to the boil, then reduce the heat to medium or medium-low, ensuring that the beans bubble gently. Cook for about 2 hours until creamy and tender, seasoning with salt in the last 5–10 minutes of cooking. Pour the beans and cooking liquid into a large bowl and wipe out the pan.

3   Heat the lard or oil in the same pan over a medium-high heat. Add the onion and cook until blistered and dark golden brown. Pour in the beans, add the bay leaf and bring to the boil. Stir in the cactus and a light sprinkling of salt, if desired. Cook for 15–20 minutes until the cactus is tender. Taste and add more salt if necessary.

4   Warm the tortillas on a *comal* or non-stick frying pan until soft and pliable, and place in a tea towel or basket. Serve the soup in shallow bowls, ladling in beans, a good amount of the cooking liquid and cactus into each bowl, along with a generous helping of Mexican rice on the side. Pass round the warm tortillas at the table.

NOPALES Y VERDURAS EN ESCABECHE
PICKLED CACTUS AND VEGETABLES

Milpa Alta, the southernmost region in Mexico City, is a massive cactus-growing region. One of my favourite ways to eat cactus there is en escabeche, or lightly pickled in vinegar. The chopped paddles are tossed with other veggies, such as broad (fava) beans, carrots or cauliflower. The mixture is so good – a balance of sweet, spicy and tangy, without being overly briny – that you can eat piece after piece, assuming you can handle the heat. Traditionally nopales en escabeche is served as a topping for your taco, or a nibble to complement whatever you're eating. I like it slightly warm, spooned into a corn tortilla and eaten as its own taco, perhaps with a soup or a little Mexican rice on the side. You can also serve this cold or at room temperature.

1   Remove the thorns from the cactus paddles (see opposite for photos), rinse and cut into 7.5cm by 2.5cm pieces. Fill a medium saucepan two-thirds full with water. Add the onion, garlic and salt and bring to a vigorous boil. Add the cactus and cook for about 2 minutes until just barely tender. Using a slotted spoon, transfer the cactus to a plate and discard the aromatics.

2   To make the *escabeche*, heat the oil in a medium, heavy-based saucepan over a medium-high heat. Add the onions and cook, stirring occasionally, for 6–8 minutes until translucent. Add the garlic and jalapeños and cook for about 1 minute until aromatic. Stir in the broad beans, carrots, cactus, salt, allspice, thyme, marjoram and bay leaves, ensuring that the vegetables are evenly coated in oil. Turn the heat to medium-low, cover and cook for about 8 minutes until the flavours combine. Stir in the vinegar and olive oil. Taste and adjust the seasonings.

3   Serve either warm or cold. The mixture will keep refrigerated in an airtight container for up to 2 weeks.

COOKING TIPS: *For pickling cactus, it's traditional to use sugar cane vinegar (vinagre de caña), a slightly sweet vinegar available from Asian supermarkets or online suppliers. If you can't find it, cider vinegar will work.*

The broad beans should not be peeled all the way, as is common in Central Mexico – locals love the beans' outer waxy skin, which adds flavour and texture. If the beans are young enough, they should not taste bitter. If you can't find broad beans, try adding cauliflower, green beans or fresh peas.

I used red jalapeños because they're slightly hotter than the green variety, and they add a burst of colour. If you can't find them or you want less heat, green jalapeños are fine.

4–5 cactus paddles (about 375g)
1 thick slice of onion
2 large garlic cloves, peeled
1 teaspoon salt

For the *escabeche*:
60ml rapeseed oil
2 medium onions, sliced into thin rounds
4 medium garlic cloves, peeled
6 red jalapeño chillies, de-stemmed and cut lengthways into 1cm-thick wedges
900g young, fresh broad beans, podded (see Tip)
2–3 large carrots, sliced medium-thick on the diagonal
1 tablespoon salt
6 allspice berries
3 sprigs of fresh thyme
2 sprigs of fresh marjoram
6 Mexican bay leaves
90ml sugar cane vinegar or cider vinegar
60ml mild olive oil

CHORIZO VERDE
HOMEMADE GREEN CHORIZO

Green chorizo – coloured green because it contains green chillies and vegetables – is typical to the city of Toluca in neighbouring Mexico State. You can find it at Mexico City markets or at certain street stalls specialising in chorizo. Typically it's crumbled and cooked, and served in a taco with a squirt of lime and a heavy spoonful of salsa.

I interviewed a half-dozen Toluca sausage makers to learn the secret behind the recipe, and all said they first create a mole-like sauce with herbs, spices and tomatillo, which they then add to the sausage. Tomatillo made my sausage too moist, so I've substituted spinach, which still gives the chorizo a nice light green colour. Some cooks also add food colouring, which makes the meat look neon green – that could be fun for holidays or for kids. This makes quite a bit of sausage; leftovers can be frozen, or used in other non-Mexican dishes such as pasta, as breakfast patties or in sauces.

1   Roast the poblano over an open gas flame until blackened in spots, then wrap in a tea towel to sweat (see page 37 for instructions). Peel off the skin and make a slit to remove the seeds and veins. Chop roughly and add to a blender with the serrano, garlic, onion, spinach, coriander, cumin, peppercorns and oregano. Blend and taste, then add ¾ teaspoon salt, or to taste, and blend again until smooth. If the sauce doesn't break down right away, scrape down the insides of the blender jug and blend again. (Water can make the sausage soggy, so try not to use any unless you absolutely have to.)

2   Place the sauce in the fridge for at least 1 hour. At the same time, place the meat, fat, meat mincer (if using) and mixing bowl in the freezer for 1 hour. If using ready-prepared minced meat, proceed to step 4.

3   Remove the items from the freezer, add the meat and fat to the mincer and mince as per the manufacturer's instructions.

4   Stir in 1¼ teaspoons salt, the peanuts and the pecans. Using a stand mixer fitted with the paddle attachment, or by hand if desired, mix the cold sauce and cider vinegar into the minced meat until fully absorbed and slightly sticky. At this point the sausage can be refrigerated in an airtight container for up to 2 days, or longer if frozen.

5   Heat a large frying pan to medium heat. Add the sausage in a more or less even layer – you may have to cook it in batches – and cook, stirring often, for 7–10 minutes until the sausage is no longer pink and slightly crisp in spots.

6   Serve in tortillas, passing round lime wedges and salsa at the table.

COOKING TIP: *If you don't have a meat mincer, ask the butcher to mince a very fatty cut of pork shoulder, or, even better, to mince 900g pork shoulder with 225g pork fat. Casings aren't needed, since you're going to crumble the sausage. If you're a more skilled sausage maker, you could try casing the sausage, let it age for 2–3 days, then cook it.*

It's important that the sausage and sauce be very cold when you're mixing it, otherwise it may not bind together correctly.

1 small poblano chilli
1 large serrano chilli, roughly chopped
1 garlic clove, roughly chopped
⅛ medium onion, roughly chopped
30g spinach leaves
2 large sprigs of fresh coriander
¼ teaspoon cumin seeds
⅛ teaspoon black peppercorns
¼ teaspoon dried Mexican oregano
900g boneless pork shoulder, cut into large cubes
225g pork fat, cut into large cubes (see Tip)
75g raw unsalted peanuts, toasted and roughly chopped
55g pecan nuts, roughly chopped
2 tablespoons cider vinegar
30 corn tortillas, warmed
7 limes, cut into wedges
salsa of choice
salt

MIXIOTES DE VERDURAS
STEAMED PARCELS OF CHICKEN AND VEGETABLES

A mixiote *is usually a steamed parcel of meat draped in a pungent, spicy chilli sauce. It's steamed in the papery peel of the maguey leaf, also called* mixiote, *hence the name.* Mixiotes *are very common in the Central Mexican states of Hidalgo, Tlaxcala, Puebla and in the State of Mexico, and you can find them throughout Mexico City, particularly at fondas or restaurants specialising in rustic food.*

It's not wholly common to find a mixiote *with so many vegetables, but I've found myself missing them every time I open a* mixiote *and find nothing but meat. This recipe, which calls for chorizo or chicken, riffs a little on the flavours and sauces found in* mixiotes *in Mexico City and speaks more to my specific tastes. I like to serve these with corn tortillas on the side.*

8 guajillo chillies

2 morita chillies

1 ripe plum tomato

2 large garlic cloves, unpeeled

¼ medium onion

120g Swiss chard leaves, chopped

200g cauliflower florets

1 large Mexican squash or courgette, cut into quarters about 1cm wide

2 cactus paddles, spines removed and rinsed (see page 146)

130g fresh or frozen peas

700g small boneless, skinless chicken thighs or cooking chorizo sausages

2 teaspoons rapeseed oil, plus more if necessary

¼ teaspoon ground Mexican cinnamon

2 cloves

1 teaspoon fresh thyme leaves

4 limes, cut into wedges

12–16 corn tortillas, warmed

salt and freshly ground black pepper

1 Cut out six squares of baking parchment roughly 35cm by 38cm each. Set aside.

2 Toast the chillies briefly on a *comal* or non-stick frying pan over a medium to medium-low heat for 15–30 seconds just until they release a spicy aroma. (Turn frequently so that they don't burn.) Transfer to a work surface, then add the tomato, garlic and onion to the *comal* or frying pan. Cook, turning occasionally, for about 5 minutes until charred in spots. Set aside to cool.

3 Snip the stems off the chillies, then make a slit to discard the seeds and veins. Place the chillies in a bowl of warm water and soak for 20–30 minutes until the skins soften. Drain and reserve the soaking water.

4 Meanwhile, add the chard, cauliflower, squash, cactus and peas to a bowl and toss with salt and pepper to taste.

5 Cut the chicken thighs into four pieces each and season liberally with salt. Heat a frying pan over a medium-high heat and add the oil. Working in batches, cook the chicken for about 3 minutes per side just until golden brown. (No need to cook them through; they'll finish in the steaming process.) Alternatively, if using chorizo, slice open the sausages and discard the casings. Crumble into large pieces and fry over a medium-high heat until dark golden brown in spots. Set aside.

6 Place the softened chillies, 240ml of the reserved chilli water, the tomato, garlic, onion, cinnamon, cloves, thyme and ¼ teaspoon black pepper in a blender. Blend into a smooth yet still slightly thick sauce. Season with salt.

7 Add water to a steamer pan and bring to the boil over a high heat.

8 Meanwhile, make a work space with the baking parchment, veggies, chicken and the sauce nearby. Place one piece of baking parchment on the work surface. Add one sixth of the vegetables, four pieces of chicken or a small handful of chorizo and a generous 4 tablespoons of the sauce, ensuring that it covers the vegetables and meat.

9 Bring up the edges of the paper to form a little parcel and tie closed tightly with kitchen string. Set aside and repeat until you have six parcels.

10 Carefully place the parcels in the steamer and cover tightly. Steam for 20 minutes or until the peas are tender.

11 Serve immediately, placing a parcel on each plate for guests to unwrap. Pass round the lime wedges and warm tortillas at the table.

COOKING TIP: *It's very hard to find* mixiote *leaves outside Mexico – and even within Mexico, they're increasingly over-harvested – so I use baking parchment, with good results. You'll also need kitchen string and a steamer pan or basket insert.*

PESCADO AL MOJO DE AJO
GARLICKY PAN-FRIED FISH

For garlic mojo sauce:
1 garlic bulb, or about 8 large cloves, roughly chopped
2 tablespoons freshly squeezed lime juice
2 tablespoons olive oil
½ teaspoon salt

700–900g firm white fish fillets such as cod, cut into 4 even pieces
2 tablespoons rapeseed oil, plus more if needed
6 large garlic cloves, thinly sliced
fresh parsley, chopped
salt and freshly ground black pepper

Driving west in Mexico City, past the city limits that end near the corporate, skyscraper-filled Santa Fe neighbourhood, a pine forest unfolds. It's jarring: just a few minutes ago, there had been a mall, and now you're in a thatch of fog, whizzing past majestic green trees. This is the State of Mexico, home to thousands of Mexico City commuters, and also home to several gastronomic delicacies – among them different preparations of trout, raised in nearby farms. In places like La Marquesa, a row of colourful roadside food stalls just beyond the outskirts of Mexico City, or in the nearby city of Malinalco, you can order trout with garlic sauce, chipotle sauce, grilled or nearly any other way you want it, with a simple lettuce and tomato salad on the side.

In the USA, it can be difficult to find this delicate freshwater fish year-round, depending on where you live. For this recipe, I've substituted cod, which has a firmer flesh but still stands up well under the mountain of garlic. Using whole fish instead of fillets would also work beautifully; that's how many fondas and restaurants do it in Mexico.

1   First, prepare the sauce. Place the garlic and lime juice in a blender and blend to a chunky purée. Add the olive oil and blend to a smooth paste. Taste and season with the salt, and blend once more. Scrape the sauce into a bowl and set aside.

2   Season the fish fillets with salt and pepper.

3   Heat a large non-stick or cast-iron frying pan over a medium-high heat and add the oil when hot. Add the garlic and cook for about 1 minute until aromatic, lightly crisp and brown, then transfer to a small bowl. Keep the oil in the pan.

4   Fry the fish fillets in two batches, about 5 minutes per side, until a golden crust forms and fish is just cooked through. Cover lightly with foil to keep warm while you fry the second batch.

5   To serve, spoon a light layer of the garlic sauce on top of the fish, and top with the fried garlic and some parsley.

COOKING TIP: *This preparation – which calls for crispy garlic and a separate garlic sauce – does not exactly mirror the mojo de ajo presentations I've seen in Mexico, which feature crispy bits of garlic and little other seasoning. I've added a bit more oomph to reflect my taste. Be careful, though – the garlic sauce is intense, and a little goes a long way.*

Use a non-stick frying pan or a well-seasoned cast-iron frying pan to cook skinned fish fillets. They tend to stick in a regular stainless-steel frying pan.

CONEJO A LA BANDOLERA
BEER-BRAISED RABBIT

Tláhuac is perhaps the hardest borough to reach in Mexico City. Driving from the Centro can take around two hours with traffic, and the subway station that opened in 2013 closed a year later due to structural problems. Thankfully, there is an oasis for Tlahuaqueños, or at least people who can afford to dine there – a large restaurant called La Playa, located at the edge of a small lake where ducks swim. The owner, a slim middle-aged man named Juan Carlos Martinez, cracks jokes with the customers and occasionally offers a free shot of tequila. The place also serves a surprisingly large variety of more rustic foods: rabbit, grilled tamales and edible insects such as maguey worms and ant larvae. This is one of the better rabbit dishes I've tried in Mexico City. The meat is fried, then braised slowly in beer until tender, giving the meat a slight yeastiness. The cook, Hortencia Zepahua, graciously explained the preparation for me.

1 Rinse the rabbit pieces and pat dry with kitchen paper. Season with salt, ensuring that you salt both sides.

2 In a large, heavy-based frying pan, melt the lard, olive oil and butter over a medium-high heat. Add the rabbit pieces in an even layer and cook, undisturbed, 4–6 minutes until a golden-brown crust forms. Be careful, as the grease may pop and splatter. Turn and fry the other side for a further 4–5 minutes until golden.

3 Add the bay leaf, fresh herbs, peppercorns, beer and 60ml water. Reduce the heat to low, cover and cook for 20 minutes. Turn the rabbit pieces and cook, covered, for a further 20–25 minutes until tender when pierced with a fork.

4 Serve warm, spooning sauce over the meat, with Mexican rice on the side.

COOKING TIP: *To prepare the rabbit, you'll need a large frying pan with deep sides and a lid. You should be able to find wild rabbit at select supermarkets and speciality butcher's shops and online suppliers – ask the butcher to cut it into pieces.*

900g wild rabbit, cut into pieces
15g lard
2 tablespoons olive oil
25g unsalted butter
1 dried Mexican bay leaf
1 sprig of fresh Mexican oregano, chopped
3 sprigs of fresh marjoram, chopped
3 sprigs of fresh thyme, chopped
2 black peppercorns
180ml light beer, such as Victoria
1 batch Mexican-style Red Rice (page 107)
salt

BARBACOA
SLOW-ROASTED MUTTON

In Mexico City, barbacoa is usually made from lamb or mutton, although occasionally you'll see it prepared with beef or goat. The dish – typically made from meat slow-roasted in a pit in the ground – is consumed with gusto at the weekends, where it's often sold in tacos or with a steaming bowl of consommé, made from the meat juices mixed with rice and chickpeas. Traditionally, the meat is freshly slaughtered and wrapped in maguey leaves while it bakes. Outside of Mexico, many of us don't have access to freshly slaughtered meat, a hole in the ground or maguey leaves. But it's still possible to re-create some of the same flavours at home, using a heavy casserole dish with a lid, or a roasting tin covered tightly in foil.

I like using mutton – the gamier flavour reminds me a little more of the countryside in Mexico. The meat slow-roasts for four hours in the oven, and from there you make an easy consommé out of the resulting juices. All you need to complete the meal are lime wedges, salsa (traditionally Salsa Borracha, recipe opposite) and good corn tortillas. It makes for a stunning, comforting meal for large groups.

1.3–1.8kg mutton or lamb shanks (see Tip)
6–7 avocado leaves (see Tip)
½ medium onion, cut into 2 pieces, plus 150g diced onion
1 dried Mexican bay leaf
2 garlic cloves, peeled
2 thick sprigs of fresh thyme
35g dried chickpeas
95g long-grain white rice
40g fresh coriander, roughly chopped
5 limes, cut into wedges
1 batch Salsa Borracha (see opposite), or salsa of choice
36 corn tortillas, warmed
salt

COOKING TIPS: *Mutton is generally available from speciality butcher's shops or online suppliers. If you can't find it, lamb is a fine (if more expensive) substitute. Avocado leaves are available from Mexican grocery stores or online suppliers.*

1   Adjust the oven shelf to the middle or lower third of the oven and preheat to 140°C/gas mark 1. Season the meat liberally with salt and set aside.

2   Heat a small frying pan over a medium-low heat and toast the avocado leaves until they smell aromatic. Set aside.

3   Place the meat in a large casserole dish (don't worry if the pieces overlap). Pour 720ml water on top and add the onion wedges, bay leaf, garlic and thyme. Arrange the toasted avocado leaves on top of the meat. Cover tightly with heavy-duty foil and place the lid on top. Cook for 3½–4 hours until the meat is tender and falling off the bone.

4   Meanwhile, place the chickpeas in a medium bowl and cover with water. Leave to soak while the meat cooks, ideally for 4 hours, then drain.

5   Remove the meat carefully from the cooking liquid and transfer to a bowl. Ladle 120ml of the cooking liquid over the meat and leave to cool slightly, then tear the meat into large pieces and cover with foil. Set the bones aside – do not discard.

6   Warm the remaining cooking liquid over a medium heat. Remove the thyme sprigs and add the bones and 2 litres water. Bring to the boil, then add the rice and soaked chickpeas. Return to the boil, then reduce the heat to medium-low. Simmer gently, uncovered, for about 1 hour until the chickpeas are soft. (If the consommé has reduced too much, add a little more water.) Season with salt – the broth should be nice and salty.

7   Place the meat on a platter and the coriander, diced onion, lime wedges and salsa on the table, with the warm tortillas. Ladle the consommé into small heatproof bowls to serve guests individually to start, and let guests make their own tacos with the mutton, garnishes and tortillas.

SALSA BORRACHA
'DRUNK' SALSA

This bitter, intense salsa traditionally calls for pulque, *the fermented, lightly alcoholic sap from the agave plant. Since* pulque *is next to impossible to find outside Mexico City (save for canned varieties, which I stay away from), I've substituted dark Mexican beer. You can make this lots of ways, but I like the textures and saltiness that come from using slightly aged cheese, pickled chillies and raw onion. If you like softer flavours, add a spritz of freshly squeezed orange juice.*

1   Toast the chillies briefly on the *comal* or in a non-stick frying pan over a medium-low heat. They should not burn – cook, turning them almost constantly, for 5–10 seconds until they release a spicy aroma. Remove, snip off the stems and shake out and discard the seeds. Fill a bowl with warm water and leave the chillies to soak for about 20 minutes until the skins soften.

2   Meanwhile, toast the garlic on the *comal* or frying pan for 5–8 minutes until soft and squishy.

3   Place the garlic, chillies, oil and beer in a blender and blend until smooth. Transfer to a bowl and stir in the pickled jalapeños and onion. (Taste and add the orange juice if you like.) Stir in the salt as desired and top with the cheese.

4   The salsa is best if eaten immediately.

5 pasilla chillies
2 garlic cloves, unpeeled
1½ teaspoons olive oil
150ml dark Mexican beer, such as Negra Modelo
4 tablespoons roughly chopped pickled jalapeño chillies
chopped onion, to taste
3 tablespoons freshly squeezed orange juice, optional
½ teaspoon salt, or more to taste
30g queso añejo, crumbled

PLÁTANO MACHO CON LECHE CONDENSADA
FRIED PLANTAIN WITH CONDENSED MILK AND JAM

I first spotted this dessert at a rustic outdoor restaurant in Texcoco, a small city northeast of the capital. A cook stood in front of a huge metal fryer set over an open flame, filled with thick slices of plantain. As a line of people watched, the cook removed a plantain slice from the bubbling oil, topped it with spoonfuls of condensed milk and finished with a dollop of chunky fruit jam. The mixture was simple but heavenly: fruity and rich, the fruit creamy-fleshed from its time in the fryer.

2 large, very ripe plantains
rapeseed oil
400g can sweetened
    condensed milk
4 heaped tablespoons
    strawberry or blackberry jam

1   Peel the plantains and cut them, from pole to pole, into three long pieces measuring 5mm–1cm thick.

2   Heat a large frying pan to medium or medium-high heat. Pour enough rapeseed oil to coat the base about 3mm deep. Line a plate with kitchen paper.

3   When hot, add the plantain slices in batches – they should sizzle, otherwise the oil isn't hot enough. Cook for 2–3 minutes per side until dark golden brown. Drain on the prepared plate.

4   Place one warm plantain on a small serving plate and spoon a generous helping of condensed milk on top. Finish with a heaped tablespoon of jam.

COOKING TIP: *At home, I've tried substituting bananas instead of plantains, but the flavour isn't the same, and bananas turn rather flaccid when pan-fried. Ensure that your plantains are as ripe as possible – the outer skin should be black. I like tart fruit jam with this, such as blackberry or strawberry.*

CHAPTER 5

AT
HOME

Even though I grew up in a Mexican-American household in Southern California, we did not eat much Mexican food. My mom was usually too busy to cook, so we ate TV dinners and hot dogs and frozen burritos, and sometimes one-pot stews with vegetables from our garden. Sometimes I wrapped our hot dogs in flour tortillas, because we didn't always have hot dog buns. Every now and then my mom bought jalapeños or canned, spicy chillies, but I stayed far away – I hated spicy food.

Once I started living on my own and cooking for myself, I realised that a homemade meal was a way to pamper myself, my friends or my boyfriend at the end of a hectic day. I began experimenting, sampling foreign cuisines, buying wine for weeknight dinners. I bought a few Mexican cookbooks that I sometimes dug out for Cinco de Mayo.

When my husband and I moved to Mexico, I thought: would they sell my organic cereal there? What about quinoa? By the time I moved back to the States four years later, my eating habits had changed. I didn't eat much quinoa anymore. I ate beans. My breakfast had morphed into roasted poblano chilli porridge, or at the very least scrambled eggs drizzled with salsa.

In New York, I craved the Mexican ingredients that had begun to taste like home to me: fresh corn tortillas (the ones made from real, nixtamalised corn), stewed beans, cactus, tomatillos, serranos, roasted poblanos, guava, dried chillies. Those cravings weaved into my pre-Mexico way of eating, which usually combined vegetables and beans and little meat. Mexican flavours permeated other culinary interests too: Indian and Middle Eastern foods, and those from the American South, where my husband is from.

At home in New York, I combine cultures as much as I want. I shop at Mexican and Indian grocery stores, Asian and farmers' markets (luckily all of these are within walking distance of my house). Most of the dishes that follow I make on a weeknight, when I'm eyeing the fridge like we all do, wondering what to cook.

PRICKLY PEAR AGUA FRESCA WITH LIME AND CHIA SEEDS

Prickly pear cactus fruit, known in Spanish as tuna, is especially abundant during Mexico City's rainy season, when you can often get 900g for less than a dollar. The flesh is moist and mildly sweet, sort of like a more floral version of watermelon. Some people peel and eat the fruit raw, and many use it in an agua fresca. At home in New York, the Mexican bodegas near my house sell prickly pear fairly inexpensively, which means I can re-create the drink most times of the year. I like adding in chia seeds and a little lime juice. The amount of fruit you include can vary, since some tunas may be riper and muskier than others.

1.3kg green or red prickly pear fruit, peeled and cut into large chunks (see panel)

2 tablespoons sugar

2 tablespoons freshly squeezed lime juice

2 tablespoons chia seeds

1 Put the fruit, sugar, lime juice and 1 litre water in a blender. Blend until smooth, taste for more sugar or lime juice and blend again. Strain into a jug using a fine-mesh sieve.

2 Stir the chia seeds into jug. Serve cold or over ice.

HOW TO PEEL PRICKLY PEAR FRUIT

Tunas have a very thick skin, which must be peeled to get to the moist, seed-dotted flesh inside. To peel, slice into the fruit from pole to pole with a paring knife. You'll want to slice deeply, almost 5mm into the fruit – don't just cut into the thin outer layer. If the tuna is ripe, you should be able to open the fruit up like a package, peeling off the thick skin like a wrapper. You will be left with a small, oval-shaped fruit, dotted with dark seeds.

SPICY CHIPOTLE BEAN DIP

I'm often looking for new ways to use leftover cooked beans in my fridge, and I threw together this dip one evening when friends were coming over to watch the basketball game. The mix of dried chipotle and chipotle in adobo sauce means you get a lot of smoke in every bite, but you don't get too much acid or vinegar, which would compete with the creaminess of the beans. This would work well in a wrap, burger or sandwich too.

1   Prepare the tortilla chips, if you haven't already.

2   Heat a *comal* or non-stick frying pan to medium-low heat, and when hot, toast the chipotle meco chillies lightly for 5–10 seconds per side until they release a spicy aroma. Place in a bowl of warm water and leave to soak for 15–20 minutes until softened. Strain and reserve about 120ml of the chilli water. Set aside.

3   Heat the lard or oil in a medium saucepan over s medium-high heat. Add the garlic and onion and cook, stirring occasionally, for about 3 minutes until dark golden and blistered on all sides.

4   Add the beans and bean liquid in one quick pour. Stir in the black pepper, cumin and a pinch of salt. Bring to the boil, then reduce the heat, cover and simmer for 5 minutes to allow the flavours to meld. Leave to cool to room temperature.

5   Pour the cooled bean mixture, chipotle, soaked chillies and the reserved chilli water into a blender and blend until smooth. Taste for more salt or cumin if desired.

6   To serve, pour the bean dip into a bowl and serve with the tortilla chips.

Baked Tortilla Chips (recipe follows)
2 chipotle meco chillies, de-stemmed and deseeded
2 teaspoons lard or rapeseed oil
2 garlic cloves, peeled
¼ medium onion
350g cooked black beans, with about 180ml bean liquid
⅛ teaspoon black pepper
½ teaspoon ground cumin
1 large chipotle in adobo sauce from a can, with seeds
salt

COOKING TIP: *The dish is very spicy, because that's how I like things. Feel free to use less chipotle or remove the seeds to reduce the heat.*

BAKED TORTILLA CHIPS

These crunchy chips are my go-to snack at home, and baking them gives them a nutty flavour. It's also a great way to use any old tortillas lying around in the fridge. I usually don't add salt, but you can if you want more punch.

1   Preheat the oven to 220°C/gas mark 7. Stack six tortillas in a pile and use a large sharp knife to carefully cut the whole stack into eight even triangles. Spread in an even layer on a baking tray. (If you have two baking trays, cut the remaining six tortillas and bake both trays at the same time.)

2   Cook, rotating the baking trays halfway through baking, for 10–15 minutes until golden brown and crispy. Season with salt if desired immediately after taking them out of the oven, then serve.

6–12 corn tortillas
salt, optional

PORRIDGE WITH CHARRED POBLANO CHILLIES AND CHEESE

In Mexico City, chilangos (the local word for Mexico City residents) put charred, peeled poblano chilli strips in quesadillas or mix them with cheese and cream. I never knew anyone who put them in porridge, but to me, the chillies and spongy cheese crumbles add electricity to what can sometimes be a boring breakfast dish. The trick is finding a good poblano. In New York, many taste bland and washed out, except in the summertime when local farmers' markets sometimes carry them.

200g rolled oats

1 teaspoon salt

4 poblano chillies, charred, peeled and deseeded (see page 37)

1 tablespoon plus 1 teaspoon olive oil

115g onion, chopped

4 small garlic cloves, very finely chopped

120g queso fresco, crumbled

freshly ground black pepper, optional

crumbled cooked bacon, optional

1 In a deep microwave-safe bowl, combine the oats, ½ teaspoon salt and 720ml water. Cook on high for 3 minutes. Stir well and cook for a further 3 minutes. Alternatively, combine the same ingredients in a medium saucepan and cook over a medium-high heat until boiling, then reduce the heat to medium-low and cook, stirring often, for about 7 minutes until all the water is absorbed and the oats are tender.

2 Cut the poblano chillies into 1cm-wide strips. Then gather and cut into 2.5cm squares. Set aside.

3 Heat the olive oil in a frying pan over a medium-low heat. Add the onion and garlic and cook for 1 minute until aromatic. Stir in the poblano chillies and the remaining ½ teaspoon salt, cooking for 4–5 minutes until the onions become translucent and the poblanos release a deep aroma.

4 Pour the porridge and crumbled cheese into the pan and stir until combined. Serve in bowls, topped with freshly ground pepper and bacon, if desired.

COOKING TIP: *Taste a small piece of the poblano before you add it to your porridge, just so you know how hot it is. It's also worth tasting the cheese beforehand, as sodium levels in packaged queso fresco can vary.*

NUTTY HOMEMADE MUESLI

For a long time I found muesli, i.e. a simple mix of grains, nuts and sometimes dried fruit, dry and boring compared to crunchy, snappy granola. Then I realised that muesli was much easier to make and possibly healthier. I'm a particular fan of stirring it into yogurt, which creates a thick, textured cereal as the yogurt seeps into the raw oats. This recipe includes the grains and seeds I used to see at the Mexico City licuado or milkshake and juice stands, plus walnuts, which are much easier to source. The result is nutty and toasty, and packed with protein and fibre.

1   Mix the oats, seeds, amaranth and walnuts in a medium bowl. To make one serving, mix 8 tablespoons of the muesli with 8 tablespoons yogurt and leave to stand for 15 minutes. Spoon over some honey or other sweetener and top with fresh or dried fruit – I like peaches, berries, cherries, raisins or dates.

2   Store leftover muesli in an airtight container in a cool, dry place for up to 2 months.

COOKING TIP: *If you can't find puffed amaranth, you can make your own from dried amaranth, which you can find at your local health food store or online. Heat a large, heavy-based saucepan over a high heat with a few grains of amaranth until those grains pop, then add 1 tablespoon amaranth to the hot pan and shake to distribute the grains in an even layer. The amaranth will start popping immediately. Give the pan a couple more shakes until all the amaranth has popped, about 30 seconds in total, being careful not to burn it. Transfer to a bowl to cool, then return the pan to the heat and repeat until you've reached your desired quantity. Four tablespoons of amaranth will yield 45g puffed amaranth.*

200g rolled oats
65g pumpkin seeds, toasted
2 tablespoons chia seeds
25g puffed amaranth (amaranth popcorn) (see Tip)
65g walnuts, chopped
natural yogurt
honey
fresh or dried fruit

HIBISCUS FLOWER QUESADILLAS

My friend Jesica served these quesadillas at her house several years ago, and I'd never seen anything like them. She plumped up dried hibiscus flowers (weren't they only used in tea?) in water, then sautéed them in a little olive oil, butter, sugar and serrano chilli. The result, layered inside a pitta bread and slathered with cheese, was tangy and creamy, salty and slightly sweet. I've made them many times since then as a wonderful starter or light meal.

85g dried hibiscus flowers
15g unsalted butter
2 teaspoons olive oil
½ medium onion, chopped
2 serrano chillies, very finely
    chopped with seeds
1 tablespoon plus 1 teaspoon
    sugar
3–4 wholemeal pitta breads
225g Monterey Jack cheese,
    sliced
salt

1   Preheat the oven to 220°C/gas mark 7. Pick over the flowers and remove any twigs or foreign matter. Rinse thoroughly in a colander under cold water.

2   Fill a medium saucepan with water and put on to boil. Add the hibiscus and turn off the heat. Leave to stand for about 3 minutes until fully hydrated. Drain and reserve the water for tea, if you like. Rinse the flowers under cold water to wash away any grit.

3   Heat the butter and olive oil in a heavy-based frying pan over a medium heat. Add the onion and chilli and cook for about 3 minutes until soft. Stir in the flowers and a pinch of salt and cook for about 2 minutes until evenly combined.

4   Add the sugar and cook a further few minutes, stirring to coat. When the flowers have darkened to a deep-purple colour, after about 3 minutes, turn off the heat.

5   Warm the pitta breads lightly in the oven or on a gently heated *comal*. Cut open the top half only, around the edge of the pittas, and tuck in a layer of cheese slices. Top with a layer of hibiscus flower filling. Place the pitta breads on a baking tray in the oven for about 4 minutes until the cheese has melted. Cut into quarters and serve immediately, while the cheese is still oozy.

COOKING TIP: *In Mexico most hydrated hibiscus flowers have a chewy texture, which I like. Elsewhere, the flowers I've found are much softer and grittier. They require a thorough rinsing both before and after you steep them, or else you get an unpleasant earthy taste in your meal. Flour tortillas can be substituted for the wholemeal pitta breads, if you prefer. (For more on dried hibiscus flowers, see page 96.)*

CRISPY COURGETTE QUESADILLAS

I make these about once a week, using courgettes in the summer and the lighter-skinned, plumper Mexican squash the rest of the year. They're very easy to cook, and the combination of sweet squash mixed with melty cheese is unbeatable. You could really use any cooked vegetable or not-too-saucy leftovers in the fridge like spinach, mushrooms, roasted poblano chillies, roasted peppers and plain shredded chicken. The key element, for me, is crisping the tortillas on the comal. *There's something about biting into a hot, crunchy quesadilla that makes it seem like you spent much more time making it than you actually did.*

2 teaspoons olive oil
3 tablespoons chopped onion
1 garlic, very finely chopped
1 medium courgette, cut into
    5mm-thick half-moons
4 corn tortillas
85g Monterrey Jack cheese,
    grated or sliced into 12 very
    thin rectangular slices
salt and freshly ground black
    pepper

1   Heat the olive oil in a medium frying pan over a medium heat. Add the onion and garlic and cook for about 3 minutes until translucent. Add the courgette and a sprinkle of salt and pepper, and cook, stirring occasionally, for about 5 minutes until the courgette softens. Taste and adjust the seasonings.

2   Warm two tortillas on a *comal*, griddle or non-stick frying pan over a medium heat. When soft and pliable, place three or four cheese slices on one side of each tortilla. Top with an even layer of courgette filling. Fold and press down, using the underside of a spatula if needed to hold the tortilla in place. Move the quesadillas to the outer edges of your pan so that they don't burn.

3   If you have room, warm the remaining two tortillas, fill and repeat. Cook, turning occasionally, for 5–7 minutes until the quesadillas are crispy on both sides and the cheese has melted. Serve immediately, while the cheese is still oozy.

CREAMY KALE SALAD

I came up with this dish after craving a vaguely Mediterranean green salad that I could scoop onto a warm piece of pitta bread. It ended up being sort of a salad dip – not quite one, not quite the other, and a sort of mischievous, light thing to eat for dinner when I was the only one at home. The dish works well as a starter, or for one person sitting alone in front of the TV. If you want less heat, use less serrano or cut out the seeds.

1   In a medium bowl, mash together the avocado, tomato, onion, chilli, lime juice and a pinch of salt, using a fork or vegetable masher. (The base of a cup also works particularly well.)

2   Press any water out of the cooked kale and chop into small pieces. If using raw kale, boil in salted water for 5 minutes or until tender. Drain well, pressing out any water. Stir into the avocado mixture and taste for more salt and lime juice. Season with pepper.

3   Top with the coriander and pumpkin seeds.

4   Warm the pitta bread on a *comal* or in a 200°C/gas mark 6 oven until hot and crisp in parts. Cut into triangles and scoop into the salad. Serve at room temperature.

1 ripe Haas avocado, peeled, stoned and diced
45g ripe tomato, diced
2 tablespoons very finely chopped onion
1 small serrano chilli, very finely chopped with seeds
juice of 1 lime, or more to taste
260g cooked curly kale, or 400g raw kale, leaves torn
1 heaped tablespoon roughly chopped fresh coriander
2 tablespoons pumpkin seeds, toasted
2 wholemeal pitta breads
salt and freshly ground black pepper

CHAYOTE SALAD WITH GREEN BEANS AND TOMATOES

I ate on the street often when I lived in Mexico City, and this was the type of dish I'd cook at home when my body couldn't take any more meat or tlacoyos. Simple blanched green beans mixed with fresh tomatoes, cooked chayote and crumbled queso fresco. It's easy and crunchy and light. Even my husband, who hates to cook, has made this salad a few times. If you can't find queso fresco, a salty, aged cheese, such as ricotta salata or feta would work too.

225g green beans, chopped into 5cm pieces

2 chayotes, diced into 1cm pieces

3 tablespoons cider vinegar

½ teaspoon Dijon mustard

¼ teaspoon agave syrup or honey

60ml olive oil

1 ripe tomato, chopped

35g fresh coriander, chopped

80g queso fresco, crumbled

salt

1   Bring a medium saucepan of water to the boil. Nearby, fill a large bowl with water and ice cubes. When you've got a vigorous boil, add the green beans and a hefty dose of salt. Cook for 3–5 minutes until crisp-tender and bright green. Using a slotted spoon, transfer to the iced water. Leave to cool for about 5 minutes to stop the cooking, then drain and dry.

2   Meanwhile, place the chayote into a microwave-safe bowl and mix generously with salt. Cover with clingfilm that's been perforated a few times with a fork. Cook on high for 2–3 minutes until crisp-tender. Alternatively, blanch the chayote in the same boiling water that you cooked the green beans in for 2–3 minutes until crisp tender, then transfer to the ice bath to stop the cooking, drain and dry.

3   Whisk together the vinegar, mustard and honey in a large bowl. Keep whisking as you add the oil in one slow stream until fully integrated. Add the cooled chayote and green beans, and toss to coat well. Add the tomato, coriander and cheese. Mix until combined and taste for more salt. Serve cold or at room temperature.

COOKING TIP: *Chayote, known as a 'vegetable pear' in English, has a thin skin and mild flavour, and you should be able to find it at Mexican, Caribbean or Asian grocery stores or at select mainstream supermarkets. The skin is so delicate that it's not worth peeling, in my opinion. Some cooks also love to eat the soft inner stone.*

HUAUZONTLE CHICKEN SOUP

Many times I've bought huauzontle at the markets because the green, fluffy stalks look so pretty. Then I've returned home and wondered: what else can I do with this? I like eating this soup, made with just huauzontle, chicken and rice, when I'm sick or craving something light for dinner. The nubby, fluffy huauzontle buds provide a fun contrast to the rice, and the taste is vegetal without being too overwhelming. The overall effect is healthy and soothing, and the soup freezes well too. I usually serve this with corn tortillas I've crisped in the oven.

1   Clean the huauzontle (see panel for detailed instructions).

2   Fill a medium saucepan two-thirds full with water, add a hefty pinch of salt and bring to the boil. Add the huauzontle and cook for 2–3 minutes or until just tender. Strain, discarding the cooking water.

3   Meanwhile, bring the stock to the boil in a medium saucepan over a medium heat. Add the rice, reduce the heat and simmer for about 12 minutes until barely al dente.

4   Add the huauzontle and chicken to the stock and season with salt and pepper. Cook, covered, over a low heat for about 5 minutes until the rice is tender and the flavours have melded. Taste and adjust the seasonings.

5   Crisp the tortillas in an oven, sprinkling on a little salt to taste. Ladle soup into bowls and serve immediately.

1 large bunch huauzuontle (Aztec spinach) (about 275g)
1.9 litres Basic Homemade Chicken Stock (page 98)
95g long-grain white rice
125g cooked, shredded chicken
6 corn tortillas
salt and freshly ground black pepper

HOW TO CLEAN HUAUZONTLES

First pluck the smaller stems from the thick centre stalk of each bunch. Then take one of the small stems and, with the tips of your fingers, gently scrape off the flower buds into a bowl. (Don't do this on your nicest tablecloth, as the buds sometimes go flying everywhere.) Discard any thicker stems, which can taste bitter. Repeat until all stalks are bare. Don't be afraid of the peppery and vaguely medicinal aroma when raw; it mellows out once cooked.

STUFFED CACTUS PADDLES

These cactus paddles are loaded like potato skins, but topped with healthier ingredients: sautéed veggies, roasted peppers, a spreading of refried black beans and a sprinkle of grated cheese. They're grilled in the oven until golden and bubbly. Depending on the size of the cactus paddles, one piece alone can make a decent meal with a side dish. Salsa also kicks things up a notch (Raw Tomatillo Salsa, page 26, goes particularly well), but it's not required.

1 batch Quick Refried Beans
   (page 45)
1 yellow pepper
6 medium cactus paddles,
   cleaned and spines removed
   (see page 146)
2 teaspoons olive oil, plus extra
   for coating cactus
2 tablespoons chopped onion
1 garlic clove, very finely
   chopped
1 courgette or Mexican squash,
   cut into thin half-moons
90g Monterey Jack cheese,
   grated
salsa of choice
salt and freshly ground black
   pepper

1   Make the refried beans, cover the pan and continue.

2   Roast the yellow pepper over a gas flame, turning occasionally, until soft and blackened in spots. Wrap in a tea towel and leave to stand for 20 minutes, then peel off the skin, remove the seeds and cut into thin strips.

3   Cut halfway into the centre of each cactus paddle, making three vertical or diagonal incisions about 5cm long. (This is for the slime to ooze out later.) Coat in olive oil and season with salt and pepper.

4   Heat a heavy-based frying pan over a medium-high heat. Working in batches, add the whole cactus paddles and cook, flipping a few times, for 5–8 minutes per batch until dark golden brown in spots on both sides.

5   Meanwhile, heat 2 teaspoons olive oil in a medium frying pan over a medium heat. Add the onion and cook for about 3 minutes until translucent. Stir in the garlic and cook for 30 seconds until aromatic. Then add the courgette or squash and a light sprinkle of salt, stirring to coat. Cook, uncovered, for about 4 minutes until just tender. Stir in the yellow pepper and warm through. Taste and adjust the seasonings. This filling can be prepared up to 2 hours in advance if necessary.

6   When ready to serve, warm the refried beans and filling and set the oven to grill.

7   Place the paddles on a baking tray. Spread with a thick layer of refried beans and top with a small mound of the filling. Finish with an even layer of grated cheese. Grill for about 3 minutes until the cheese is golden brown and bubbly.

8   Serve immediately, passing round the salsa at the table.

COOKING TIP: *You can find cactus at Mexican grocery stores. Choose firm, green paddles that don't have any brown spots.*

CACTUS FAJITAS WITH CECINA, SPINACH AND MUSHROOMS

A few years ago, while at a Tijuana restaurant with my mom, a waiter brought us a sizzling skillet of cactus, mushrooms, salty cecina steak and rectangles of grilled panela cheese. I'd never seen anything like it in Mexico City, and I couldn't wait to try it at home. Back in New York, I added tomatoes, spinach and avocado, and swapped out the panela for Dominican queso de freir, a mild, not-too-salty cheese that doesn't melt when fried (and is much easier for me to find in my neighbourhood). The tumble of vegetables and smoky meat feels sort of Tex-Mex, which is why I call them fajitas.

1   Heat a large cast-iron frying pan over a medium-high heat. Working in batches, add the steak in a single layer and cook for about 2 minutes per side until dark golden brown and the meat starts to release clear juices. Transfer to a plate and leave to cool. Slice into 1cm by 5cm strips.

2   Cut the cactus paddles into 1cm by 5cm strips. Place in a medium bowl and season with salt and pepper. Toss with about 1 tablespoon of the olive oil to coat.

3   Heat a large frying pan over a medium-high heat. Working in batches, add the cactus in a single layer and cook, undisturbed, for about 2 minutes until it begins to brown. Then cook, uncovered, stirring occasionally, for about 6 minutes until golden brown on both sides and tender. Transfer to a bowl and set aside.

4   In the same pan, heat the remaining 1 tablespoon olive oil over a high heat. Add the mushrooms and cook for about 5 minutes until tender and browned. Toss in the spinach, tomatoes and salt to taste. Turn up the heat if necessary to evaporate some of the juices.

5   Meanwhile, heat the rapeseed oil in a medium non-stick frying pan over a medium heat. Add the cheese slices in an even layer. Cook, turning once, for 4–6 minutes until a dark golden crust develops on both sides. Transfer to a plate.

6   Add the cactus and steak to the vegetables, and stir to combine. Taste for more salt and cook until warmed through. Transfer to a platter, draining off some of the juice if necessary. Top with the fried cheese and coriander.

7   Heat the tortillas on a *comal* or non-stick frying pan until soft and pliable. Place in a tea towel or basket to keep warm. Serve the platter at the table, passing round the tortillas, avocado slices, lime wedges and salsa for guests to make their own tacos.

450g *cecina* steak (see page 80), cut into large pieces
450g cactus paddles, spines removed and rinsed (see page 146)
2 tablespoons olive oil
225g chestnut mushrooms, sliced 5mm thick
1 large bunch of spinach, washed and spun dry
1 large tomato, cut into chunks
1 tablespoon rapeseed oil
225g panela cheese or Dominican queso de freir, cut into rectangles
15g fresh coriander, roughly chopped
20 corn tortillas
1–2 ripe Haas avocados, peeled, stoned and sliced
5 limes, cut into wedges
salsa of choice
salt and freshly ground black pepper

COOKING TIP: *You may find panela cheese in Mexican grocery stores. Queso de freir is generally sold in square blocks at Caribbean grocery stores (I like the Tropical brand). If you can't find either of these, you could use Halloumi instead.*

CURRIED CAULIFLOWER TACOS WITH ROASTED TOMATILLO CHUTNEY

One thing I learnt in Mexico is that you can taco anything. (There's actually a verb for it, taquear.) Taco-ing not only stretches the meal – tortillas require smaller portions – but foods just seem more complete when wrapped in a tortilla, even if you're only serving one ingredient.

I visited India while I was living in Mexico, and when I got back, I made tacos from all sorts of curries. (One of my friends teased me about opening an 'Indo-Mex' food van someday.) This one, made with roasted, browned cauliflower, makes a lot of sense in New York, where the variety of fresh vegetables drops severely in the winter. The chutney-salsa hybrid mixes tomatillos with grated coconut – creamy, sweet and acidic – and is mandatory with this dish.

1 teaspoon black mustard seeds
2½ teaspoons spicy curry powder
1¼ teaspoons salt
120ml olive oil
1 large cauliflower or two small, chopped into florets
2 medium onions, quartered
12 corn tortillas

For the chutney:
5 small tomatillos, husked and rinsed
1 serrano chilli
3 tablespoons grated fresh coconut, or 4 tablespoons unsweetened dried coconut flakes
1 teaspoon rapeseed oil
½ teaspoon black mustard seeds
1 teaspoon *urad dal* or raw unsalted peanuts
4 fresh curry leaves
salt

1 Preheat the oven to 230°C/gas mark 8. In a large bowl, mix the mustard seeds, curry powder and salt until well combined. Add the olive oil in a slow pour, whisking everything together. Taste and adjust the salt.

2 Add the cauliflower and onion, breaking apart the onion pieces with your fingers and mixing everything together thoroughly with your hands, until the vegetables are evenly coated. Transfer to a baking tray and roast for 30–40 minutes until dark golden brown and crispy in spots.

3 Meanwhile, prepare the chutney. Roast the tomatillos and chilli on a *comal* or non-stick frying pan until blackened in spots. Transfer to a bowl to cool, then chop into smaller pieces. Place in a blender with the coconut and blend until smooth, adding a little water if necessary to help the blades turn. Transfer to a small bowl.

4 Heat the rapeseed oil in a small frying pan over a medium-high heat. Add the mustard seeds and *urad dal*. When the seeds begin popping, immediately remove from the heat and add the curry leaves. Add to the chutney and mix well. Season with salt.

5 Warm the tortillas on a *comal* or non-stick frying pan and place in a tea towel or basket to keep warm. Transfer the curried cauliflower to a serving bowl, and pass round the tortillas and chutney at the table so that each guest can make their own tacos.

COOKING TIP: *You can find black mustard seeds, fresh curry leaves and* urad dal *– a type of nutty lentil – at Indian grocery stores, or you can substitute peanuts for the urad dal. Don't leave out the fresh curry leaves if you can help it, and use the smallest tomatillos you can find – they'll blacken more easily on the* comal.

FISH TACOS WITH CREAMY PASILLA OAXACA SAUCE

I can never decide which type of fish tacos I like better: battered and fried, for the crunch and texture, or pan-fried because they're healthier and only need a few minutes to make. So I'm giving you both versions here, both topped with a pile of fresh cabbage and a creamy, hot salsa. The latter is my favourite part of the dish, made from the smoky Oaxacan pasilla chilli, not the pasilla generally sold in Mexican markets. You want the one that is berry-coloured, wrinkly and extremely hot, found online – and you'll want to stockpile them because they're that good.

1   To make the battered fish, in a medium bowl, whisk together the flour and 1 teaspoon salt. Pour in the beer, whisking until a thick batter forms; it will be lumpy. Set aside in the fridge.

2   Heat the oil in a deep saucepan to 180°C. Place about 4 tablespoons flour on a plate, and season the fish on both sides with salt and pepper.

3   When the oil is ready, dredge the fish pieces lightly in flour and shake off any excess. Dunk the fish pieces in the beer batter one at a time and place in the hot oil. Fry for about 3 minutes per side until golden. Drain on kitchen paper.

4   To make the pan-fried fish, rinse and pat the fish dry. Season with salt and pepper. Pour the oil into a non-stick frying pan and heat to medium. Add the fish and cook for 3 minutes per side until the flesh is juicy and flaky, and the fish is golden brown.

5   To serve, warm the corn tortillas on a *comal* or non-stick frying pan. Place one piece of battered fish, or a generous helping of pan-fried fish, in a tortilla and drizzle with lime juice. Top with chilli pasilla cream sauce and thinly sliced cabbage. Serve immediately, passing round additional sauce at the table.

COOKING TIP: *I've made these tacos with trout, hake and pollock, and all have worked well. If you can't find Oaxacan pasilla chilli, substitute chilli morita. Also, if you don't like very spicy salsas, double the amount of yogurt and mayo.*

For battered and fried fish tacos:
125g flour, plus extra for dredging
300ml light beer, preferably Modelo Especial
rapeseed oil
450g fish fillets, cut into 5–7.5cm fingers

For pan-fried fish tacos:
450g fish fillets, sliced into 4 pieces
1 tablespoon olive oil

12 corn tortillas
3 limes, sliced into wedges
Chilli Pasilla Cream Sauce (see below)
150g cabbage, thinly sliced
salt and freshly ground black pepper

CHILLI PASILLA CREAM SAUCE

1   Make an incision in the chilli and scrape out the seeds and veins with a small spoon or butter knife. (Don't use your fingers, as the chilli is very hot.) Cover the chilli in hot water and leave to soak for about 20 minutes until the skin has softened.

2   Add the chilli, garlic, yogurt and mayonnaise to a blender with 1–2 tablespoons water. (Using chilli water in this instance would make the sauce extremely spicy – if you do it, proceed with caution.) Blend until as smooth as possible. Taste for salt and add if necessary. Refrigerate until ready to use.

1 Oaxaca chilli pasilla
1 garlic clove, very finely chopped
2 tablespoons natural yogurt (not Greek)
1 tablespoon mayonnaise
salt

PASTA WITH ANCHO CHILLIES, MUSHROOMS AND GARLIC

This recipe is a twist on champiñones al ajillo, *the Spanish dish of garlicky, slightly spicy mushrooms. The anchos here almost act as a vegetable, lending a hint of sweetness and creaminess. A lot of garlic is necessary: it infuses the olive oil at the start of the dish, which then coats the mushrooms and the chillies. I like topping this with a slightly aged cheese (Parmesan or Mexican queso añejo) and chopped, lightly briny black olives, which brings out the bitter notes in the chillies. If you don't eat gluten, this also works excellently as a taco filling without the pasta.*

3 large ancho chillies

11 garlic cloves

225g dried fettuccine noodles

60ml olive oil, plus extra
    if needed

380g oyster mushrooms, torn
    into very thin strips

65g lightly brined pitted black
    olives, chopped, to garnish

60g queso añejo or Parmesan
    cheese, grated, to garnish

salt

1   Snip the stems off the anchos and cut an incision in each. Scrape out the seeds and veins with a spoon or knife. Place the chillies in a bowl and cover with warm water. Leave to soak for about 20 minutes until the flesh has softened.

2   Meanwhile, peel the garlic cloves and slice thinly.

3   Bring a saucepan of water to the boil. Add the pasta and cook for 10–12 minutes until al dente. Drain and set aside, reserving 120ml of the pasta water.

4   Cut the softened chillies into 1cm strips – I do this by rolling them up like a burrito first, and then chopping widthways.

5   Heat the oil in a heavy-based frying pan over a medium-high heat. Add the garlic and cook for about 2 minutes until slightly browned. Add the chillies and stir quickly, ensuring that the garlic doesn't burn. Reduce the heat if you need to.

6   Once the chillies have become aromatic, stir in the mushrooms and cook for 5–10 minutes until softened, adding salt once the mushrooms have released their juices.

7   Add the pasta to your mushroom mixture, with a little of the reserved pasta water and extra oil to make it more saucy if you like. Serve immediately in shallow bowls, topped with the chopped olives and a dusting of cheese.

COOKING TIPS: *I chose oyster mushrooms because they're abundant in Mexico and because I like their chewy texture. If you can't find them, substitute shiitake or chestnut. Also, if you can find ready-peeled garlic cloves, use them – peeling is the step that takes the most time.*

    Look for soft, pliable dried chillies. Brittle chillies won't rehydrate well and the flesh won't break down while cooking. You can also soften them on a comal beforehand in order to remove the seeds.

SOPA WITH SPINACH AND CHEESE

We ate my mom's sopa at least once a month growing up, which was sort of like Fideo Noodles in Chipotle-Tomato Sauce (page 102), except less complicated. It calls for canned tomato sauce (see Tip), a little onion and salt. I dress mine up to my own tastes by adding sautéed spinach or chard, and some crumbled cheese. The pasta is still fried in oil beforehand, and because they're shells, little bits of sauce cling to their insides. In Mexico, sopa seca is a side dish. In my house, we've always eaten it as a main meal.

2 teaspoons rapeseed oil, plus more for cooking greens

4 thin slices of onion

200g dried small pasta shells

227g can American-style tomato sauce, such as Hunt's

180–240g spinach leaves, rinsed and dried

1 hunk queso fresco, or any other mild white cheese, crumbled

salt

1 Heat the oil in a medium saucepan over a medium-high heat. When hot, add the onion and pasta shells and cook, stirring constantly, for 5–8 minutes until the pasta is toasty, and the edges turn a deep golden brown. (It's okay if the onion burns a little.)

2 Add the tomato sauce and 720ml water in one quick pour. (The pot may hiss and splatter.) Season with salt, cover and reduce the heat. Simmer gently for about 12 minutes until the pasta shells are al dente and have soaked up the sauce. If you're unsure, take off the lid and peek in on it once in a while. It won't hurt the dish.

3 Heat a small amount of oil in a large frying pan over a medium heat. Add the spinach and sauté until wilted but still a deep green colour. Season with salt. Scrape the spinach into four separate bowls, and top with a few scoops of *sopa* and cheese. Serve warm.

COOKING TIP: *American-style canned tomato sauce is not spaghetti sauce. It's just puréed tomato and salt, generally sold in small cans, and is available from online. Small pasta shells are widely available, but you can use any other pasta or noodle you like.*

AMARANTH AND PUMPKIN SEED-CRUSTED CHICKEN WITH CREAMY POMEGRANATE DIPPING SAUCE

Some days I don't crave any acidity or heat at all. (Can you believe it, after reading this book?) On those days, I eat something simple like roast chicken and vegetables, or these baked chicken escalopes, coated in a crunchy, mild mix of puffed amaranth, pumpkin seeds and panko breadcrumbs. They're like a more elegant chicken finger, served with a fun (purple-coloured!), slightly sweet, slightly smoky dipping sauce. This dish is easy to throw together, and if you know you'll be pressed for time, you could mix the dry ingredients a day or two beforehand. Salad or roasted or steamed vegetables work just fine as a side.

1 First make the creamy pomegranate sauce. Pour the pomegranate juice into a small saucepan over a medium-high heat and reduce for 15 minutes; you should end up with about 60ml syrup. Transfer to a bowl and leave to cool. Stir in the rest of the sauce ingredients and set aside.

2 Preheat the oven to 180°C/gas mark 4. In a medium bowl, mix together the panko breadcrumbs, puffed amaranth, pumpkin seeds, ¾ teaspoon salt, ¼ teaspoon pepper, thyme and oregano.

3 Season the chicken escalopes with salt.

4 Pour the flour onto a plate, and place the beaten egg and the amaranth mixture nearby in two shallow bowls. Grease a baking tray lightly with olive oil.

5 Dredge one chicken escalope in the flour, shaking off any excess. Dip in the egg, then press into the amaranth and pumpkin seed mixture, covering the escalope evenly.

6 Place the escalope on the baking tray and repeat with the remaining escalopes. Bake for 20 minutes or until the chicken is juicy and no longer pink. For a crispier crust, finish under the grill for 2 minutes.

7 Serve with the room-temperature creamy pomegranate sauce.

COOKING TIP: *You can find amaranth – a native Mexican grain – at health food stores or online. If you can't find puffed amaranth (amaranth popcorn), you can make your own from dried amaranth (see page 163).*

For the creamy pomegranate sauce:
240ml unsweetened pomegranate juice, such as POM brand
4 tablespoons soured cream
⅛ scant teaspoon smoked paprika (not sweet)
freshly ground black pepper

30g panko breadcrumbs
45g puffed amaranth (amaranth popcorn – see Tip)
65g pumpkin seeds
1½ teaspoons fresh thyme
1 teaspoon dried Mexican oregano
700g chicken breast escalopes (or pound chicken breast fillets between 2 sheets of clingfilm to flatten and thin)
40g all-purpose flour
2 medium eggs, lightly beaten
olive oil
salt and freshly ground black pepper

CABBAGE ENCHILADAS

I remember the day when my husband came home from work and asked, 'What's for dinner?' I said, 'Cabbage enchiladas!' And he grimaced. Yet after a few bites, he was a convert. Cooked cabbage, naturally sweet, pairs well with spicy enchilada sauce, and the dish is spunkier than the usual cabbage offerings of coleslaw, salads and salt beef. These are inspired by enchiladas queretanas, *a dark red enchilada native to the state of Querétaro. They're traditionally served topped with fried potatoes, lightly pickled jalapeños and carrots.*

1   Fill a medium saucepan two-thirds full with water and bring to the boil. Add the potatoes and cook for about 20 minutes until just tender when pricked with a fork. Drain and set aside to cool, then cut into small dice.

2   Meanwhile, heat a *comal* or non-stick frying pan to medium-low heat. Toast the chillies lightly, turning frequently, for about 20 seconds until they release a spicy aroma. Place the garlic cloves near the edge of the pan and roast for 5–10 minutes until soft and squishy. Transfer the chillies to a clean work surface, snip off the stems and remove the seeds. Place the chillies in a bowl of warm water and leave to soak for about 20 minutes until the skins soften. Peel the garlic and set aside.

3   While the chillies soak, warm 2 teaspoons oil in a large frying pan over a medium heat. Add the onion and cook for about 3 minutes until translucent. Add the finely chopped garlic and cook for about 30 seconds until aromatic. Add the cabbage and 120ml water and bring to the boil. Season with salt, reduce the heat to low and simmer, covered, for about 10 minutes until the cabbage is soft and tender. Taste and adjust salt. Keep warm, covered.

4   In a medium frying pan, heat 1 tablespoon oil to medium heat and add the potatoes. Season with salt and cook, undisturbed, for about 4 minutes or until a golden-brown crust forms on the underside. Flip and cook the other side, seasoning lightly with salt. Once both sides are crisp, reduce the heat, cover and cook for 12–15 minutes until the potatoes are crunchy on the outside but soft in the middle. Keep warm.

5   Place the chillies, garlic and 360ml water in a blender and blend until smooth but fairly thick, not thin and soupy. Heat 1 teaspoon lard (or oil) in a medium saucepan. When hot, add the sauce in one quick pour, stirring. (Careful, it may splatter.) Season with ¾ teaspoon salt and cook for about 5 minutes until the flavours meld. Keep warm.

6   In a small frying pan, heat 2 teaspoons oil over a medium heat. Add one tortilla and cook, flipping once, for 20–25 seconds until slightly tougher but not crisp. Using tongs, quickly dip in the warm enchilada sauce, ensuring that the sauce coats both sides. Transfer to a plate and add a generous amount of cabbage. Roll into a tube, then repeat with another tortilla. Top the enchiladas with fried potatoes, pickled jalapeño, queso fresco and chopped coriander. Serve immediately, and then repeat with the remaining enchiladas.

2 large, waxy potatoes
5 guajillo chillies
4 ancho chillies
2 garlic cloves, unpeeled, plus
   1 clove, very finely chopped
4 teaspoons plus 1 tablespoon
   rapeseed oil, plus more for
   frying
1 small onion, chopped
1 small cabbage, sliced into very
   thin shreds
1 teaspoon lard or oil
8 corn tortillas
1 small can pickled jalapeño
   strips
120g queso fresco, crumbled
25–40g fresh coriander,
   chopped
salt

COOKING TIP: *Enchiladas should be served immediately, which means that the cook is often stuck in the kitchen while everyone else is eating. For that reason, it's helpful to have a friend (or significant other) in the kitchen helping stuff and assemble, if possible.*

TOMATO MILPA PIE

I hadn't heard of tomato pie until I married my husband, whose family is from South Carolina. It's a typical Southern dish of fresh tomatoes sliced and layered in a cooked pastry case. The tomatoes are blanketed with cheese and mayonnaise, then baked. To help round the dish out, I like throwing in squash and sweetcorn, two items traditionally found in the Mexican farming plot known as a milpa, an ancient multi-crop farming system, in which three items – beans, squash and corn – are farmed together to work synergistically. I don't use beans in this recipe, but a sprinkle of cooked black or pinto beans might be fun, now that I think about it.

For the pastry:
155g plain flour
½ teaspoon salt
½ teaspoon sugar
115g cold unsalted butter

For the filling:
900g fresh, ripe tomatoes
2 tablespoons olive oil
½ medium onion, chopped
1 garlic clove, minced
1 small Mexican squash or
    courgette, cut into thin
    half-moons
175g fresh sweetcorn kernels
80g mayonnaise
115g Monterey Jack cheese, or
    a mix of Monterey Jack and
    Gruyère, grated
15g fresh coriander, chopped
salt

COOKING TIPS: *This recipe traditionally calls for much more mayonnaise, but I've cut back to save a few calories. This means that the topping is more mottled than smooth. It's still delicious.*

Any cheese would work here – mozzarella, Gruyère or Emmental. Or mix them up.

1   Fill a small bowl with 120ml water and add a few ice cubes.

2   In a medium bowl, whisk together the flour, salt and sugar. Using a pastry blender, or two knives, cut in the butter until it breaks into uneven, more-or-less pea-shaped pieces. Add 1 tablespoon iced water at a time to the mixture until the dough just comes together when squeezed. Shape the dough into a ball and wrap in clingfilm. Flatten into a disc and refrigerate for at least 1 hour. (You can freeze the dough for less time if you're in a hurry, but if you overfreeze, the dough will be impossible to roll out.)

3   Place the dough on a well-floured work surface. With a floured rolling pin, roll the dough into a 28cm circle, gently peeling the dough off the work surface and rotating in a circle as needed. Transfer the dough to a 23cm pie plate or dish and trim any excess. Pinch or crimp the ends. If the pastry case has softened too much and feels greasy, chill in the fridge for about 30 minutes. Meanwhile, preheat the oven to 200°C/gas mark 6.

4   Cover the pastry case with a layer of foil (this will prevent it from browning too soon in the oven), and weigh it down with a layer of dried beans. Bake for 20 minutes, then remove the foil and bake for a further 5–10 minutes until the pastry is golden brown. Leave to cool while you make the filling. Reduce the oven to 180°C/gas mark 4.

5   Cut the tomatoes into 5mm slices and sprinkle with salt (you can blanch and peel them first if you're picky about skins). Place in a colander and leave to sit for at least 20 minutes to help the tomatoes release their juices, which will make the pie less soggy.

6   Heat the oil in a medium frying pan over a medium heat. Add the onion and cook for 4–5 minutes until translucent. Add the garlic and cook for about 30 seconds until aromatic. Stir in the squash and sweetcorn and cook for 6–7 minutes until the squash is just tender. Season with salt and set aside.

7   Pat the tomatoes dry with kitchen paper. Mix together the mayonnaise and cheese in a small bowl. Place half the tomatoes in an even layer in the pastry case. Top with half the squash mixture and a sprinkle of coriander. Repeat layers with the remaining tomatoes and squash, then slather the mayonnaise-cheese mixture evenly over the top.

8   Bake for about 25 minutes or until lightly browned. Leave the pie to cool slightly, then serve warm. The pie is best the day it's made – it will become soggy in the fridge.

DARK CHOCOLATE CHICHARRÓN COOKIES

I love anything sweet and savoury, so this snack makes perfect sense to me: chicharrón *– fluffy, salty, fried pork skin – is mixed with dark chocolate in a buttery, dense cookie. It's not too far removed from chocolate and bacon (another fabulous combination), but with a heartier crunch. My sense is that most* chilangos *would be weirded out by this pairing, because in Mexico City,* chicharrón *is always used in a savoury context.*

You may find chicharrón *at some Mexican grocery stores, and they may offer a couple varieties: thinner, lighter sheets, and thicker sheets curled at the edges, speckled with bits of meat. For the purposes of this cookie, it's best to use the lighter, meatless variety. (The meatier stuff is great with salsa, though.) If you can't find it,* chicharrón *in packets works, which is available online from specialist Mexican food suppliers.*

1   Whisk together the flour, bicarbonate of soda and salt in a medium bowl. Set aside.

2   In the bowl of a stand mixer fitted with the paddle attachment, beat together the eggs and both sugars for about 3 minutes until light and fluffy and doubled in volume. Reduce the speed and mix in the butter and vanilla until well combined.

3   Using a wooden spoon or rubber spatula, stir the dry mixture into the wet until just combined. Gently stir in the chocolate and *chicharrón*, being careful not to over-mix.

4   Cover the dough with clingfilm and refrigerate until firm – at least 2 hours, or ideally overnight.

5   When ready to bake, preheat the oven to 180°C/gas mark 4. Drop the cookies by mounded tablespoonfuls onto an ungreased baking tray, spacing them 5cm apart. Bake for 10–12 minutes or until the edges just start to brown and the middles are still soft.

6   Leave the cookies to cool on the baking tray for 1 minute, then remove to a wire rack to cool completely.

COOKING TIPS: *To crumble the* chicharrón, *if it's very hard, place it in a plastic bag and whack it with a meat mallet or the base of a heavy frying pan.*

The cookies taste best if you chill the dough overnight in the fridge – resting time allows the dough to develop more flavour. They'll keep for 4 days in an airtight container.

275g plain flour
1 teaspoon bicarbonate of soda
1 teaspoon salt
2 medium eggs
150g caster sugar
165g light soft brown sugar
225g unsalted butter, melted and cooled to room temperature
1 teaspoon vanilla extract
200g dark chocolate (at least 70% cocoa solids), chopped into 5mm chunks
115g *chicharrón* (Mexican pork crackling or scratchings), crumbled

INDEX

A

achiote 11, 121–3
adobo, roasted chicken in 82–3
amaranth (puffed)
    amaranth and pumpkin seed-crusted chicken with
        creamy pomegranate dipping sauce 181
    mamey milkshake 62
    nutty homemade muesli 163
amaranth greens, 'sweated' Mexican greens 79
ancho chilli 11
    ancho chillies stuffed with beans and cheese
        118–19
    cabbage enchiladas 183
    pasta with ancho chillies, mushrooms and garlic
        178–9
árbol chilli 10, 11
    árbol chilli and peanut salsa 29, 46–7
    red taco-stand style salsa 27
    sour cactus fruit salsa 134–5
    toasted árbol chilli salsa 133
avocado
    cactus fajita, *cecina*, spinach and mushroom 174–5
    chicken in chipotle-tomato sauce 32–3
    creamy kale salad 167
    fideo noodles in chipotle-tomato sauce 102–3
    prawn and octopus cocktail 66–7
    prawn quesadillas with avocado 40–1
    raw tomatillo salsa 26
    stewed Swiss chard 111
    turkey tortas with chipotle salsa 48
avocado leaf, slow-roasted mutton 154
ayocote (runner) beans with cactus 146

B

bacon, porridge, poblano chilli and cheese 162
banana leaf, slow-cooked citrusy pork 121–3
bean(s) 11
    ancho chillies stuffed with beans and cheese
        118–19
    basic cooked beans 107
        recipes using 106, 110, 113, 118–20
    bean and cheese *tlacoyos* 42–3
    bean filling for steamed tacos 46–7
    beans and eggs 106
    quick refried beans 45
        recipes using 44, 74–5, 104, 118–19, 138–9,
        172–3
    spicy chipotle bean dip 161
    see also broad bean; green bean
beef
    cactus fajita, *cecina*, spinach and mushroom 174–5
    meatballs in chipotle sauce 113
    mole from the pot 108–9
    steak in chilli pasilla sauce 112
    steak and chorizo tacos 80
    steak flautas 72
beer
    beer-braised rabbit 153
    'drunk' salsa 155
    fish tacos with creamy pasilla oaxaca sauce 177
    sweetened fermented pineapple juice 63
beetroot
    creamy beetroot soup 100–1

roasted chicken in adobo 82–3
biscuits, sweet cream 53
black beans
    basic cooked beans 107
    bean filling for steamed tacos 46–7
    quick refried beans 45
    spicy chipotle bean dip 161
blenders 15
blue corn
    blue corn *sopes* 138–9
    blue corn tortilla masa 139
broad bean
    fresh broad bean salad 68–9
    pickled cactus and vegetables 147
burritos, squash flower 44

C

cabbage
    cabbage enchiladas 183
    fish tacos with creamy pasilla oaxaca sauce 177
    steak flautas 72
cactus fruit, sour cactus fruit salsa 134–5
cactus paddles
    cactus fajita, *cecina*, spinach and mushroom 174–5
    cactus salad 76–7
    chicken, chilli and vegetable parcels 150–1
    cleaning 76
    grilled fish tamales 142–3
    pickled cactus strips 42–3
    pickled cactus and vegetables 147
    runner bean with cactus 146
    stuffed cactus paddles 172
calcium hydroxide (*cal*) 23, 25
carnitas 38–9
carrot
    crispy carrot tacos 114–15
    Mexican-style red rice 97
    pickled cactus and vegetables 147
cauliflower
    chorizo, chilli and vegetable parcels 150–1
    curried cauliflower tacos with tomatillo chutney 176
cecina steak
    cactus fajita, *cecina*, spinach and mushroom 174–5
    steak and chorizo tacos 80
chard
    chorizo, chilli and vegetable parcels 150–1
    stewed Swiss chard 111
chayote
    chayote salad, green bean and tomato 168–9
    mole from the pot 108–9
cheese
    ancho chillies stuffed with beans and cheese
        118–19
    bean and cheese *tlacoyos* 42–3
    cheesy enchilada parcels 116–17
    porridge, poblano chillies and cheese 162
    sopa with spinach and cheese 180
    see also specific cheeses
chia seed
    nutty homemade muesli 163
    prickly pear *agua fresca*, lime and chia 160
chicharrón (pork crackling or scratchings)
    dark chocolate *chicharrón* cookies 186–7
    fideo noodles in chipotle-tomato sauce 102–3
    homemade *chicharrón* 136–7
    white *pozole* 65
chicken

amaranth and pumpkin seed-crusted chicken with
    creamy pomegranate dipping sauce 181
basic homemade chicken stock 98
    recipes using 33, 97, 99, 101, 111–13, 121,
    144–5, 171
chicken stock 11, 98
chicken, chilli and vegetable parcels 150–1
chicken in chipotle-tomato sauce 32–3
green chicken enchiladas 50–1
green *mole* with chicken 124–5
huauzontle chicken soup 170–1
roasted chicken in adobo 82–3
squash flower and vegetable soup 140–1
chicken feet, basic homemade chicken stock 98
chickpeas, stewed Swiss chard 111
Chihuahua cheese
    corn smut quesadillas 31
    squash flower burritos 44
chilli
    water 71
    see also specific chillies
chipotle chilli, dried 11
chipotle chilli in adobo sauce (canned) 11
    chipotle sauce 113
    fideo noodles in chipotle-tomato sauce 102–3
    spicy chipotle bean dip 161
    tinga sauce 32–3
    turkey tortas with chipotle salsa 48
chipotle meco chilli, spicy chipotle bean dip 161
chocolate
    dark chocolate *chicharrón* cookies 186–7
    thickened Mexican hot chocolate 54–5
chorizo
    fried chorizo and potato sandwiches 70–1
    homemade green chorizo 148–9
    steak and chorizo tacos 80
chutney, roasted tomatillo 176
cinnamon-spiked coffee 60–1
clotted cream
    clotted cream substitute 53
    sweet cream biscuits 53
coconut, roasted tomatillo chutney 176
coffee, sweet cinnamon-spiked 60–1
comals 15
comida corrida menus 93, 94, 101
cookies, dark chocolate *chicharrón* 186–7
coriander 11
    ancho chillies stuffed with beans and cheese
        118–19
    cabbage enchiladas 183
    cactus fajita, *cecina*, spinach and mushroom 174–5
    fresh broad bean salad 68–9
    fresh tomato salsa 81
    green *mole* with chicken 124–5
    purslane in tomatillo sauce 110
    slow-roasted mutton 154
    tomato *milpa* pie 184–5
corn husks 12
    grilled fish tamales 142–3
    mushroom and green salsa tamales 144–5
    roasted poblano chilli tamales 36–7
    sweetcorn tamales 87
corn kernels
    corn smut quesadillas 31
    squash flower and vegetable soup 140–1
    tomato *milpa* pie 184–5
corn tortillas 159

ancho chillies stuffed with beans and cheese 118–19
baked tortilla chips 161
battered stuffed tortillas 84–5
bean filling for steamed tacos 46–7
beans and eggs 106
cabbage enchiladas 183
cactus fajita, *cecina*, spinach and mushroom 174–5
chicken, chilli and vegetable parcels 150–1
corn smut quesadillas 31
crispy carrot tacos 114–15
crispy courgette quesadillas 166
curried cauliflower tacos with roasted tomatillo chutney 176
fish tacos with creamy pasilla oaxaca sauce 177
fried huauzontle patties 120
green chicken enchiladas 50–1
green *mole* with chicken 124–5
homemade corn tortillas 22–4
homemade green chorizo 148–9
huauzontle chicken soup 170–1
marinated, spit-roasted tacos 49
meatballs in chipotle sauce 113
Mexican-style eggs 86
mole from the pot 108–9
Montuleño-style egg 104
mushroom quesadillas 30
prawn quesadillas with avocado 40–1
purslane in tomatillo sauce 110
roasted poblano chillies with Mexican *crema* 78
runner bean with cactus 146
slow-cooked citrusy pork 121–3
slow-roasted mutton 154
squash flower and vegetable soup 140–1
steak in chilli pasilla sauce 112
steak and chorizo tacos 80
steak flautas 72
stewed Swiss chard 111
'sweated' Mexican greens 79
costeño chilli, *mole* from the pot 108–9
courgette
    battered stuffed tortillas 84–5
    chicken, chilli and vegetable parcels 150–1
    crispy courgette quesadillas 166
    mole from the pot 108–9
    squash flower and vegetable soup 140–1
    stuffed cactus paddles 172
    tomato *milpa* pie 184–5
cream 12
    creamy corn soup 99
    creamy orange jelly with mezcal 88–9
    homemade crema 139
        recipes using 33, 50, 65, 70–2, 74–5, 78, 80, 87, 101–3, 114–15, 138–9
    roasted poblano chillies with Mexican *crema* 78
    see also clotted cream
curried cauliflower tacos with roasted tomatillo chutney 176

D

dip, spicy chipotle bean 161
dipping sauce, pomegranate 181

E

egg
    ancho chillies stuffed with beans and cheese 118–19
    battered stuffed tortillas 84–5
    beans and eggs 106
    fried huauzontle patties 120
    meatballs in chipotle sauce 113
    Mexican-style eggs 86
    Montuleño-style 104
enchiladas
    cabbage enchiladas 183
    cheesy enchilada parcels 116–17
    green chicken enchiladas 50–1
epazote 12
    basic cooked beans 107
    green *mole* with chicken 124–5
    grilled fish tamales 142–3
    mole from the pot 108–9
    squash flower huaraches 74–5
    squash flower and vegetable soup 140–1
    street corn in a cup 52
equipment 15
escabeche, pickled cactus and vegetables 147
Escuela de Gastronomía Mexicana 8

F

fajitas, cactus fajitas with *cecina*, spinach and mushrooms 174–5
fideo noodles in chipotle-tomato sauce 102–3
fish
    fish tacos with creamy pasilla oaxaca sauce 177
    garlicky pan-fried fish 152
    grilled fish tamales 142–3
flautas, steak 72
flour tortillas, squash flower burritos 44
fondas (homestyle restaurants) 93

G

Garduño, Miguel 115
garlic
    chilli morita salsa 75
    chilli pasilla cream sauce 177
    chilli pasilla salsa 73
    creamy jalapeño salsa 96
    crispy garlic 152
    garlic mojo sauce 152
    garlicky pan-fried fish 152
    pasta, ancho chilli, mushroom and garlic 178–9
    roasted habanero salsa 123
gelatine, creamy orange jelly with mezcal 88–9
green bean
    battered stuffed tortillas 84–5
    chayote salad, green bean and tomato 168–9
    mole from the pot 108–9
guajillo chilli 12
    árbol chilli and peanut salsa 29
    cabbage enchiladas 183
    cheesy enchilada parcels 116–17
    chicken, chilli and vegetable parcels 150–1
    mole from the pot 108–9
    red taco-stand style salsa 27
    sauce for fried chorizo and potato sandwiches 70–1
Gutiérrez, Luis Buenrostro 48

H

habanero chilli 12
    pickled onions and habanero 29, 46–7
    roasted habanero salsa 121, 123
ham, Montuleño-style egg 104
hibiscus flower

hibiscus flower quesadillas 164–5
hibiscus flower tea 96
hominy, nixtamalised 65
huaraches, squash flower 74–5
huauzontle
    fried huauzontle patties 120
    huauzontle chicken soup 170–1
huitlacoche, corn smut quesadillas 31

J

jalapeño chilli 12
    cabbage enchiladas 183
    cheesy enchilada parcels 116–17
    creamy jalapeño salsa 96, 142–3
    fresh tomato salsa 81
    pickled cactus and vegetables 147
    roasted poblano chilli tamales 36–7
jam and condensed milk with fried plantain 156–7
jelly, creamy orange with mezcal 88–9

K

kale, creamy kale salad 167

L

lambs quarters or fat hen, 'sweated' Mexican greens 79
lard 12
lime
    cactus fajitas, *cecina*, spinach and mushroom 174–5
    chicken, chilli and vegetable parcels 150–1
    crispy carrot tacos 114–15
    fish tacos with creamy pasilla oaxaca sauce 177
    fresh tomato salsa 81
    garlic mojo sauce 152
    grilled fish tamales 142–3
    homemade green chorizo 148–9
    lime and brown sugar cooler 131
    marinated, spit-roasted tacos 49
    mole from the pot 108–9
    pickled red onions 123
    prawn and octopus cocktail 66–7
    prickly pear agua fresca, lime and chia 160
    slow-roasted mutton 154
    sour orange substitute 123
    steak and chorizo tacos 80
    steak flautas 72
    stewed Swiss chard 111
    street corn in a cup 52
    white *pozole* 65
López, Janneth 108

M

mamey milkshake 62
marrow bone(s), *mole* from the pot 108–9
Martinez, Juan Carlos 153
masa
    fresh tamales masa 12, 35, 87
        basic savoury coarse-ground masa 34, 36
        mushroom and green salsa tamales 144–5
        sweetcorn tamales 87
    fresh tortilla masa 12
        bean and cheese *tlacoyos* 42–3
        cheesy enchilada parcels 116–17
        fresh nixtamal 25
        squash flower huaraches 74–5
        thickened Mexican hot chocolate 54–5
masa harina 12, 159
    bean and cheese *tlacoyos* 42–3

blue corn *sopes* 139
homemade corn tortillas 22–4
masa made with 87, 144–5
pinole atole 132
sweetcorn tamales 87
tamales 35
thickened Mexican hot chocolate 54–5
mayonnaise
    chilli pasilla cream sauce 177
    street corn in a cup 52
    tomato *milpa* pie 184–5
meatballs in chipotle sauce 113
mercados (markets) 57–8
mezcal with creamy orange jelly 88–9
Mexican bay leaf 11
Mexican cinnamon 12
Mexican oregano 14, 65
Mexican squash 14
    battered stuffed tortillas 84–5
    chicken, chilli and vegetable parcels 150–1
    mole from the pot 108–9
    squash flower and vegetable soup 140–1
    stuffed cactus paddles 172
    tomato *milpa* pie 184–5
milk
    condensed milk and jam with fried plantain 156–7
    creamy beetroot soup 100–1
    homemade requesón cheese 64
    mamey milkshake 62
    masa 87
    pinole atole 132
    thickened Mexican hot chocolate 54–5
Milpa Alta 127, 128, 132, 141, 147
milpa farming system 184–5
mixiotes 150–1
mole
    green *mole* with chicken 124–5
    mole from the pot 108–9
Montaño, Graciela 89
Monterey Jack cheese
    battered stuffed tortillas 84–5
    corn smut quesadillas 31
    crispy courgette quesadillas 166
    green chicken enchiladas 50–1
    hibiscus flower quesadillas 164–5
    mushroom quesadillas 30
    roasted poblano chilli tamales 36–7
    roasted poblano chillies with Mexican crema 78
    stuffed cactus paddles 172
    tomato *milpa* pie 184–5
Montuleño-style egg 104
Morelos 127, 128
morita chilli
    chicken, chilli and vegetable parcels 150–1
    chilli morita salsa 74–5
    creamy chilli morita salsa 44–5
    dried 14
mote, street corn in a cup 52
muesli, nutty homemade 163
mulato chilli (dried) 14
mushroom
    cactus fajita, *cecina*, spinach and mushroom 174–5
    mushroom and green salsa tamales 144–5
    mushroom quesadillas 30
    pasta, ancho chilli, mushroom and garlic 178–9
    squash flower huaraches 74–5
    squash flower and vegetable soup 140–1

mustard seeds, black 176
mutton, slow-roasted 154

N

nixtamal
    fresh nixtamal 25
    homemade corn tortillas 22–4
    nixtamalised corn flour 22–5, 34, 159
    nixtamalised hominy 65
noodles in chipotle-tomato sauce 102–3
nopal 14
nutty homemade muesli 163

O

oat(s)
    mamey milkshake 62
    nutty homemade muesli 163
    porridge, poblano chillies and cheese 162
Oaxaca chilli pasilla, chilli pasilla cream sauce 177
octopus and prawn cocktail 66–7
onion 14
    pickled onions and habanero 29, 46–7
    pickled red onions 121, 123
orange
    creamy orange jelly with mezcal 88–9
    'drunk" salsa 155
    pickled red onions 123
orange, sour (Seville)
    slow-cooked citrusy pork 121–3
    sour orange substitute 123

P

panela cheese, cactus fajitas 174–5
pápaloquelite, turkey tortas with chipotle salsa 48
Parmesan, pasta, chilli, mushroom and garlic 178–9
parsley, pineapple-parsley cooler 131
pasilla chilli 14
    chilli pasilla cream sauce 177
    chilli pasilla salsa 72–3
    'drunk" salsa 155
    mole from the pot 108–9
    steak in chilli pasilla sauce 112
pasta
    pasta, ancho chilli, mushroom and garlic 178–9
    sopa with spinach and cheese 180
patties, fried huauzontle 120
peanut
    árbol chilli and peanut salsa 29, 46–7
    homemade green chorizo 148–9
    marinated, spit-roasted tacos 49
    toasted árbol chilli salsa 133
pea(s)
    chorizo, chilli and vegetable parcels 150–1
    Mexican-style red rice 97
    Montuleño-style egg 104
Peña Sotres, Rosa 42
pickles
    pickled cactus strips 42–3
    pickled onion and habanero 29, 46–7
    pickled red onion 121, 123
pie, tomato *milpa* 184–5
pig's trotters, white *pozole* 65
piloncillo (unrefined cane sugar)
    fideo noodles in chipotle-tomato sauce 102–3
    grating/chopping 61
    lime and brown sugar cooler 131
    sweet cinnamon-spiked coffee 60–1

sweetened fermented pineapple juice 63
pineapple
    marinated, spit-roasted tacos 49
    pineapple-parsley cooler 131
    sweetened fermented pineapple juice 63
pinole atole 132
pinto bean
    basic cooked beans 107
    bean filling for steamed tacos 46–7
    quick refried beans 45
pitta bread
    creamy kale salad 167
    hibiscus flower quesadillas 164–5
plantain
    fried plantain with condensed milk and jam 156–7
    Montuleño-style egg 104
poblano chilli 14
    charring 37
    porridge, charred poblano chilli and cheese 162
    roasted poblano chilli tamales 36–7
    roasted poblano chillies with Mexican crema 78
    squash flower huaraches 74–5
pomegranate dipping sauce 181
pork 7
    homemade green chorizo 148–9
    marinated, spit-roasted tacos 49
    meatballs in chipotle sauce 113
    purslane in tomatillo sauce 110
    slow-cooked citrusy pork 121–2
    slow-cooked pork 38–9
    white *pozole* 65
pork skin see *chicharrón* (pork crackling)
potato
    cabbage enchiladas 183
    fried chorizo and potato sandwiches 70–1
    potato filling for steamed tacos 46–7
    roasted chicken in adobo 82–3
    steak in chilli pasilla sauce 112
pots and pans 15
pozole, white 65
prawn
    prawn and octopus cocktail 66–7
    prawn quesadillas with avocado 40–1
prickly pear agua fresca, lime and chia 160
pumpkin seed
    amaranth and pumpkin seed-crusted chicken 181
    creamy beetroot soup 100–1
    creamy kale salad 167
    green *mole* with chicken 124–5
    nutty homemade muesli 163
purslane in tomatillo sauce 110

Q

quelites (Mexican greens), 'sweated' 79
quesadillas
    corn smut quesadillas 31
    crispy courgette quesadillas 166
    hibiscus flower quesadillas 164–5
    mushroom quesadillas 30
    prawn quesadillas with avocado 40–1
quesillo, squash flower huaraches 74–5
queso añejo 14
    chicken in chipotle-tomato sauce 32–3
    creamy corn soup 99
    'drunk' salsa 155
    Montuleño-style egg 104
    pasta, ancho chilli, mushroom and garlic 178–9

street corn in a cup 52
queso de mano, creamy corn soup 99
queso fresco 14
    ancho chillies stuffed with beans and cheese
        118–19
    blue corn *sopes* 138–9
    cabbage enchiladas 183
    cactus salad 76–7
    cheesy enchilada parcels 116–17
    crispy carrot tacos 114–15
    fideo noodles in chipotle-tomato sauce 102–3
    Montuleño-style egg 104
    porridge, poblano chillies and cheese 162
    sopa with spinach and cheese 180
    steak flautas 72
Quiroz Pérez, Victor Hugo 38

R
rabbit, beer-braised 153
radish, white *pozole* 65
ranchera sauce 105
    recipes using 84–5, 104, 120
Rendón, Amparo Reina 106
requesón cheese, homemade 42–3, 64
rib (beef), *mole* from the pot 108–9
rib (pork)
    purslane in tomatillo sauce 110
    white *pozole* 65
rice, Mexican-style red rice 97
    recipes containing 113, 146, 153
ricotta salata, street corn in a cup 52
Romano, street corn in a cup 52
runner bean with cactus 146
Ruvalcaba, Alonso 82

S
salads
    cactus salad 76–7
    chayote salad, green bean and tomato 168–9
    creamy kale salad 167
    fresh broad bean salad 68–9
salsa
    acidity 28
    árbol chilli and peanut salsa 29, 46–7
    chilli morita salsa 74–5
    chilli pasilla salsa 73
    creamy chilli morita salsa 44–5
    creamy jalapeño salsa 96
    'drunk' salsa 154, 155
    fresh tomato salsa 80, 81
    how to salsa guide 28
    mushroom and green salsa tamales 144–5
    raw tomatillo salsa 26
        recipes using 38–9, 46–7, 114–16, 138–9
    red taco-stand style salsa 27
    roasted habanero salsa 121, 123
    saltiness 28
    sour cactus fruit salsa 134–5
    toasted árbol chilli salsa 133
salt 14
San Luis Potosí 116
San Pedro Atocpan 127, 128
sandwiches, fried chorizo and potato 70–1
serrano chilli 14
    fresh tomato salsa 81
    purslane in tomatillo sauce 110
    ranchera sauce 105

sieves 15
sopa with spinach and cheese 180
sopes, blue corn 139
soup
    creamy beetroot soup 100–1
    creamy corn soup 99
    huauzontle chicken soup 170–1
    mole from the pot 108–9
    squash flower and vegetable soup 140–1
spice grinders 15
spinach
    cactus fajita, *cecina*, spinach and mushroom 174–5
    homemade green chorizo 148–9
    sopa with spinach and cheese 180
squash (and courgette) flower
    squash flower burritos 44
    squash flower huaraches 74–5
    squash flower and vegetable soup 140–1
steak
    steak in chilli pasilla sauce 112
    steak and chorizo tacos 80
    steak flautas 72
stock 51
    basic homemade chicken stock 98
        recipes using 33, 97, 99, 101, 111–13, 121,
            144–5, 171
    low-salt 98
    ready-made 98
sunflower seeds, toasted árbol chilli salsa 133
sweetcorn
    creamy corn soup 99
    mole from the pot 108–9
    street corn in a cup 52
    sweetcorn tamales 87
    see also corn husks; corn kernels; corn tortillas
Swiss chard, stewed 111
Swiss cheese, tomato *milpa* pie 184–5

T
tacos 7
    crispy carrot tacos 114–15
    curried cauliflower tacos with roasted tomatillo
        chutney 176
    fish tacos and creamy pasilla oaxaca sauce 177
    marinated, spit-roasted tacos 49
    steak and chorizo tacos 80
    steamed tacos 46–7
tamales
    basic savoury coarse-ground masa 34, 36
    grilled fish tamales 142–3
    mushroom and green salsa tamales 144–5
    roasted poblano chilli tamales 36–7
    sweetcorn tamales 87
    tamales recipe 35
tea, hibiscus flower 96
telera rolls
    fried chorizo and potato sandwiches 70–1
    turkey tortas with chipotle salsa 48
tequila, creamy orange jelly with mezcal 88–9
tianguis (markets) 57–8, 127, 128
tinga sauce 32–3
tlacoyos 7
    bean and cheese *tlacoyos* 42–3
Tláhuac 153
tomatillo 14
    buying 26
    green chicken enchiladas 50–1

green *mole* with chicken 124–5
mushroom and green salsa tamales 144–5
preparation 26
purslane in tomatillo sauce 110
raw tomatillo salsa 26
    recipes using 38–9, 46–7, 114–16, 138–9
roasted habanero salsa 123
roasted tomatillo chutney 176
sour cactus fruit salsa 134–5
steak in chilli pasilla sauce 112
tomato 14
    ancho chillies stuffed with beans and cheese
        118–19
    cactus salad 76–7
    chayote salad, green bean and tomato 168–9
    cheesy enchilada parcels 116–17
    chicken in chipotle-tomato sauce 32–3
    chilli morita salsa 74–5
    chilli pasilla salsa 73
    chipotle sauce 113
    fideo noodles in chipotle-tomato sauce 102–3
    fresh tomato salsa 80, 81
    Mexican-style eggs 86
    Mexican-style red rice 97
    mole from the pot 108–9
    ranchera sauce 105
    red taco-stand style salsa 27
    roasted poblano chilli tamales 36–7
    sopa with spinach and cheese 180
    squash flower burritos 44
    stewed Swiss chard 111
    tomato *milpa* pie 184–5
tortas rolls, turkey tortas with chipotle salsa 48
tortilla chips, baked 161
tortilla presses 15
tortillas 14
    see also corn tortillas; flour tortillas
tostadas
    chicken in chipotle-tomato sauce 32–3
    prawn and octopus cocktail 66–7
    white *pozole* 65
trompos (roasting spits) 7
turkey tortas with chipotle salsa 48

U
urad dal 176

V
Valle, Erick 141
veal bone(s), *mole* from the pot 108–9
Velázquez de León, Josefina 99
Villanueva Buendía, Abel 146
Villanueva Buendía, Emma 146

X
Xochimilco 132, 133
xoconostles (sour cactus fruit) salsa 134–5

Y
yogurt
    chilli pasilla cream sauce 177
    homemade crema 139
Yucatán 104, 121

Z
Zepahua, Hortencia 153
Zukin, Nick 113

ACKNOWLEDGEMENTS

So many people helped make this cookbook a reality. My editor, Anja Schmidt, believed in the idea from the beginning, and I'm grateful to her and the team at Kyle Books. Thanks to Blair Richardson for her hard work on the design and to my agent Jeff Ourvan for his guidance and support. My cooking assistant and friend, Girelle Guzmán, kept me motivated, as did recipe testers Mira Evnine and Anna Stockwell, my brother Chris Téllez (who prepared the dishes with gusto for his three children) and Josh Keller. Jesica López Sol shared her enthusiasm for Mexican cuisine with me early on, and let me know it was okay to share this culture even if I didn't grow up in it.

Special thanks to Mexico City food vendors and friends who lent me their recipes, walked me through a technique or directly inspired a dish: Erick Valle, Luís Buenrostro Guitérrez, Victor Hugo Quiróz Pérez, Amparo Reina Rendón, Jorge León, Juan Carlos Martínez, Angélica Nápoles, Abel Rodriguez and Emma Villanueva Buendía, Miguel Garduño and his mother Sra. Paty, Janneth López, Nick Zukin, Alonso Ruvalcaba, Graciela Montaño and the staff at Burrería a Todo Mecate, Con Sabor a Tixtla and Tacos Don Guero, Sra. Rosa Peña Sotres and her daughter Delia and Sra. Margarita of the *tortillería* on Calle Aranda. *Gracias* to Arturo Anzaldo for doing the legwork when I couldn't be in DF, and to my team at Eat Mexico Culinary Tours for holding down the fort while I slogged away writing recipes. I'm grateful, too, to Marcela Landres, Katherine Fausset and Penny De Los Santos, who listened to my ideas about this book several years ago and encouraged me to pursue it. I'm immensely grateful to Liz and Erik Vance for giving me a home in DF.

Thank you to the Escuela de Gastronomía Mexicana for teaching me about the cuisine of my *antepasados*. To my parents, who taught me to be curious and take pleasure in food, I owe you homemade tortillas every day for the rest of my life. And finally, thanks to Crayton, whose early morning trips to the *tortillería*, grocery buying and all-around cheerleading made this project possible.

ONLINE RESOURCES

You can find many of the specialist ingredients used in this book in Mexican and other speciality food stores and markets or online. Here is a list of online suppliers, which should be useful when sourcing some of the more unusual ingredients.

Mexican/Latin American
www.casamexico.co.uk
www.coolchile.co.uk
mexika.co.uk
www.mexgrocer.co.uk
www.mexifood.co.uk
mextrade.co.uk
gringadairy.com – for cheese
labodeguita.co.uk
latiendita.co.uk
www.otomi.co.uk - for kitchen equipment
veneshop.co.uk
vivaperu.co.uk

Specialist food
www.amazon.co.uk
finefoodspecialist.co.uk
www.healthysupplies.co.uk – puffed
    amaranth/health food store
www.melburyandappleton.co.uk
mmm-glug.co.uk
www.souschef.co.uk
greenpasturefarms.co.uk – lard

Chillies
www.justchillies.co.uk
www.southdevonchillifarm.co.uk